Ready to Print

Handbook for Media Designers
Kristina Nickel

gestalten

Preface   05

1. Paper   06

2. Printing Technology   60

3. Composition and Typography 96

4. Trapping   146

Preface

Technical books have to be translated twice: once from one language into another, and again from one technical language into another. The history of printing and typesetting is full of developments that took place in German-speaking countries. Even to this day, German printing machine manufacturers retain a worldwide market share of over 80 percent. Accordingly, printing terminology developed independently in Germany and is more precise and comprehensive than anywhere else. However, the emergence of software at the end of the twentieth century created terms that hadn't existed before, and thus had no equivalents in other languages. The world of graphic design increasingly speaks English, which is due in large part to the dominance of the programs made by Adobe, such as InDesign, Photoshop, and Illustrator. After all, Adobe redefined the parameters of prepress with the first universal page description language, PostScript. The fact that the developers hung on to several obsolete terms from hot metal setting—"leading" for line spacing, for example—leads to new uncertainties for the translator.

There is also the problem of different standards throughout the world to define color spaces, format sizes, paper weight, and so on. With the exception of Liberia and Burma, only the United States does not use the metric system, sticking instead to their version of what the British call the Imperial system. In order for this book to be understood in the United States, we have included American measures and sizes along with the metric figures, either in the text or as endnotes. Hence this book is not only useful for work in one system of measurements or the other, but also as a reference for conversion between the two.

Berlin and London, winter 2010.
Erik & Dylan Spiekermann

1. Paper

Paper is an extremely versatile material with unique properties. It is more durable than digital technology, which has
the outstanding characteristic of beeing able to change pace
quickly. What is it that makes paper so unique? It is material, palpable, and therefore sensual. These are big words for
a medium that not only informs us of great truths every day
but also bombards us with meaningless advertisements.

Paper is our work's constant companion. Everything
begins with paper—as a scribble or an inspiration—and
everything ends with paper—as a printed work, as evi-
dence of our creation. This is reason enough to have
a closer look at this medium. How much should someone
reading this really know about paper, someone who
perhaps works at an advertising agency or as a paste-
up artist or designer?

This chapter will begin by looking at the basics.
Here we will answer some general questions, such as:
What is paper? What is it made of and what properties
help discern different grades of paper? Following on
from this we will look at what paper can be used for.
How is it processed? How does this topic relate to the
requirements of practical work on a computer? If the
approach does not basically differ in the individual programs, the practical part is always limited to the pre-
ferred program of Adobe Creative Suite, although the
book as a whole deals with Adobe InDesign, Illustrator
and Photoshop.

<u>1.1 Basics</u> If one wants to describe a certain type of paper, one cannot restrict oneself to appearance alone. The feel of its surface, its consistency, and its weight are also significant characteristics. What determines the properties of a paper is its composition, its finish, its color or whiteness, its weight, and its volume. Other features, such as non-aging properties or the paper grain, may also have some bearing on the selection and processing of a particular kind of paper.

Handmade deckle-edge paper has an uneven edge.

Yellowed paper is common in old books. Above, detail of the half title of a book from 1958.

<u>Papermaking</u> Knowledge of papermaking spread to Europe from China around 1100 AD through trade routes to the Mediterranean region, first reaching Italy and Spain. The first paper mill in Germany was constructed in Nuremberg in 1390. The raw material for paper production at that time was rags or textile fibers. Only later, in the nineteenth century, when rags became scarce due to the increase in demand for paper, did paper fibers begin to be obtained from wood.

Paper consists mainly of organic material known as pulp. Pulp consists largely of cellulose, wich makes up plant cells. Cellulose is connected to the cell wall—the substance that contains lignin, among other things. This structural substance from plant cells is in fact undesired, since paper that contains wood turns yellow markedly faster than woodfree paper.

Paper made from pulp is called wood-free paper, and when it is made from groundwood it is called wood-containing paper because it contains a relatively large proportion of wood pulp. In the paper industry fibers are obtained from the wood of coniferous trees, such as firs, spruces, and pines, and of deciduous trees, such as birches, poplars, and beeches. The wood is dissolved into the individual fibers using chemicals so that the pulp is almost entirely freed from the cell walls and the lignin that they contain.

Other possible kinds of pulp are, for example, semi-chemical pulps which contain only a small amount of wood, straw pulp, which is usually made from rye or wheat straw, and, of course, recovered waste paper. Even today paper may still contain textile fibers, i.e., rags made from linen or cotton. These are the most precious pulp materials for papermaking. Rag paper is particularly age-resistant and strong.

Paper is seldom made purely from one type of fiber. Its material composition is divided into five families: The first family is composed solely of rags such as linen, hemp, or cotton. The second family is composed of rags and up to 50 percent chemical pulp, but without any wood pulp. The third family is composed of any type of material, but again without wood pulp. The fourth family is composed of pulp with up to 50 percent wood fibers. The fifth family is composed of wood pulp with more than 50 percent wood fibers. The proportion and quality of the various fibers are essentially responsible for the non-aging properties and subsequent use of a type of paper.

Further ingredients of paper are known as additives. These include fillers, which are largely composed of mineral materials, such as talcum, gypsum, or chalk. These materials fill the gaps between the paper fibers, giving the paper a closed surface. They make it more opaque and improve smoothness, ink resistance, and printability. The kind of filler used determines the softness and flexibility of the paper.

Water and size also count as additives, as do synthetic resins, dyes, and optical brighteners, where necessary. Glues used for sizing make the paper less absorbent and more ink-resistant. Size makes the paper absorb less water from the air, which affects printability and processing. Only certain kinds of paper that are meant to be especially absorbent are made without size. These include blotting paper and filter paper. Dyes are required to be as lightfast, rub-proof and heatresistant as possible. The water used is also subject to special requirements. It ought to be as soft as possible and free of impurities, such as suspended matter, iron or manganese.

Paper may be produced by a machine or handmade. Handmade paper is more expensive to produce than machine-made paper, which is why it is seldom used today. Deckle-edge paper, also known as vat paper, was originally handmade in oval wooden vats. The diluted wood pulp was scooped by hand with the help of a sieve. One can recognize this kind of paper by its uneven edge. Nowadays machine-made imitation deckle-edge paper is sold; the uneven edge is punched.

Non-aging properties

Thanks to its relative durability, paper is not only useful for short-lived advertisements, but also for documents that need to last a long time. Take for example a DVD that, depending on quality and storage, may only last a few years, while paper can easily last 400 years. Its non-aging properties depend on its composition and method of production. Every kind of paper will eventually turn yellow before it finally crumbles.

Paper from the sixteenth, seventeenth, and eighteenth centuries is particularly age-resistant because its chief ingredient is rag. At the end of the eighteenth century paper use was so high that wood was increasingly needed as a resource. This uncoated paper had a shortened lifespan of some 100 to 200 years.

There are various reasons for such rapid decay. One of the main reasons is the pH value of the paper. Paper produced industrially after 1840 is composed of several acidic ingredients that lead to faster decay. Among these acidic ingredients are chemicals that were introduced to split the wood fibers and separate the resin. Size contains alum, a double sulfate made of potassium sulfate and aluminum sulfate, which also adds to the paper's acidic pH value. Moisture in the air turns the remains of these sulfates into sulfuric acid. Lignin that is contained in the wood pulp's cell walls also forms acids over the course of many years, meaning that the paper virtually destroys itself. Today books from this period are neutralized in order to preserve them. In addition, an alkaline reserve is used to help slow decay.

Around 1985, or 1990 in East Germany, production was changed so that paper, with the exception of recycled paper, was made with considerably fewer acidic substances, and in fact had an alkaline pH value. With a neutral sizing agent and a calcium carbonate buffer, paper can last 400 years. This is due mainly to the alkaline method of production, the use of alkaline fillers, ceasing the use of acid-forming wood fibers, and the exclusive use of bleached pulps.

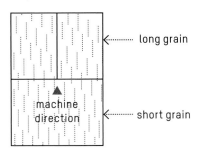

Paper reel

long grain

machine direction

short grain

The direction of the paper fibers always runs at a right angle to the web width.

However, there are other causes of paper decay that can not always be avoided. These include the use of optical brighteners and synthetic binding agents for coated paper. Outside environmental influences may also play a part. All of these things can contribute to the formation of acids that cause paper decay. Coated super white art paper is not necessarily the best choice for a product that ought to last as long as possible.

If longevity is particularly important for the choice of paper, one should check the durability standards. A German paper industry standard divides the non-aging properties of paper and paperboard into three durability classes (Lebensdauerklassen, LDK): paper with LDK 24–85 lasts several hundred years, LDK 6–70 lasts at least 100 years, and LDK 6–40 lasts at least 50 years. However, only paper and cardboard with LDK 24–85 can be called "age-resistant." Most importantly, these include uncoated kinds with a pH value between 7.5 and 9.5 that are exclusively made from bleached pulp and/or rags.

Machine direction

The machine direction determines the paper grain. In handmade paper the fibers do not face any particular direction.

However, in machine-produced paper the fibers mostly face the direction in wich the web runs through the machine. Thus the machine direction is always at a right angle to the web width of the paper reel. The grain might be of little significance for final artwork or layouts, but it is vital when it comes to processing all kinds of paper. For this reason, both printers and bookbinders must pay attention to the grain.

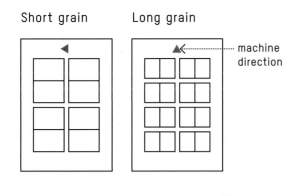

Short grain · Long grain · machine direction

coating color applied to one or both surfaces in order to improve the surface smoothness, gloss, whiteness, and printability like, for instance, art paper. Glazed paper has a smooth and glossy surface, pressed smooth between rollers. Paper may be either coated or glazed, or both.

Paper finish is classified as following:

Machine finished paper Paper without a surface finish is called machine finished paper. It has a relatively rough surface and has only been smoothed in the paper machine calender. This type of paper may also be described as uncoated.

Glazed paper Glazing gives machine finished or coated paper a closed, smooth, and glossy surface. The paper is fed through a rolling press with several hot pairs of rollers and pressed smooth under high pressure. This rolling press is also known as a calender. When fed through the press a second time, the paper can be glazed to a high gloss.

Embossed paper An embossing calender can give paper a particular surface texture. These embossing calenders have different patterns, so that the surface may be ribbed, grained, veined, or hammered, for example. This technique is also known as goffering.

Coated paper The surface of coated paper is even more closed and smooth than glazed paper. It is evenly coated with a coating color made of pigments, binders and additives in coating machines, before being

Print sheets are cut from the reel either in long grain or short grain. In the latter the machine direction runs parallel to the shorter side, while long grain runs parallel to the longer side. Where possible, long grain is used for multicolor offset printing, as registration inaccuracies are thus minimized due to the smaller risk of distortion.

Care must be taken during processing to ensure that the fold runs parallel to the grain. In book production, sheets with the fold at a right angle to the grain are only used in exceptional cases. Thus the paper fibers normally run parallel to the spine. If the machine direction is wrong, it will be hard to leaf through a book with adhesive binding.

There are different methods for determining the grain. One method is the bending test, where the paper is easier to bend or curl when parallel to the grain. In the tearing test, the paper tears easier along the grain. In the droop test, after one side of the paper is moistened it will curl up parallel to the grain. The fingernail test consists of sliding fingernails along the edges of a sheet. The paper parallel to the grain will remain relatively smooth, while the cross direction will be noticeably wavy.

The surface of the paperboard on the right has what is known as a felt grain, which occurs due to the use of felts in production in the paper machine wet press. The paperboard on the right got its hammertone texture in an embossing calender.

Finish The finish is a considerable distinguishing feature of the many kinds of paper. It influences their appearance and performance, making it an important factor when selecting paper. Paper that has not had a finish applied to it is called uncoated paper. On the other hand, coated paper has a

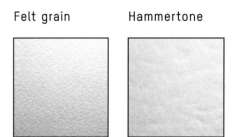

Felt grain · Hammertone

The surface of the paperboard on the left has what is known as a felt grain, which occurs due to the use of felts in production in the paper machine wet press. The paperboard on the right got its hammertone texture in an embossing calender.

dried and glazed. Depending on the method employed, the paper can be given a gloss or matte surface. Paper coated on one side has coating color applied to one side only. The surface of coated paper is considerably denser than that of exclusively glazed paper, making it excellent for high-quality print products and especially well suited for reproducing pictures.

Laminated paper By coating paper or paperboard with plastic or varnish, it can be made water-, smudge-, and aroma-proof. Laminating entails sealing the material by bonding it with synthetic or metal foil.

Paper weight[1] Another distinguishing feature of paper is its weight. In the metric system, its basis weight is called grammage and is given in grams per square meter (gsm, or g/m²) or kilograms per 1,000 sheets, which is customary in the trade. Weight and thickness—also called caliper—determine whether one is dealing with paper, cardboard, or paperboard. Grammage between 7 and 150 g/m² denotes paper. Grammage between 150 and 250 g/m² may be paper or paperboard, depending on thickness. This is not clearly defined. Grammage in excess of 250 g/m² is paperboard, although heavier paperboard is often generically referred to as cardboard.

The choice of a specific paper weight depends on the requirements of the print product. For example, if the paper used for a folded leaflet is too thick, the leaflet will not close properly. On the other hand, if the paper is too thin, the printed elements will show through too clearly on the other side or the leaflet will appear altogether too flimsy. In general, thick paper appears to be of higher quality than thin paper. The choice of paper is often a compromise between functionality, quality, and cost efficiency.

Paper volume Paper volume is the sheet thickness in relation to its weight. Different kinds of paper with the same weight can have different thicknesses; in other words they can have a different volume. The higher the volume, the easier to grip hold of material becomes at the same weight. In the metric system paper is normally 1-fold, 1.25-fold, 1.5-fold, 1.75-fold, 2-fold, and 2.2-fold volume. For instance, a 100 g/m² machine finished book paper with a 1.5-fold volume has a thickness of 0.15 mm, and a 2-fold volume has a thickness of 0.2 mm.

Paper volume is indicated by the manufacturer or by the retailer. If not, then it has to be estimated, which is often the case with glossy coated paper, since it is often much thinner than its grammage would suggest.

Grades of paper and paperboard

There are many different types of paper and paperboard. A paste-up artist or a designer at an advertising agency or a publish house rarely needs to select the type of paper. Either the choice of paper is more or less limited to a particular type, as is the case for a newspaper advertisement or a billboard, or else the paper is already determined in advance during the development of a corporate design. Often the choice of paper is given little thought due to cost. This means that certain standard grades of paper have managed to prevail by being cheaper due to the very fact that they are used a lot. In many cases, the types of paper that are used are always available at the printer's and do not need to be specially ordered, thus avoiding extra costs. This is because special grades of paper have to be bought in minimum quantities, which can incur disproportionately high paper costs for small orders.

In general, however, it is to be commended when paper choice is due to a conscious decision and plays an important role in design. A special type of paper can improve a printed product and help fulfill a design concept. It can also help a product stand out, something that is especially advantageous in advertising. However, that does not mean that a standard paper cannot satisfy high demands.

The following alphabetical lists provide an elementary insight into the various grades of paper and paperboard, which differ in their composition, manufacture, and use. The lists show what characteristics the different grades have and what they are used for, without going into detail about the many kinds of paper from the manufacturers' extensive ranges. Each paper type may contain many different grades of paper, sometimes only differing slightly. Paper samples provided by manufacturers offer broad support for choosing a specific type of paper.

Paper grades[2]

Affiche paper is the term for heavily sized wood-free paper used for printing large format posters. Its reverse side is blue, in order to avoid such things as posters pasted underneath from showing through. Formerly, low-grade, wood-containing paper was pasted onto the reverse side of posters or pictures to achieve flatness. "Affiche" is French for poster or placard.

Art paper is a wood-free or slightly wood-containing paper with a finish applied to both sides. The surface has a matte or gloss coating. It has an absolutely even and completely closed surface, and is particularly suited for printing pictures with a very fine screen.

Banknote paper is extremely resilient to mechanical stress, and in addition has special UV fibers and security marks.

Bible paper is also called lightweight printing paper. It is very thin yet also relatively opaque, and is used for substantial works such as bibles or lexicons. It is white or slightly yellowish and is preferably made from high-quality pulp or purely from rag. It contains a high proportion of filler pigments that give it its opacity, which in some cases is also due to the inclusion of groundwood.

Book paper is a wood-free and fully sized writing paper. It is made from high-quality pulp and is highly resistant against mechanical stress.

Bookbinding paper consists of different kinds of paper that are used specifically for bookbinding. These include endpaper, cover paper, and colored endpaper.

Book endpaper is a special tear-resistant bookbinding paper that is glued between the cover and the book block. It normally consists of a double sheet, with one sheet glued to the inside of the cover while the other is free and placed before and after the book block. Endpaper is usually colored, often light, and may be smooth, ribbed, or hammered.

Book printing paper is machine finished paper used for printing books. Its surface is porous and unglazed, so that the printing ink is absorbed well. It is very bulky due to the amount of fillers used and makes books appear thicker. However, coated paper should be used instead of book printing paper to faithfully reproduce photos and pictures in multicolor offset printing.

Bulky paper, also called bulking paper, is a soft, flexible, thick, heavily coated paper with a high 1.5 to 2.2-fold volume. It allows small books to appear thicker.

Coated paper is the generic term for paper that has been coated on one or both sides with a pigment- or synthetic-based compound. This improves the surface smoothness, printability, gloss, and whiteness. There are various different kinds. In special web offset and gravure paper, a distinction is made between ULWC (ultra lightweight coated), LLWC (light lightweight coated), LWC (lightweight coated), MWC (mediumweight coated), and HWC (heavyweight coated).

Colored endpaper has been used at binderies since the very beginning as a cover for the book block. As opposed to plain endpaper, it is multicolored or patterned. A distinction is made between paste, marble, Turkish marbling, stencil wipe, colored, wash, and silkscreen cover paper. All of these have a different method of production. Paste paper is probably the oldest technique for making colored paper. The paper is coated with dyed paste using a brush. Patterns are created using different techniques, such as by placing together two freshly pasted sheets that produce squishy patterns when pulled apart. Patterns may also be produced by sprinkling water or soap onto the pasted paper.

Copying paper is a wood-free, uncoated paper for copiers and laser printers. It is made drier than printing paper, which means that its pile humidity is lower than room humidity.

Cover paper is used at binderies to cover the cardboard for hardcovers. Cover paper, or stock, is usually very durable and age-resistant. It should be as scratch and rub-proof, and as lightfast and colorfast as possible.

Deckle-edge paper is synonymous with quality. It can be handmade or mold-made in a cylinder paper machine. The paper fibers in handmade paper have no particular grain. Imitation deckle-edge paper is made in a fourdrinier machine. It has the texture of deckle-edge paper, but the edges do not taper like they do with the pulp dilution used for the genuine article. Deckle-edge paper is made from high-quality pulp. It is used as writing paper, paper for personal stationery, cover paper at printing houses, end- and cover paper at binderies, and as lining paper for drawers and boxes.

Glazed paper is the generic term for paper that has not merely been glazed in a calender at the end of the paper machine. Its surface is given an additional glaze or gloss in a separate calender. A calender consists of several rollers through which the paper is fed.

Gravure paper is a largely wood-containing glazed paper that is very absorbent and strong.

Gummed paper has an adhesive layer on one side. It is used for postage stamps, for example.

Halftone printing and gravure paper is medium-fine or wood-free glazed paper for commercial web offset or gravure printing. It is very soft and absorbent. Rotogravure paper must have a high tensile strength and opacity, due to the fluidity of gravure ink that penetrates deep into the paper.

HWC paper (heavyweight coated) is an improved, heavier, white LWC paper. Like the latter, it is coated on both sides, and is used in gravure printing and web offset.

Art paper is a relatively high-quality paper, coated on both sides. Its surface is closed and absolutely even.

Handmade paste paper may be used at binderies as covering paper.

It is smoothed using a viscous coat and is either matte, semi-matte, or glossy. It is often printed with multiple colors in offset or web printing. There are many different grades of illustration printing paper with varying quality.

Imitation parchment paper is not as strong as parchment paper. It is used for such things as technical drawings or sandwich paper.

Japanese vellum is a handmade paper from Japan. It is made from high-quality plant pulp, such as bast fiber from the kozo (mulberry tree) or mitsumata (daphne shrub). Japanese vellum is unsized and very strong. There are white, yellowy, dyed, patterned, and printed varieties with different textures and strengths. They are used, for example, as endpaper or cover paper.

Label paper is sized on one side or foliated. It has good printing characteristics and meets certain special requirements, such as being tear-, water-, and stamp durability.

LWC paper (lightweight coated) is coated on both sides and particularly light. It is used in gravure and web offset printing and is relatively opaque despite its light weight. ULWC stands for ultra lightweight coated.

Machine finished paper has a surface that is only glazed in the calender in the end section of the paper machine.

Machine finished coated paper is produced mainly from groundwood. Its grammage can be between 40 and 80 g/m² and it is sometimes produced in bulk quantities.

Marbled paper is colored paper whose patterns imitate marble. Marbling techniques originated in the Orient.

Offset paper is wood-containing or wood-free paper, and machine finished. Because of the need for accuracy it requires ample surface sizing and minimum possible stretch, improving the printability in wet printing.

Paper for personal stationery is wood-free, partially rag-containing paper with a closed and smooth semi-matte or embossed surface. It is used for portfolios or envelopes, and is sometimes used book jackets.

Parchment paper is a translucent paper that is as grease-resistant, airtight, and waterproof as possible. Its surface is sealed in such a way that it is particularly good for packing greasy foods.

Poster paper is paper coated on one or both sides that is especially light- and weatherproof, and relatively impermeable to glue.

Rag paper is made 100 percent from linen or cotton rags, although nowadays cotton waste from the textile industry is often used. It is the most expensive type of paper. Rag paper is very strong and age-resistant. Rag-containing paper is more common than pure rag paper.

Recycled paper is the generic term for paper that is produced chiefly from recovered paper.

Sized paper is less absorbent due to the addition of size. It is therefore useful for sticking to other grades of paper or for writing with ink.

Standard newsprint paper is a standard paper for newspaper printing on web offset machines. Newsprint paper is relatively low quality. It is wood-containing and uncoated. In newspaper printing using heatset web offset, the total ink application is limited to 260 percent. This is slightly more than newspaper printing using coldset web offset machines, seeing as heatset printing machines have a drier built in.

Supercalendered (SC) paper is a heavily calendered, or glazed, paper made largely from groundwood and recovered paper. Its surface is heavily compacted due to the extreme glazing in a supercalender. Its thickness is reduced and it is used in web offset and rotogravure. It is particularly glossy due to its having been so heavily pressed. The counterpart to the supercalender is the soft calender, which exerts little pressure on the paper, meaning that the paper remains bulkier.

Tissue paper is a very thin and light paper used for packing and decoration. Its grammage is $30 \, \text{g/m}^2$ or less.

Uncoated paper has a machine finished surface, which means that it has not had any additional glazing. It is made from fibers and additives, and can be wood-containing or wood-free. Its matte surface has a different feel than coated paper.

Web printing paper is used for newsprint on web offset—also called rotary offset—machines. It is a white or slightly colored machine finished or slightly glazed uncoated paper with a high wood fiber content. It is used for producing newspapers or other publications. It is very absorbent, making it suitable for fast web printing where ink needs to be absorbed quickly. Because of its high dot gain plus the short amount of time printing ink has to dry in coldset web offset machines, the total ink application is limited to 240 percent.

Wood-containing paper is made to a large extent from groundwood with very little pulp. It is less strong than paper made from pure pulp, and is less age-resistant and turns yellow faster.

Wood-free paper is made exclusively from pulp. It decays considerably more slowly than paper that contains wood, and is better for having a finish applied, seeing as it is stronger.

Writing paper is particularly good for writing on both sides, thanks to the surface sizing and glazing which give it a smooth surface.

Paperboard grades

Beverage packaging board is board laminated with plastic for the production of milk and juice cartons. It sometimes has aluminum foil on the inside.

Bristol board is an uncoated, unbleached board. It is made of different layers. The top layers are wood-free, while the middle layers are wood-containing. It is very sturdy and good for printing and processing. It is often used for envelopes and packaging.

Cardboard is a generic term for thick paperboard. Roughly speaking, cardboard is paperboard with grammage over $500 \, \text{g/m}^2$, although it is sold by millimeter width rather than weight. It is commonly used for packaging and bookbinding.

Chromo board is a folding boxboard with a smooth coating on one side and a strong wood-containing middle layer. It is especially good for printing

Paper types

HWC	heavyweight coated
LLWC	light lightweight coated
LWC	lightweight coated
MF	machine finished
MFC	machine finished coated
MWC	medium-weight coated
SC	supercalendered
SNP	standard newsprint (for heatset web offset)
ULWC	ultra lightweight coated

Commonly used abbreviations.

Duplex board

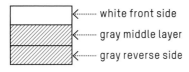

white front side
gray middle layer
gray reverse side

Triplex board

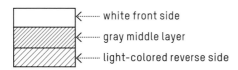

white front side
gray middle layer
light-colored reverse side

and varnishing, and excellent for punching, creasing, and scoring.

Corrugated board consists of fluted packing paper stuck to smooth packing paper in multiple lines. Corrugated board is a stiff but lightweight board often made into shipping cartons.

Duplex board is a triple-ply board made from two different layers plus a gray middle layer and a gray reverse side, and a wood-free or low wood-content

smooth coating that can be either white or colored. It is frequently made from recovered paper and often made into folding boxboard.

Folding boxboard is a duplex or triplex board made from pulp. It is good for printing and varnishing. Its surface may be coated or uncoated.

Gray board is a solid board made from recovered paper.

Hard board is a particularly bend-resistant, multi-ply solid board made of pulp. Folder boards or bookbinder's boards are hard boards, but game boards and picture boards may also be made of hard board.

Leather board does not contain leather, but brown mechanical pulp (steamed groundwood), which gives it a leathery appearance. It is used a lot in the packaging industry. Nowadays leather board also contains recovered paper.

Multi-ply board consists of at least two layers that either have a different composition, weight, or color from one another. It is often used for packaging.

Packaging board is the generic term for paperboard, wood board, gray board, and solid board used for packaging.

Paperboard is made from pulp or from recovered paper, with or without groundwood. It can be composed of several layers. Paperboard is thicker than paper and thinner than cardboard. If the grammage is in excess of $250\,\mathrm{g/m^2}$ it is paperboard, although sometimes it can be as low as $150\,\mathrm{g/m^2}$.

Postcard board is a machine finished coated or glazed board that is good for writing.

Pulp board is a triple-ply folding boxboard. Both the front and reverse sides as well as the middle layer are wood-free and white.

Solid board is the generic term for all solid board that has no recesses like, say, corrugated board has. Solid board is mainly used for packaging.

Triplex board is a triple-ply board made from three different layers, with a white coating and a white

Paper types

Paper type 1	Gloss coated paper, wood free
Paper type 2	Matte coated paper, wood free
Paper type 3	Gloss coated LWC (lightweight coated)
Paper type 4	Uncoated white paper, offset
Paper type 5	Uncoated slightly yellowish paper, offset

Newspaper paper

Newsprint	Coldset web offset, daily newspapers
Standard newsprint	Heatset web offset, weekly newspapers

or light-colored reverse side and a gray middle layer. The front and reverse sides may also be colored.

Wood pulp board is a solid board made from wood pulp and used for such things as packaging.

Paper types The many different grades of paper are divided into five paper types. They are limited to the classification of basic characteristics, such as paper finish or whiteness. Paper grades are defined in the ISO standard for offset and included under color profile specifications.

Newsprint is grouped into uncoated paper for coldset web offset and coated paper for heatset web offset. Newsprint for coldset web offset is used for daily newspapers. It is a very low-quality paper with a relatively high groundwood content. Its high lignin content makes the thin newsprint relatively strong and opaque. Newsprint is not at all age-resistant and will rot on a compost heap in a matter of months.

Endnotes for USreaders

1 – see below "Basis weight of paper in lbs., US"

2 – see below "Paper grades, US"

Basis weight of paper in lbs., US

Grade of paper						
Book 25 x 38 in	Bond 17 x 22 in	Cover 20 x 26 in	Bristol 22.5 x 28.5 in	Index 25.5 x 30.5 in	Newsprint 24 x 36 in	TAG 24 x 36 in
30	13	50	67	90	22	100
40	16	60	80	110	28	125
45	20	65	100	140	30	150
50	24	80	120	170	32	175
60	28	90	140	220	34	200
70	32	100	160		35	250
80	36	110				300
90	40	130				
100		160				
120						

Paper weight in the United States is given in pounds (lbs.) and calculated with the help of the basis weight. The basis weight denotes the weight of a ream of 500 sheets. One must know the paper grade in order to calculate the basis weight of a paper. The classification of different types of paper is based on the pulp, treatment, and end use of the paper. Some common grades are book, bond, cover, vellum bristol, index, newsprint, and TAG.

Paper grades, US

Grade	Brightness in %
Premium	88–95
1	85–87.9
2	83–84.9
3	79–82.9
4	73–78.9
5	72.9 and below

US paper grade specifications: The paper grades are organized into six categories classified from the highest level, premium, to the lowest level, 5. More than anything, they determine the level of brightness, i.e., what percentage of light is reflected.

Notes

<u>1.2 Print sheet production</u> Untrimmed print sheets are often many times larger than the end product. As a rule several copies—known as multiple-ups—or pages are pasted up onto a print sheet and then cut or folded where necessary to the trimmed size after printing. In the old days the individual components of a sheet or page were assembled manually at a light table. Nowadays printing plates are normally prepared digitally with the help of imposition software.

Above all, a print sheet must allow room for printing aids. These include register marks and the print control strip, the trim, fold, and collating marks, and the sheet title, all of which are needed for processing the sheet. In addition, a sheet has to have room for the gripper edge—the front edge to be fed through the printing machine—which must remain unprinted.

There are different print sheet formats. The type of format is determined by the size of the printing machine, among other things. When choosing a format one must ensure that only thin papers without irregularities or creases are folded as 24- and 32-page sheets. For thicker paper, 24-page sheets must be halved to 12-, and 32- to 16-page sheets. The sheet format of coated illustration printing paper for sheet-fed offset in the medium format category would be, for example, 70 x 100 cm, and 43 x 61 cm in the small format category.[3]

Knowledge of sheet formats is important for the optimum use of paper if costs need to be taken into account. The tables on the next page give examples of maximum formats for fitting pages onto sheets. If there is no bleed, pages may be a couple of millimeters wider or longer. However, for four-color printing, pages have to be a little smaller in order to accommodate the print control strip.

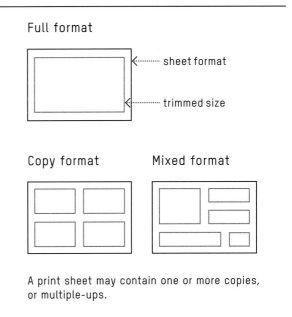

Full format

sheet format

trimmed size

Copy format   Mixed format

A print sheet may contain one or more copies, or multiple-ups.

Register marks
Register marks ensure that printed images are in register. This means keeping images on the front and reverse of the sheet aligned and making sure that everything is printed in its proper place on the page. Color registration marks help control the precise overprinting of all colors and coatings in multicolor printing. In manual sheet assembly, register marks serve as a visual aid for assembling the individual color films, which must overlap exactly. The printed register ought to be so accurate that any misregister is undetectable by the naked eye. The overprinting of colors is tested using a special magnifying glass called a linen tester to check the register marks and the print image. Automatic register measuring devices make the printer's work easier. If a color is not printed in register, the misalignment is easily spotted at the register marks. This test is repeated continually during the printing process so that the printing machine can be adjusted when necessary.

Register inaccuracies may occur in conventional printing processes if, for example, the sheet assembly has mistakes, the printing machine has not been correctly adjusted, or if the paper stretches when it is pulled from the blanket cylinder after the first color has been applied. Register inaccuracies are much rarer in digital printing, and are impossible with computer-to-plate during the plate-making process.

An agreement should be made with the printer as to whether the register marks need to be included in the print PDF. Where required, they should be placed 2 to 4 mm from the margin. If the file contains bleed marks they should be placed directly on the picture margin, so that if the bleed is 3 mm, they should be 3 mm from the paper edge. The line weight of register marks should be no thicker than 0.1 mm unless otherwise specified.[4]

Trim marks
Trim marks indicate where the sheet is to be cut to size after printing. Like register marks, they should be placed 2 to 4 mm from the margin, usually 3 mm. Unless otherwise specified, they should be 5 mm long and no thicker than 0.1 mm. If the pages or copy have a bleed the trim marks may be placed directly on the picture margin. For example, at a bleed of 5 mm the distance to the paper edge is likewise 5 mm, and at a bleed of 3 mm it is 3 mm.[4, 5]

In case marks are placed using manually drawn lines rather than automatically, the color of the trim marks should already be used in the document,

Print sheet with printer marks

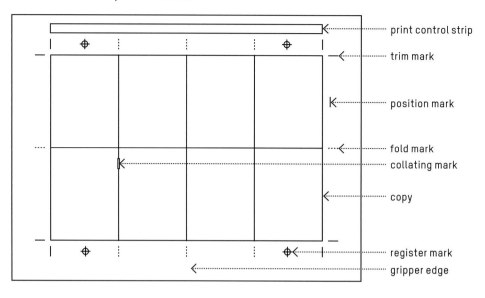

- print control strip
- trim mark
- position mark
- fold mark
- collating mark
- copy
- register mark
- gripper edge

The print sheet contains the individual pages and printer marks necessary for printing.

Number of pages per sheet on printing machines up to 500 x 700 mm [6]

Blank sheet	8 pages	12 pages	16 pages	24 pages	32 pages
610 x 860	204 x 299	204 x 197	146 x 204	95 x 204	99 x 146
630 x 880	209 x 309	209 x 204	151 x 209	98 x 209	101 x 151
640 x 900	214 x 314	214 x 207	154 x 214	100 x 214	104 x 154
700 x 1000	239 x 344	239 x 227	169 x 239	110 x 239	116 x 169

Number of pages per sheet on printing machines up to 700 x 1000 mm [6]

Blank sheet	8 pages	12 pages	16 pages	24 pages	32 pages
610 x 860	294 x 280	209 x 294	136 x 294	209 x 194	144 x 209
630 x 880	304 x 287	214 x 304	140 x 304	214 x 200	149 x 214
640 x 900	309 x 294	219 x 309	143 x 309	219 x 204	151 x 219
700 x 1000	339 x 327	244 x 339	160 x 339	244 x 224	166 x 244

Trim marks, fold marks, and bleed

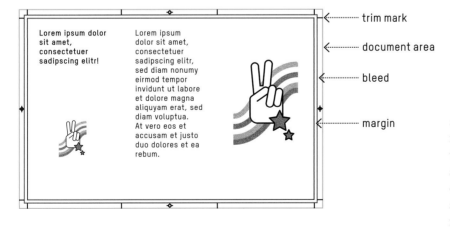

fold mark
trim mark
bleed
trimmed size

Different register marks

Out of register

Letterfold flyers with trim, fold, and register marks

Lorem ipsum dolor sit amet, consectetuer sadipscing elitr!

Lorem ipsum dolor sit amet, consectetuer sadipscing elitr, sed diam nonumy eirmod tempor invidunt ut labore et dolore magna aliquyam erat, sed diam voluptua. At vero eos et accusam et justo duo dolores et ea rebum.

trim mark
document area
bleed
margin

Fold marks

Fold marks indicate the position of the fold. They are automatically included by imposition software in sheet assembly for multipage publications, such as brochures or books. Sometimes fold marks are already put in manually during final artwork. This is the case with flyers folded to DIN, for instance. The fold marks must also be included in the print PDF.

Like trim and register marks, fold marks should be placed 2 to 4 mm from the margin, 3 mm being the norm. Unless otherwise specified, they should be 5 mm long and no thicker than 0.1 mm.[4,5] If the pages or copy have a bleed of, say, 5 mm, the fold marks should also be 5 mm from the paper edge. Unlike trim marks, they are dashed.[5]

Bleed

Bled-off objects, such as colored backgrounds that cover the whole sheet or pictures that go right up to the edge, have to run over the trimmed size. This overlapping area outside of the trimmed size is called bleed. This is needed when the sheet is only trimmed to the final size after printing. Since it is technically impossible to cut exactly on the specified spot, bleed helps avoid white gaps on the edge.

When a sheet that has already been trimmed to size is printed, for instance with a color printer on an A4 sheet, the elements cannot go right up to the paper

like black, for instance. "Registration Color" is equally useful. It is normally found in the color palette in all programs, and is composed of all the print colors used, so that objects of that color are found on all color separations.

Business cards sheet without spaces between multiple-ups

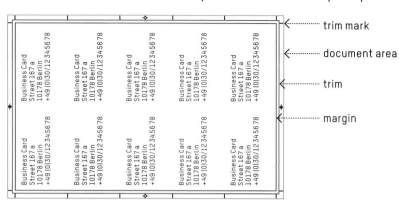

The document format contains 10 multiple-ups of different business cards at 55x85mm. There is no space between the individual multiple-ups, seeing as the background joins together seamlessly.

Setting trim and slug in InDesign[7]

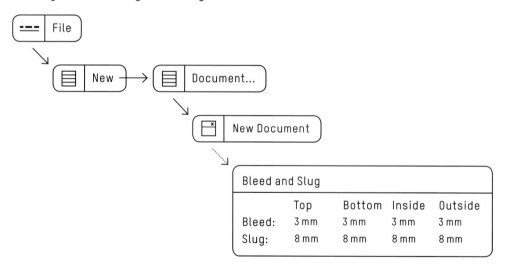

The bleed and document area are defined in InDesign in the document setup. The Smart Guides feature helps arrange multiple-ups and manual trim marks.

edge. In such a case the layout should provide a white margin, as a printer or a printing machine cannot print exactly up to the paper edge. At most, if at all possible, the page may be printed in a reduced size.

Unless otherwise specified, the bleed must be at least 3mm. A bleed of 5mm is often required for multi-page products with an adhesive binding. There is no need for bleed between multiple-ups if they are seamlessly connected, like on a plain-colored background, for

example. However, seeing as paste-up artists do not normally do sheet assembly, they do not necessarily need to take this into account, and may insert a bleed on all multiple-ups, as it will be needed on the outside in any case. The printer can always remove the bleed where required.

The bleed may be defined when setting up the page in InDesign, where it can be inserted more easily outside of the format by using the automatic Smart

Collating marks sequence

right   wrong   missing sheet   double sheet

Signature title

prime   second

7 Ready to Print   7*

serial sheet number · abbreviated book title · serial sheet number and asterisk

Guides. A document area may also be set outside of the bleed, where manually created fold or trim marks can be placed.

signature title is on the third page of the print sheet and is called the second. It consists of a serial sheet number and a asterisk.

Collating marks Collating marks are book-binders' aids. The little black bars are visible in a particular place on the book spine once the print sheet has been folded. When all the individual sheets are assembled into a book, the step-like collating marks lying on top of one another indicate that the sheets are in the correct order. Collating marks are exclusively used during sheet assembly and, unlike trim and register marks, cannot be inserted by a layout program.

Signature title The signature title is a mark for identifying the correct order of folded print sheets in large-scale works, particularly books. It is always put in the same place on the spine of the folded sheet or, if it has already been done in the layout, on the first page of the document below the type area, or outside of the trim, which is preferable. The first signature title is on the first page of the print sheet and is called the prime. It consists of an abbreviation of the book title, and a serial sheet number. The second

Print control strip The print control strip is for checking the print result. The strip contains the various color measurement and control swatches, which allow the result to be tested visually and have its density measured. It is printed on the sheet at a right angle to the print direction and across the entire sheet width. (The print control strip is explained more thoroughly in the chapter "Printing Technology," in the section "Quality Control," p. 90ff.)

Imposition Multipage products are collated into print sheets with 4, 8, 12, 16, 24, or 32 pages, for example. The arrangement of pages or multiple-ups on the print sheet is known as imposition. The type of arrangement used is determined by the page orientation, the type of bookbinding process, the folding method, and the sequence. As a rule, arranging pages or multiple-ups is done directly at the printer's using special programs. Pages are distributed on the

Different swatches on a print control strip

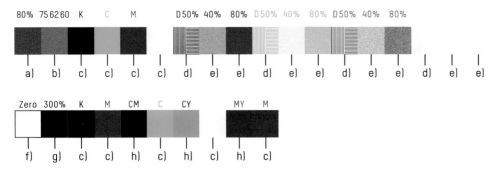

a) 80% true gray
b) gray balance swatch composed of 75% cyan, 62% magenta, and 60% yellow to monitor the color balance
c) spot color swatch to monitor coloration
d) dot slur and doubling swatches to monitor cylinder progression
e) halftone swatches to monitor dot gain
f) paper color
g) 3-color overprint swatches to monitor trapping
h) 2-color overprint swatches

Inner form

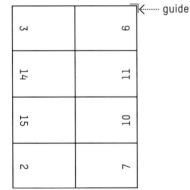

Outer form

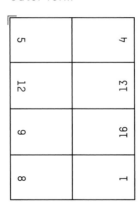

16-page upright format in two forms for front and reverse side printing, imposed for work and turn.

Work and turn

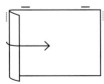

Work and tumble

Work and twist

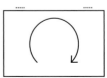

In turning, the side stop changes, whereas in tumbling the front stop changes, and in twisting both the side and front stops change.

sheet in the manner that optimizes surface space. After folding and cutting, the pages have to be put in the right order.

The imposition scheme also depends on how the print sheet looks after the front side has been printed, in order to print on the reverse side. There is a difference between work and turn, and work and tumble. In the seldom-practiced work and twist, the sheet is printed twice on the same side of the page after turning, instead of on the other side, which is more common.

One can print a plain sheet or a double sheet. For a plain sheet the printing block, or form, has to be changed after the first printing session, so that the reverse side of the sheet can be printed. Each printing block contains half the pages of a folded sheet. When printing a double sheet, the printing block contains all the pages of the folded sheet, meaning that it does not need to be changed to print the reverse side. In order to obtain two folded sheets, the sheet is cut down the middle after both sides have been printed. One only needs half the press passes when using the double sheet size.

In multipage documents, care must be taken to make sure that pages are distributed in the sheet in their entirety. A print sheet has at least four pages. The four cover pages do not count if the cover is printed on a different kind of a paper. The printers can give information as to how many pages are on each sheet. Normally there are 4, 8, 12, 16, 24, or 32 pages. Accordingly, the extent of the work must be divisible by the number of pages per sheet, or else there will be empty pages at the end.

In addition, in saddle stitching the inner pages are always somewhat shorter due to technical reasons. The imposition software automatically takes into account paper displacement, known as creep, and inner margin adjustment, depending on weight. Nevertheless, this may still work out badly under inconvenient circumstances, for instance in a layout with a white or colored margin. In such a case the margins would vary due to creep.

Bleed across signatures

Creep

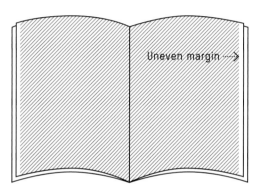

The thicker the paper, the shorter the inner pages are in saddle stitching. This can lead to problems with a peripheral margin, for example.

Endnotes for USreaders

3 – 70 x 100 cm = 28 x 40 in
     43 x 61 cm = 14 x 20 in

4 – 2 to 4 mm = 6 to 12 pt or 0.08 to 0.16 in or $^{5}/_{64}$ to $^{5}/_{32}$ in
     3 mm = 8.5 pt or 0.125 in or $^{1}/_{8}$ in
     0.1 mm = 0.25 pt

5 – 5 mm = 0.2 in or $^{13}/_{64}$ in

6 – see below "Number of pages per sheet on printing machines up to 19.5 x 27.5 in, US" and "Number of pages per sheet on printing machines up to 27.5 x 39.0 in, US"

7 – 3 mm = 0.125 in or $^{1}/_{8}$ in
     8 mm = 0.3125 in or $^{5}/_{16}$ in

Number of pages per sheet on printing machines up to 19.5 x 27.5 in, US

Blank sheet	8 pages	12 pages	16 pages	24 pages	32 pages
24.0 x 33.8	8.0 x 11.7	8.0 x 7.7	5.7 x 8.0	3.7 x 8.0	3.8 x 5.7
24.8 x 34.5	8.2 x 12.2	8.2 x 8.0	5.9 x 8.2	3.8 x 8.2	3.9 x 5.9
25.1 x 35.5	8.4 x 12.3	8.4 x 8.1	6.0 x 8.4	3.9 x 8.4	4.0 x 6.0
27.5 x 39.0	9.4 x 13.5	9.4 x 8.9	6.6 x 9.4	4.3 x 9.4	4.5 x 6.6

Number of pages per sheet on printing machines up to 27.5 x 39.0 in, US

Blank sheet	8 pages	12 pages	16 pages	24 pages	32 pages
24.0 x 33.8	11.5 x 11.0	8.2 x 11.5	5.3 x 11.5	8.2 x 11.5	5.6 x 8.2
24.8 x 34.5	11.9 x 11.2	8.4 x 11.9	5.5 x 11.9	8.4 x 7.8	5.8 x 8.4
25.1 x 35.5	12.1 x 11.5	8.6 x 12.1	5.6 x 12.1	8.6 x 8.0	5.9 x 8.6
27.5 x 39.0	13.3 x 12.8	9.6 x 13.3	6.2 x 13.3	9.6 x 8.8	6.5 x 9.6

Convert fractions to decimal equivalents, US

1/64	= 0.015625	1/4	= 0.25	1/2	= 0.5	3/4	= 0.75	1	= 1.0
1/16	= 0.0625	5/16	= 0.3125	9/16	= 0.5625	13/16	= 0.8125		
1/8	= 0.125	3/8	= 0.375	5/8	= 0.625	7/8	= 0.875		
3/16	= 0.1875	7/16	= 0.4375	11/16	= 0.6875	15/16	= 0.9375		

<u>1.3 Finishing</u> Finishing includes folding, punching, perforating, surface finishing, binding, and cutting. As soon as a sheet has been printed and the ink is completely dry it can be processed. Ink dries by absorption and in part by applying hot air or infrared heating or ultraviolet radiation. The duration of the drying phase varies, particularly in sheet-fed offset, depending on the type of printing process, ink, and carrier material employed.

Folding Folding is defined as bending sharp-edged paper along a straight line called the fold. The paper is folded along this line. The fold cannot be undone, because the paper surface has already been broken there. As a rule, a print sheet is folded first and then trimmed to size.

Folding itself is done on special machines at the bindery or printer's. In rare cases, folding is done manually. Handsheets, which give customers or printers a first look, are folded manually. These handsheets may also be cut first and then folded. A folding or creasing tool is used. These used to be made of bone but are now made of plastic. One can also run a fingernail along the fold, so that the sheet will close easier.

Types of fold An unfolded sheet is called a broadsheet, as opposed to a folded sheet. A print sheet may be folded once or several times.

Folding a two-page sheet once is known as single folding. Quire folding consists of folding several sheets laid on top of one another at the same time.

In multiple folding, the two basic methods are cross folding and parallel folding. In the latter, the folds are only parallel to each other. In cross folding the folds cross each other at right angles, and one always folds the longer side.

A printed sheet may be folded from one to four times: One-, two-, three-, and four-directional folded sheets. A sheet cannot be folded endlessly. The amount of folds depends on the strength of paper.

Parallel folding is usually employed for leaflets. Here the main distinction is made between a fan fold—also called an accordion fold or a zigzag fold—and a letter fold. Cross- and parallel folds may also be used together in combination.

In some types of fold, care must be taken to make sure that folded pages are at least 2 mm shorter, as otherwise brochures or leaflets cannot be closed. Either the type area or margin ought to be set smaller on these pages; choose whichever is less obtrusive. One can also set both the type area and the margin at half the size. In this case the page components must be shifted or reduced as required. In doing so one must be careful to avoid mistakes in line breaks and word separations.

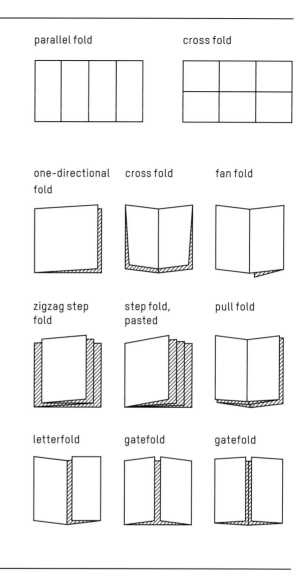

Creasing At a surface weight in excess of 170 g/m², paper and paperboard should be creased prior to folding, in order to avoid wrinkles, as well as the coating and ink breaking up. Coating breaking up is especially troublesome if the fold is printed in stark contrast to the paper color. In such a case the broken coating is clearly recognizable as a bright line on a dark color.

To make creases, a recess is pressed into the paper, making a bulge on the reverse side, which is on the inside when folded. The paper is then squeezed along the fold, making it easier to fold without its surface being affected. Creasing need not have any special marks for final artwork, as it is done automatically during processing.

Dimensions of a folder punch (in mm)[8]

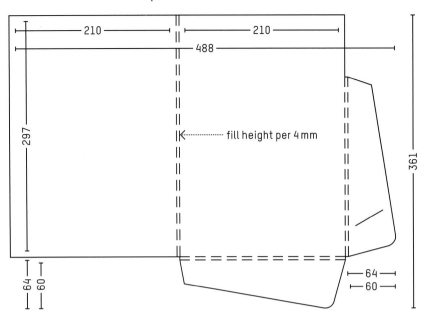

Closed form

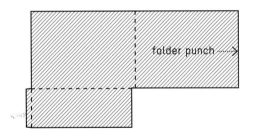

folder punch ------->

Open form

register punch ------->

Blank
inside

Cutting (scrap)
outside

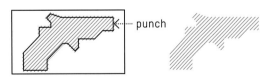

<----- punch

Blank
outside

Cutting (scrap)
inside

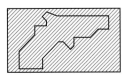

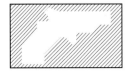

Overprinting in InDesign or Illustrator

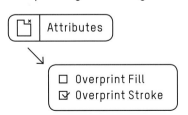

[ ] Attributes

☐ Overprint Fill
☑ Overprint Stroke

The cutting die has to print over the objects lying underneath it.

Folder punch

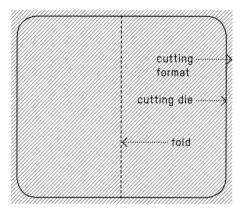

Printed background when the cutting die does not overprint (wrong)

Printed background when the cutting die overprints (right)

It is important not to choose too thick a paperboard. Paperboard over a certain grammage cannot be folded. As a rule the limit is around $350\,g/m^2$, although some creasing machines can process paperboard up to $600\,g/m^2$.

<u>Punching</u> A print sheet may be punched, or die-cut, to size, in addition to being cut in the form. The difference between punching and cutting is that in punching the dividing rule is not normally exclusively straight. A cutting die is often a closed form for cutting paper sheets. There are also open cutting dies used for index cutting or for rounding off book block edges, for example. Other classic examples of punching are labels with rounded-off edges, individually shaped stickers, carry folders, coasters, and index sheets.

There are two methods of punching: If, for example, one punches a circular hole in a piece of paper, the circle can either be the resulting blank or scrap. The scrap is also called a cutting. If the circle is the blank, the cutting is around the hole. On the other hand, if the circle is the cutting, the blank is around the hole.

<u>Setting the cutting die</u> The cutting die must be drawn during the final artwork and provided as a separate ink form. There are cutting dies that the printers or producers have in digital form because they are used relatively frequently. These cutting dies have the advantage of being considerably cheaper, seeing as they do not need to be specially made, plus they are tried and tested.

The cutting die must be placed on the page in order to make sure that all the elements are in the right place. If there is no digital cutting die available, an exact measurement will suffice. This may also be requested from the printing house. A cutting die may be drawn in Adobe Illustrator or InDesign, for example. It is set up as a closed form with an outline or as an open line, depending on what the cutting die should look like. The line or outline boldness is relatively meaningless, although a 0.25 to 0.5 pt line is normally used.

The amount of color in the punch outlines is of secondary importance. A dark-colored cutting die on a light background is optimal, as it is easier to see.

Definition in InDesign

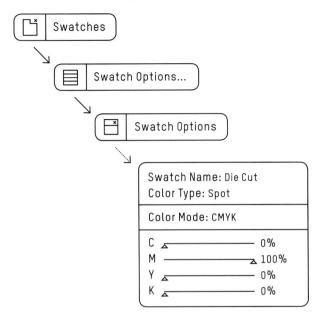

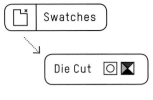

Definition in Illustrator

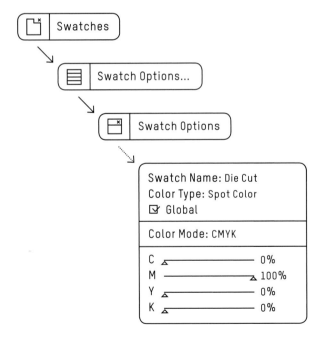

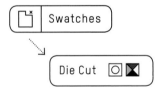

Perforation as a continuous line

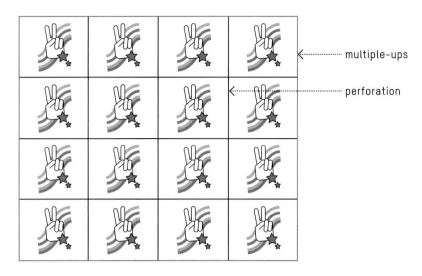

multiple-ups ←

perforation ←

Narrower folding pages

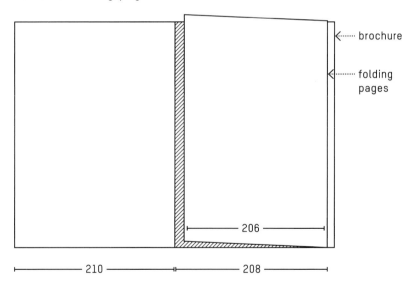

brochure ←

folding pages ←

206

210   208

Folding pages have to be narrower than the other pages. The first folding page may be exactly as wide as the brochure if it is bound after being cut.

reversed out and possibly cause white gaps. If the cutting die is on a colored background, it must not be copied onto the background in negative during color separation. Since a cutting die consists of outlines, the line has to be set manually to Overprint. The settings for this are slightly different in each program.

Laser punching

Laser punching is a newer process for very small or delicate punching on paper or board. It can work out cheaper than the conventional method for small runs. Using this method, filigree logos and halftone images can be punched. However, the motifs must not be smaller or finer than 0.3 to 0.5 mm. Nearly all kinds of paper and board can be laser punched.

Perforating

Perforation consists of punching little holes or slits along a line to make tearing or separating a part of the paper easier. Like folds, perforations are labeled by perforation marks outside of the format. Alternatively, a continuous line over the entire page may also be drawn.

Like a cutting die, a perforation must be given in a separate spot color, logically called "perforation." It must overprint all objects lying underneath it if it is to be drawn as a continuous line. (See "Setting the cutting die," p. 33 ff.)

It ought to have a spot color that can be separated from other colors and not printed along with them. The spot color should logically be called "punch" or "cutting die."

In the final artwork, care must be taken to ensure that the cutting die prints over all of the objects lying underneath it. If not, the colors underneath would be

Cutting The finished print sheet is cut to size on a cutting machine. In most cases this is done once the book block or booklet has already been folded and bound. That is why pages with a flap have to be narrower than other pages, because otherwise the flap will be cut off. Also, the folding page has to be narrower than the page next to it. The pages should be shortened by around 2 to 3 mm.

Endnotes for USreaders

8 – see below "Dimensions of a folder punch (in inches)"

Dimensions of a folder punch (in inches)

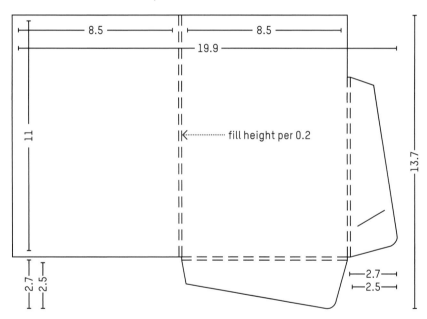

Notes

<u>1.4. Paper formats</u> The format of a print product is a working basis for a layout or final artwork. It has a decisive influence on the positioning and size of all objects. That is why the page format should be checked at the beginning of the final artwork to make sure that all elements are processed in the correct proportion and position in relation to the page format.

Test sheets

A test sheet, or dummy, is a handmade sample of the end product, typically required for producing booklets or packages. It shows errors that are not obviously apparent on a screen and highlights the weak points of the layout and the tricky parts for the paste-up artist.

There are many examples of mock-ups having proven useful. Before the final artwork is done, a test sheet can be made using low-resolution pictures. Once the final artwork is done, checking its high-resolution data will show any faults in the image processing. Test sheets are indispensable for products that need folding. It will show, for instance, when the folding page of a letterfold flyer has not been set slightly narrower, or when the type area on the folding page needs to be readjusted so that the fold runs right through the middle of both type areas. A dummy is a great help in general to printers and bookbinders for checking the folding and page sequence.

Size specifications

Size specifications may be given in different formats depending on the type of work. The best way is with clearly designed and easy to grasp tables.
The advertisement formats are also included in the publisher's media details. This consists of a collection of any relevant technical information pertaining to a publication. One can look up the circulation figures of a newspaper, the kind of paper used, the relevant color profile, the file format used for the ad copy, and ultimately, all formats. Media details are revised every year by the publishers and sent to the agencies. They are also often found on the internet.

The size is normally given as width by height, usually in millimeters. In most cases it is a trimmed format. Both the open and closed formats are relevant when it comes to folded works, such as flyers. The open format gives the size of the unfolded flyer; the closed format gives the size of the folded flyer.

Both page format and type area format are used for advertisements. The distinction between these two is vital for the final artwork. If pictures or colored backgrounds are supposed to go up to the edge, a bleed will have to be set when using page format. This is not necessary for newspaper advertisements, as newspapers are never printed with bleed. Sometimes it is necesssary to set a border around the format, in case the layout has not taken it into consideration.

Standard formats

There are a few formats that do not need to be given precisely in millimeters. These include the standard DIN formats, where "DIN A4 portrait" and "DIN A4 landscape" will suffice. In order to avoid any mistakes, "DIN long" should be given in millimeters.[9]

Along with the final formats within the DIN A series, there is also the DIN RA and SRA series with untrimmed sheet sizes. Along with these DIN formats there are, for instance, oversize A4+ and A3+ for laser or inkjet printers, onto which an A4 or A3 sheet with trim may be printed.

The DIN sizes of the A, B, and C series can be worked out by repeatedly halving the surface of a DIN A0 sheet, which has a surface area of one square meter. The number indicates how many times the A0 format has been halved. The sides of the rectangle are always like the side of a square to its diagonal.

Because wallets and various other types of card holders are standardized to it, most business cards are made to credit card size. There are two official credit card sizes: one for Europe and an international standard.

9 – See endnotes for USreaders, p. 42

Advertising information[10]

Formats

Type area:	370.5 mm high x 528 mm wide	Price list: 36
Advertisement columns:	8	Valid from: 01/10
Text columns:	6	Sheets: 3
Conversion factor:	1.333	

Column widths	Advertising section	Text section
1 column:	45.0 mm	58.5 mm
2 columns:	91.5 mm	120.9 mm
3 columns:	138.0 mm	183.3 mm
4 columns:	184.5 mm	245.7 mm
5 columns:	231.0 mm	308.1 mm
6 columns:	277.5 mm	370.5 mm
7 columns:	324.0 mm	–
8 columns:	370.5 mm	–

Media details contain all the technical information relevant to a publication.

Work sheet

Job
Customer: Company X
Job number: 12345-10
Description: Flyers
Account: X Flyers
Responsible: CD, TX, AD, RZ

Contacts
Customer 1: Thomas Regular, Company X
Customer 2: Laura Fisher, Company X
In-house 1: Melissa Brown, Accounts
In-house 2: Joe Mouse, contact

Deadlines
Text: 8/12, 12 p.m.
Photo: 8/15, 10:30 a.m.
Layout: 8/16, 2 p.m.

Print
Print run: 6 m
Size: A4, folded DIN long[11]
No. of pages: 2
Colors: 4/4
Grid: 70
Material: Offset, white
Processing: DIN long fold
Printing method: Offset
Proof: Litho X
Printers: X Printers
Processing: X Printers

Notes
Priority: 2a

A work sheet has all the relevant information at a glance.

10, 11 – See endnotes for USreaders, p. 42

AO sheet

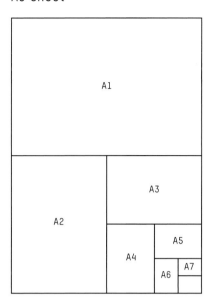

DIN A4

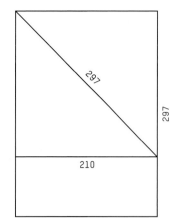

DIN sizes

Series	A	B	C
0	841 x 1189	1000 x 1414	917 x 1297
1	594 x 841	707 x 1000	648 x 917
2	420 x 594	500 x 707	458 x 648
3	297 x 420	353 x 500	324 x 458
4	210 x 297	250 x 353	229 x 324
5	148 x 210	176 x 250	162 x 229
6	105 x 148	125 x 176	114 x 162
7	74 x 105	88 x 125	81 x 114
8	52 x 74	62 x 88	57 x 81
9	37 x 52	44 x 62	40 x 57
10	26 x 37	31 x 44	28 x 40

DIN oversizes

Row	RA	SRA
0	860 x 1220	900 x 1280
1	610 x 860	640 x 900
2	430 x 610	450 x 640
3	305 x 430	320 x 450
4	215 x 305	225 x 320

Wrapping sizes

C6	114 x 162
DIN long	110 x 220
C5	162 x 229
C4	229 x 324
B4	250 x 353

DIN long

Cover	220 x 110
Short message	210 x 105
One third of A4	210 x 99
Usual	210 x 100

Credit card sizes

EU	85 x 55
ISO/IEC 7810	85.6 x 53.98

All figures in mm.

Endnotes for USreaders

9 –   There are a few sizes that do not need to be given precisely in inches. These include the standard paper sizes, such as letter, legal, ledger, and tabloid. Along with these standard sizes there are the ANSI (American National Standard Institute) paper sizes. One gets the sizes of series A, B, C, and D by repeatedly halving the surface of an ANSI E sheet, although the page ratios alternate between 1:1.30 and 1:1.55. The standard business card size in the US is 3.5 x 2 in.

10 – see below "Advertising information, US"

11 – 11 x 8.5 in, tri-fold brochure

12 – see next page

Advertising information, US

Formats

Type area:	11.55 in high x 21 in wide	Price list: 36
Advertisement columns:	8	Valid from: 01/10
Text columns:	6	Sheets: 3
Conversion factor:	1.333	

Column width	Advertising section	Text section
1 column:	1.40 in	1.80 in
2 columns:	2.85 in	3.75 in
3 columns:	4.35 in	5.70 in
4 columns:	5.75 in	7.65 in
5 columns:	7,00 in	9.60 in
6 columns:	8.50 in	11.55 in
7 columns:	10.00 in	–
8 columns:	11.55 in	–

ANSI E sheet, US

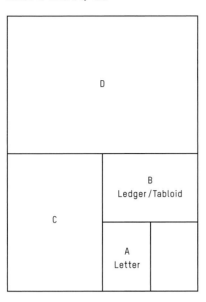

ANSI paper sizes, US

Name	in x in
ANSI A	8.5 x 11
ANSI B	17 x 11
	11 x 17
ANSI C	17 x 22
ANSI D	22 x 34
ANSI E	34 x 44

Paper sizes, US

Letter	8.5 x 11
Legal	8.5 x 14
Junior legal	8.0 x 5.0
Statement	5.5 x 8.5
Executive	7.25 x 10.5
Quarto	8.46 x 10.8
Folio	8.5 x 13
Ledger, tabloid	11 x 17
Foolscap	13.5 x 17

Basic ream sizes, US

Paper Type	Paper Size
Bond, writing, ledger	17 x 22
Manuscript cover	18 x 31
Blotting	19 x 24
Box cover	20 x 24
Cover	20 x 26
Bristol and tag	22.5 x 28.5
Tissue	24 x 36
Newsprint	24 x 36
Hanging, waxing, bag, etc.	24 x 36
Book, text, offset	25 x 38
Index bristol	25.5 x 30.5
Paperboard (all types)	12 x 12

Sheath sizes, US

Standard	
Business commercial	4.13 x 95
Monarch	3.88 x 7.5
Mini-lope	3.63 x 2.13

Credit card size, US

3.370 x 2.125 in
3.375 x 2.125 in

<u>1.5 Surface finishing</u> There are different finishing techniques to enhance print products. A varnish applied to the paper surface will make paper glossy and intensify its color effect. This optical effect makes the product appear more luxurious. By applying a finish, such as a partial varnish, or by embossing, an effect is created which is meant to attract the attention and make the viewer want to touch it and buy it.

Product packaging is a good example of the application of finishing techniques for specific markets. Products generally fare better if their packaging is appealing. A finish can elevate a product from the masses, making it appear unique and no longer interchangeable. This effect suggests to the user that the product is high quality. Effects such as relief-like embossing, special print lacquers, and glitter foil are often applied, as are inks with pearl luster or sparkle effects. Printing special gold or silver inks is not exactly surface finishing, but it serves the same purpose. Silver ink may also be mixed with other ink colors to produce metallic colors.

Apart from its optical effects, surface finishing is also applied to protect against wear and to preserve the paper. A coat of varnish protects against scratch marks that would otherwise be noticeable during further processing where the ink has been applied. A coating also prevents certain products, such as packages or labels, from becoming moist. The same holds true for surface dirt due to oils and fats, where a varnished finish is used on packets, menus, and so forth. Even metallic paints are often sealed with a varnish coating. Absolute protection against moisture is only possible using film-laminated material, short of using foil or glass packaging.

Finishing techniques should be used sparingly because they become less effective if they are overused. The following selection of surface finishes shows which techniques are commonly used, what their characteristics are, and what they are normally used for.

Print varnishing

In print varnishing, a transparent coat of varnish is applied to the already printed sheet. A general distinction is made between varnish for effect and for protection. In the latter, a sheet of paper is entirely varnished, leaving it rub-proof while brightening colors and making them more lightfast. Varnishing for effect entails varnishing the paper in certain places only, hence it is called spot varnishing. As a rule it improves paper gloss. Matte varnish, on the other hand, is usually applied to make paper more rub-proof, but it is sometimes used for an optical effect on shiny surfaces. One particular effect occurs when a motif is exclusively varnished and not printed, meaning it can only be faintly recognized. Print varnishing is often applied to logos and headlines. These are printed first and then coated. Shadow varnishing offers the added possibility of screening the spot varnishes, depending on image density.

In the end a varnish coating makes processing the print material easier. For instance, in sheet offset, the sheets are dusted with a powder to aid the drying process. The powder can soil the processing machines. Varnished sheets, however, may be stacked in the delivery using little or no powder, meaning that sheets can be processed faster and with fewer problems.

Print varnish is applied using either the inking unit or a special varnishing unit of the offset machine. In general, a distinction is made between oilprint varnish, dispersion varnish, and UV varnish. It is important to note that all print varnishes alter the ink's color tone to some degree. In many cases it is wise to do a proof print.

Oilprint varnish

In principle, oilprint varnish is colorless offset ink. It is applied in the printing machine and dried by absorption and oxidation. High-gloss varnish is mostly used to emphasize ink gloss, while matte and semi-matte are used for special matte effects. Oilprint varnishing can turn yellow, although the optical effect is relatively small due to the thinness of the coating.

Dispersion varnish

Due to its relatively thick coating, dispersion varnish has a strong optical effect and is highly protective. It is water-based and dries very quickly when the water evaporates. It has to be applied using a special varnishing unit in the printing machine. It is odorless and does not turn yellow. Colorless dispersion varnish is available as matte, semi-matte, high-gloss, and finishing varnish, while colored varnish is available in silver, gold, and Iriodin. Iriodin is a pearl luster pigment in different colors that changes color depending on the viewer's angle and produces a silky shimmer, sparkle or glittery effect, depending on its size. The thicker the varnish coating, the stronger the effect becomes.

UV varnish

UV radiation gives this varnish a rub-proof, high-gloss, or matte surface within seconds that can hardly be distinguished from laminated film. It is faster to process, durable and clearly enhances brightness and color depth. It can be applied both in-line using the printing machine varnishing unit, and off-line using special varnishing machines. Its relatively thick coating means that its gloss effect is generally higher than dispersion varnish.

Nitro varnishing

As opposed to print varnishing, nitro varnishing is exclusively carried out by specialists without using printing machines. The coating is thicker than print varnishing. This gives it a stronger effect and makes it relatively rub- and scratch-proof. This solvent-containing varnish loses out on ecological grounds, not least because similar results can be achieved with dispersion varnish.

Effect coating

Special effect coating is mixed with reflective or absorbent color pigments. These mainly include metallic pigments, such as bronze for gold effects and aluminum for silver effects and similar metallic color pigments, which are immersed in water lacquer. Good results can be achieved using pigments with pearl-like reflections. These kinds of coatings can be applied in unusually thick layers with screen printing, adding a special touch.

Spot varnishing

Spot varnishing achieves its effect by contrasting against the unvarnished areas, thus enabling combinations of gloss and matte effects. The coated areas are glossy and the matte effect accentuates the uncoated areas. Spot varnishing has to be applied very precisely, as even the slightest misalignment is noticeable.

Scented coating

Scented coating leaves a special sensory impression. The scented materials are put into the print varnish in microcapsules that open and release their scent only when rubbed or touched. This works particularly well if the paper and ink are as aroma-free as possible.

Digital print varnishing

Digital print varnishing is an economical and high-quality alternative to film laminating and print varnishing. It likewise offers smear-proof surface protection or a partial effect coating. A 3-D coating produces a tangible, raised effect. The effect increases with the opacity of the coating. A varnish with 50 percent opacity is thus less raised than one with 100 percent opacity. Using this method, textures with different elevations can be created.

Film laminating

A print sheet can be given a finish with a full-page covering of gloss or matte film or foil. This makes the paper shiny and protects it at the same time. This technique is often employed when products needs to be durable or are used a lot, such as business cards or covers. The film makes print products weatherproof, protects them against dirt and grease, and makes them extra aroma-proof and puncture-resistant. There are smooth or textured foils that imitate things such as linen or leather, and foils with granules that give them a texture.

Blind embossing

Blind embossing describes the inkless embossing of certain forms on paper. The embossing may be raised or depressed. The distinctions are: high-relief embossing, deep embossing, multiphase embossing, and relief embossing. The interesting thing about blind embossing is its shadow effect. Typical examples are old books adorned with blind-embossed patterns, or business cards with decorative blind embossing to complete the logo. It is important to note that the reverse side should not be printed, as the paper is distorted. Also, thick uncoated paper is better for embossing than thin uncoated paper.

Die stamping

Die stamping is a very high-quality method of print finishing. A steel engraving is made, which is coated with ink that is then wiped off, leaving the thicker ink in the recesses of the form. The form is then pressed onto the paper at high pressure. After that the coating is dried using infrared light. The thick layer of ink makes the printed image look as though it has been raised. Matte, varnish, and metallic inks may be used. Die stamping is used for the most diverse purposes. As it is particularly useful for fine lines and type, it is frequently employed for logos or headlines in brochures or invitations. Its high opacity makes it well suited to dark backgrounds.

Thermo relief printing

Thermo relief printing is a cheaper and less high-quality alternative to die stamping. Synthetic granules are sprinkled onto the fresh ink. The granules are melted under infrared light into a raised, transparent covering. Business cards are very often relief-printed.

Applying a partial surface finish

An all-surface varnish or film lamination does not have to be indicated in the final artwork, but it does need to be requested. On the other hand, a spot varnish or embossing, or a cutting die, is given as a separate ink form. The ink may be specified to preference. It is important that it be defined as an overprint spot color in order for it to have color separation. The spot color ought to have a logical name like "blind embossing" or "varnish." It is also important, as with cutting dies, that the finishing form overprints the objects underneath it, but does not print over things that must be left blank instead.

Here is an example to illustrate the point: A logo is to be printed and then have a transparent coating applied. When the logo is an Illustrator file, two

Varnish in Illustrator

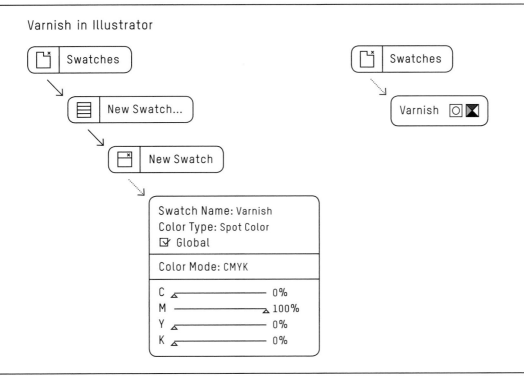

Hot foil stamping

Foil is stamped onto the print material at a temperature between 100 °C and 200 °C (212 °F and 392 °F) using a brass or magnesium printing plate. There are glossy or matte foils with or without texture, metallic foils, pearly foils, and multicolor foils. Holograph foil is often used to prevent forgery. However, hot foil is not available in many colors, and this limits its design potential. Foil stamping is often done in combination with blind embossing.

forms of the logo are needed: one form for the printing ink and one for the varnish. The varnish has to be specified as a spot color. It makes no difference in principle what color tone the varnish receives. However, it tends to look better in the layout when the varnish is mixed to look like the ink.

Both logos are then placed exactly over one another. The bottom logo is filled with ink, for example magenta and yellow, while the top logo has the spot

Mixed ink in InDesign

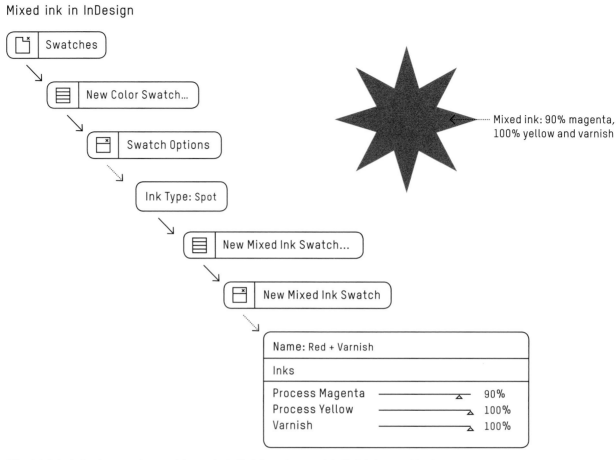

Mixed ink: 90% magenta, 100% yellow and varnish

Mixed ink in InDesign can be used to apply both ink and a varnish finish to an object.

color "varnish." Because the top varnish form is set to Overprint, the color of the logo underneath will not be canceled out so that the color separation for both logos will appear on the print. In the illustrated example, the logo is shown once in magenta and yellow color separations, and once in varnish color separation.

Alternatively, the top logo could be ink and the bottom logo varnish; what matters is that the top form prints over the one underneath. Overprinting is set in Illustrator in the Graphic Attribute Palette. If the logo or form was designed in InDesign, overprinting can be found in the Attribute Palette. This process also works for all other finishing methods.

In InDesign it is also possible to specify mixed printing ink. For instance, for a print varnish one can specify mixed ink that is made from a combination of printing ink and varnish. In this case, two separate forms are not needed; only one form would have the mixed ink.

Two forms in Illustrator

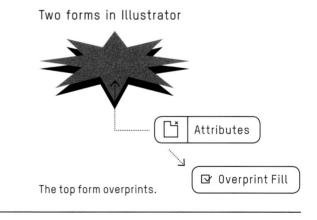

The top form overprints.

The color of the varnish should always be mixed so that its form is recognizable in the layout.

Notes

<u>1.6 Bookbinding</u> Binding the print products is among the last links in the production chain. It takes place either at the printing house or in an independent book-bindery. Binding multipage works makes them handy, protects them from damage and dirt, and serves as decoration.

Product groups A bound work may be made from many different materials. These include paper and board, but also cloth, leather, parchment, plastic, glue, sewing thread, and stapling wire. The products are accordingly diverse, and can mainly be divided into four groups: single leaf broschures, insert brochures, booklets, and cover bindings. These groups are distinguished by their binding. The brochures have a simpler binding compared to covers, usually with a paper or card cover, whereas cover binding deals with more elaborately bound books with hardcovers.

Single leaf brochure A single leaf brochure consists of several cut single leaves that can be bound with a pair of half covers. There is the spiral brochure with a spiral binding, comb brochure with a comb binding, ring brochure with a ring binder mechanism, and the cord brochure where the sheets are bound with a cord. The mechanics can be constructed so that it is easy to undo like booklets, or using book screws. These are useful for producing cheap goods where single pages are changed every now and again.

Insert brochure An insert brochure consists of one or several folded sheets usually bound together with a cover on the spine using wire or thread. An insert brochure is bound with saddle stitching. A wire saddle-stitched brochure is bound to the spine with wire, and a thread saddle-stitched brochure is bound with thread.

Booklet without endpaper A booklet without endpaper is an assembled block made of several signatures of folded sheets put together. The cover made of flexible card is called a soft cover. It is usually the same size as the inner pages and is attached directly to the book block. It can be wire side- bound or thread-bound, thread-sealed, or adhesive-bound. The block is bound without endpaper to the cover, which can be 2- or 4-fold creased and may consist of two half-covers that are stapled or glued together and back-stripped.

Single leaf brochure

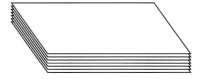

Insert brochure

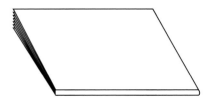

Booklet

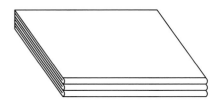

A brochure may contain single leaves, inserts, or multisection sheets.

Cover   Book block with endpaper

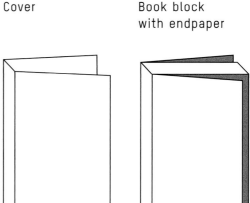

Endpaper joins a booklet block to its cover.

Cover binding

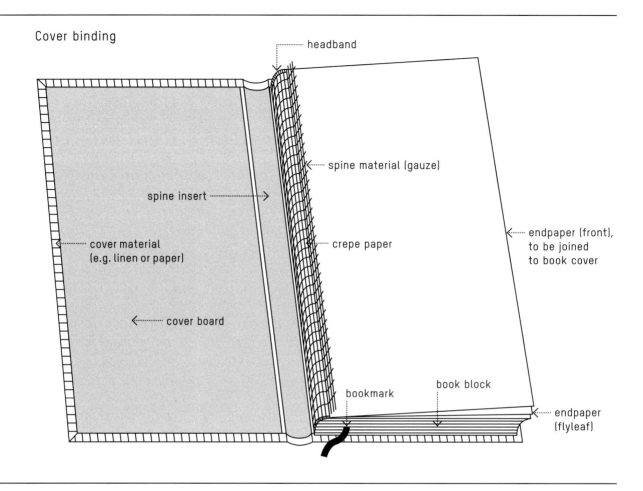

This group contains the simple brochure and the folding brochure. In the former, the card cover is placed around the book block while the pages are being glued. Paperbacks are bound in this way. The unique characteristic of folding brochures is that the cover is creased and folded down to individual cover parts, making it easier to unfold. The ensuing bulge close to the edge by the spine must be taken into account by the designer, who should avoid placing elements too close to the edge.

Booklet with endpaper The book block of a booklet may have endpaper attached to it. The endpaper is a folded sheet of paper glued to the first and last sheets of a block, and also connected to the cover. This type of brochure is either a cover brochure, which is covered with flexible binding material (soft cover), or a stiff brochure, where the endpaper is laminated onto board and covered with cover paper (hard cover). Hard cover booklets will often have a jacket made of paper.

English, French, and Swiss brochures
English, French, and Swiss are all types of brochure. The English brochure has an additional overlaying cover that has two stamped flaps on the front that hang loose around the tighter, often unprinted binding, or is glued to the spine. A printed dust jacket is sometimes pulled over it. The French brochure has the book block joined only to a mostly overlaying cover, and can also have a jacket. In the Swiss brochure the book block is not joined to the cover at the spine, but to a narrow adhesive strip on the inner edge of the last page of the book block. That way the book may be completely opened and lie flat. The book block is bordered with gauze at the spine.

Half binding A half bind is a stitched or glued book block that is mounted onto the case together with the endpaper. It is known as half binding because the binding is not composed of one piece and instead has a different material on the spine than on both covers. There is half laminate, half fabric, half leather and half parchment binding. In half laminate binding the cover is composed of two cardboard covers and a spine insert. The book block is cased in with laminate to the spine. Two half covers, often made of paper, are put over the cover boards. The book block is joined to the spine with binding fabric in half fabric binding, and with leather in half leather binding. The covers normally have paper or fabric half covers put over them. This is also true for half parchment binding where the book block is joined to the spine with parchment, and the covers are in a pair of paper half covers.

Full binding Like half binding, full binding also has a stitched or glued book block joined to the cover. However, unlike half binding, the covering paper over the covers and spine is all one piece. There is paperback, laminate, full fabric, full leather, and plastic binding. With the exception of plastic binding, the cover consists of two boards and a spine insert. Paperbacks are entirely made of paper; laminate binding is made of laminate, such as imitation leather, fabric binding is made of fabric, and leather binding of leather. The plastic-bound cover is made of two hard PVC sheets covered entirely by soft PVC sheets, or two board covers reinforced between two soft PVC sheets.

Binding techniques As opposed to newspapers or similar print products where folded sheets are merely placed together and not bound, there are numerous techniques for binding together many single pages or print sheets. In general a distinction is drawn between binding single leaves, binding folded print sheets, and making and finishing book blocks. Single leaves can be bound using various systems of binding or they can be glued. Folded print sheets are collated and stitched to the spine with wire or thread, or they are glued. In book production there are different methods for binding the assembled book block.

Swiss brochure

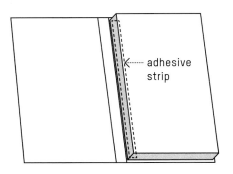

adhesive strip

Book thread stitching

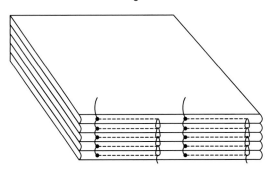

Thread stitching is used for high quality books or much-used textbooks.

Spiral binding Spiral binding belongs to single leaf binding systems. Here a wire or plastic spiral is screwed into pre-drilled or punched openings in the block. One has to take care not to have any text or design elements too near the binding margin, so that they are not close to the holes and covered by the spiral. The disadvantage of this kind of binding is that spiral causes the open pages to be misaligned.

Wire comb binding Wire comb binding also belongs to single leaf binding systems. Here wire combs are put into pre-punched holes on a block and pressed together. This kind of binding is popular for booklets, because small amounts can be bound quickly. Like spiral binding, the danger here is of print elements being too close to the holes.

Spiral binding

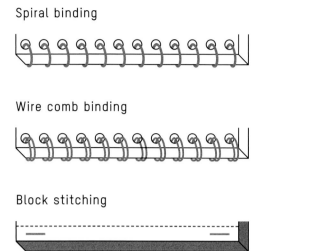

Wire comb binding

Block stitching

Wire stitching   Thread stitching

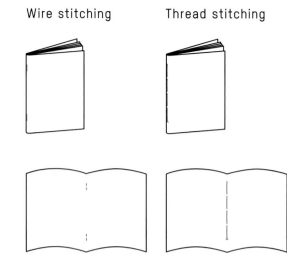

Block stitching In block or side stitching, individual leaves or sections are stapled together. The staples are close to the binding and can be covered with a card cover that is put around the block. Block stitching makes it more difficult to hold brochures open, but it is good way to bind notepads.

Book thread stitching Book thread stitching starts with multisection products being bound to a book block using textile thread. The individual folded sheets within a section are bound, and then all the folded signatures are bound together. This binding is subsequently reinforced by glue, gauzing, backing, and so forth. Thread stitching is very robust and good to use, as books bound in this way open out completely, unlike brochures.

Thread sealing Thread sealing is an alternative to stable but costly stitch binding and to the less stable but cheaper glue binding. The thread ends are melted together in the binding and sealed on the paper. The folded sheets assembled together are bound to a book block using adhesive binding.

Saddle stitching In saddle stitching, a single section brochure is bound with wire or thread through the spine fold. The product is known as a saddle-stitched brochure. It has no book spine. The innermost pages should always be somewhat narrower than the outside ones in saddle stitching. This effect is called displacement. How strong it is depends on the size of the work and the paper grammage and volume. Books or brochures with many pages may also have multiple sections processed together. Several sections of assembled folded paper sheets are laid on top of one another and saddle-stitched together. Booklets are usually thread-stitched.

Knot stitching Here the sheets of a single section block are bound with thread. A thread is put through the gutter margin and knotted. This method of binding is often used for school folders, as the thread allows them to be opened out flat.

Wire stitching Wire stitching is a kind of saddle stitching where staples are driven through the gutter margin of a single section block from front to back or vice versa. The resulting product opens very easily but not out flat. Wire stitching is relatively robust and is used a lot for magazines.

Adhesive binding Adhesive binding—also called perfect binding—is the most popular binding technique in use today for book and brochure production. This method is also known as the Lumbeck process, after Emil Lumbeck, who developed it in 1936. This led to routing adhesive binding in 1950. The spine folds of the assembled book block are routed off and glued. The book block is joined to a brochure cover or backing material. The cover can be bound tighter to the book block with an extra side gluing close to the spine.

Adhesive binding is used for single leaves as well as booklets and hardbacks. As opposed to any other binding method it allows any combination of different collections of sheets, so that a book block could be composed of 32-, 16-, and 8-page sheets in addition to single leaves. However, single leaves should not be put at the front or back of the book block, because they might not be registered by the machine or might slip during processing. If individual pages made of special paper need to be bound in a book block, it is advisable to speak with the binder in order to clarify their position.

The quality of this binding technique depends on the types of paper and glue used. Damage due to ink leaking into the binding is another consideration. Therefore it is good where possible to leave a blank area around the spine of fully printed inner pages. In general, uncoated papers are easier to work with than coated varieties, where the paper surface does not adhere as well to the glue. For books, gauze is glued in to reinforce the connection between the book block and the cover.

An adhesive bound product cannot be opened out completely, so important elements must not be too close to the fold. The safety margin to the fold should be compared to a similar product or measured on a sample. As a rule it is at least 5 to 6 mm.[13]

To take a practical example: if the side margins of a one-sided advertisement are to have the same width, the binding margin will have to be a little wider because a part of the page disappears into the fold. One must also know whether the ad will appear on a left- or a right-hand page. The position of advertisements can normally be booked with the publisher. In case the position should remain unknown, a safety margin should be set on both sides. This applies in particular when there are important design elements, which could include a dropped line with the agency logo. In a double-page design the binding margin must also be heeded. One example is a headline that goes across the fold. In this case, the words or letters have to be spaced apart slightly more than usual. Where

possible, any sort of bleed close to the fold ought to be avoided in adhesive binding.

If a bleed cannot be avoided, then the final artwork must at least include a fold trim that is slightly larger than usual. The reason for it lies in the spine fold trim, which depends on the sheet strength. Therefore an extra bleed in the spine of 2 to 5 mm[14] is required so that a bleed of 5 to 10 mm[15] can be set at the gutter margin. For the sake of simplicity, publishers and printers usually request the larger bleed for all pages.

The cover design has to take into account not only the front and back but also the spine. The width of the spine depends on the amount of pages and the paper weight and volume. There is a formula for calculating the thickness of a book block: (paper weight/1000) x (number of pages/2) x paper volume. An example sum: the spine width of a 64-page book block with a paper weight of 90 g/m^2[16] and a volume of 1 would be: (90/1000) x (64/2) x 1 = 2.88 mm. However, the spine width is a bit larger than the size of the unbound book block because the grammage of the cover that is bound

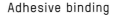

Adhesive binding

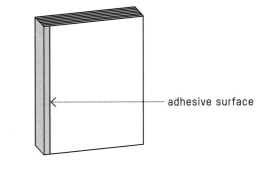

adhesive surface

around the book block has to be taken into consideration. If the grammage of the covering paper is between 200 to 300 g/m^2[17], add 1 mm to the thickness of the block to get the spine width. It is best to ask the printer or binder about the exact width, and make a dummy using production paper.

The thickness of the cover board depends on the number of pages. The thinner the block is, the thinner the board has to be, otherwise the block would not be easily pressed into the cover. That would cause a hollow or curved spine, which would damage the connection between block and cover. In general, the cover board should be no stronger than 350 g/m^2.[18]

The paper should also not be too heavy, as stiffness increases with weight, creating more mechanical demands. This can cause glue to come unstuck. Due to the extra leverage, paper over $130\,\text{g/m}^2$[19] should be bound using a different method. Something to watch out for in adhesive binding is that glue does not stick to paper with a synthetic coating or to certain inks and varnishes. The smoother and denser a paper is, the less suitable it is for adhesive binding. The best choice is machine finished paper up to $90\,\text{g/m}^2$,[16] with the adhesive area unprinted and unvarnished.

Book cover

A book is composed of several parts produced independently from one another. These include the book block, which has a casing called a cover, which in turn may also be covered with a book jacket. In addition, advertising and information material may also be inserted or glued to the finished product. Other elements, such as endpaper, spine material, head- and tailband, and crepe paper, are required. A bookmark may also be worked into the book block.

As a rule, the collated book block is bound with thread stitching. In industrial book production the subsequent book block processing takes place fully automatically or in sections in book production lines. First, the block is put through the crimping machine and pressed in the smashing machine. The fold is pressed down on both sides, making the stitching holes smaller. Then the whole book block is pressed to remove the air from the stitching and so maintain an even block width.

Afterward, endpaper is added to the block, the spine is glued, dried, trimmed on three sides, or rounded and pressed as required. The glue makes the stitches in the individual signatures form a spine shape together that prevents the signatures from shifting during processing. By allowing glue to seep between the individual signatures, it becomes impossible to tell where the signatures lie on top of each other in an opened book. At the same time, the glue has to be flexible enough for the book block to be rounded so that the book may be opened up to the binding.

After it is trimmed, the book block can be rounded off at the spine and front. On a straight book block the sections lie exactly on top of one another, whereas on a round spine the sections are stacked. Curving the spine is advisable for books in excess of $30\,\text{cm}$[20] thickness because otherwise the straight foredge will lose its shape after little use.

Other materials are used to strengthen the book block and to curve the spine. These include backing with gauze, which consists of a wide mesh finished fabric. A headband or tailband may also be inserted. This is a colored or multicolored ribbon made from cotton or artificial silk that is stuck to the spine and covers the top and bottom ends of the block spine. It is decorative, plus it pads a hollow book spine and creates a transition to the book cover. The top of the spine is called the head, and the bottom is the tail.

Furthermore, a backing tube can be glued along the spine. The tube is made from thin but firm paper and reinforces the spine and the connection between the book block and cover, thereby preventing anything from shifting.

Binding margin

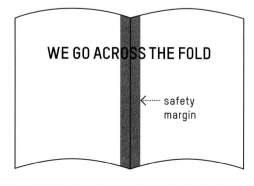

WE GO ACROSS THE FOLD

←----- safety
margin

PDF of a cover with spine

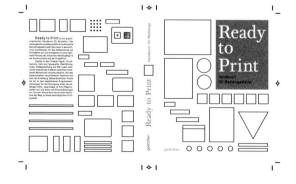

In the end the book block has to be joined to the book cover. This is called "casing-in." Endpapers are attached to the case, and the sleeve is attached to the cover spine insert. The book block is held in a device and has glue applied to both sides as it moves upwards. The book block is then pressed onto the cover. Meanwhile, the cover spine is either rounded or broken if it is a straight spine in order to make joining it to the block spine easier.

The connection is then secured in the pressing station and pressed into form. Burning-in is a way of stabilizing the book block form and creating a firm joint between the cover and the endpaper or back strip by using heat. The back- or lining strip is a connecting strip made of paper or fabric.

The book block and cover may have additional elements applied. These include different book edges, headbands, colored papers, bookmarks, and various decorative techniques. In principle book design knows few boundaries. Economic reasons are more often than not behind any constraints. Design techniques that have to be carried out by hand are falling into disuse and are no longer so important. One such example is old, elaborately adorned book covers fitted with a leather inlay that has a leather cover with a hand-cut different-colored leather inlay or leather mosaic, whose edges might be gold bordered. Gold leaf decoration is another time-consuming task; or a textured overlay, in which a decorative shape or type that has been cut from thin paperboard is glued onto the cover board and covered.

On the other hand, there are now so many finishing techniques used on a cover to help sell a title. These include the use of different varnishing or embossing methods, plus special metallic or glitter ink.

One can still find colored or gilded edges. Telephone directories, for instance, use edge stamping, where the edge of the book is used for advertising. Colored and metallic edges are not used merely for decoration. They also keep pages from yellowing, and protect the book block from dust and grime. They also strengthen the leaf edges. There are many gilding techniques that have almost disappeared today. Among them is graphite edging, in which graphite is rubbed on the book edges before being glazed. The use of colored paper is equally uncommon now. This can be used as covering paper for book covers or boxes, and also as multicolored endpaper. **(More about colored paper under "Colored endpaper" in the list of paper grades, p. 14.)**

Backing tube

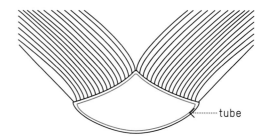

A backing tube is a tube made from thin but strong paper that is glued to the head and tail of the rounded spine. It reinforces the spine.

Straight spine

Curved spine

A bookmark accentuates the valuable character of a book. It is normally a colored cotton, silk, or synthetic fiber band, which is glued to the head of the spine. The little band is glued to the last page before the cover in brochures. For advertising purposes it can be covered on one or both sides with printed card, which must be inserted by hand.

Endnotes for USreaders

13 –   5 to 6 mm = 0.2 in

14 –   2 to 5 mm = 0.08 to 0.2 in or $^{5}/_{64}$ to $^{13}/_{64}$ in

15 –   5 to 10 mm = 0.2 to 0.4 in or $^{13}/_{64}$ to $^{25}/_{64}$ in

16 –   90 g/m^2 = 60 lbs book

17 –   200–300 g/m^2 = 80 to 130 lbs cover

18 –   350 g/m^2 = 130 lbs book

19 –   130 g/m^2 = 90 lbs book

20 –   ca. 30 cm = ca. 12 in

Notes

2. Printing Technology

The invention of the printing press by Johannes Gutenberg in the fifteenth century and the use of movable type are without doubt among the achievements that have changed our civilization the most. It was not until the advent of printing technology that the reproduction and mass distribution of information and knowledge became a reality—a milestone in the development of humankind. A world without printed matter is barely imaginable today. And even though the means of communication are in an age of digital change, the printed word and image still maintain their meaning and justification.

This chapter gives an insight into the history and present state of printing technology. It answers some basic questions about different printing processes, color reproduction, and the possibilities for quality control. It will also look at different printing processes and will explain which of these produce proofs, what the difference is between computer-to-press, computer-to-plate and computer-to-print, how colors are reproduced, what printing inks are really made of, and how to print a continuous gradation.

<u>2.1 Printing process</u> Since the first printing press was invented, several different methods of printing have become established. The main kinds are letterpress, gravure, flat, screen, and digital printing. All of these have one thing in common: a form composed of printing and non-printing elements is inked in order to transfer the image onto the carrier, be it analog or digital.

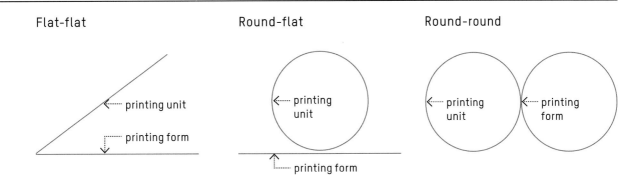

In general, printing processes are divided according to the geometric design of the form and the counterpressure elements of the printing unit. There are flat and round printing units and forms. The first printing machine consisted of a flat printing press that was pressed onto a flat printing form. Over time they found that by using increasingly round bodies the printing process could be sped up. So round cylinders were rolled on flat forms until the combination of round press rollers and round forms managed to maximize speed.

How press rolls and forms are used basically depends on whether it is a direct or indirect printing process. In direct processing the form carries the image straight onto the material, whereas in indirect processing the image is carried via an intermediary onto the print material. Accordingly, the print image has to be placed wrong-reading (mirror image) on the form for direct processing, while it has to be right-reading for indirect processing. Direct processing includes letterpress, gravure, and screen printing, with a few exceptions such as pad printing. Indirect processing includes planographic printing, with the exception of lithography and dilitho printing.

An important thing to consider when it comes to classifying the different processes is the horizontal view of the printing form: the printing elements are either higher, lower, or on almost the same level as the non-printing elements. Being the newest type of process, digital printing is different from analog methods in that it does not need fixed printing plates, seeing as dynamic forms can be used. The information on the plate can be erased, meaning that a whole new form no longer has to be prepared for each print product. Some digital print methods do not need a form at all, because the ink is sprayed directly onto the paper, as with an inkjet printer.

Comparing the different processes, there is no one method to favor in general. The type of product and the size of the print run are decisive when it comes to selecting the process, although it normally hinges on technical and financial considerations. One can print using metal plates at speeds that digital printing cannot yet attain, meaning that analog printing is still cheaper for large print runs. The classic, mainly analog processes continue to play a major role, although digital technology has of course become integrated into them, for example, in the shape of digitally created printing plates for an analog printing process—also called computer-to-plate (CTP).

One thing has changed more than anything with the introduction of digital technology: products can now be made more quickly. Digital processing has cut production time by doing away with or automating work stages. All of the different methods are geared around high-quality print products. Analog sheet-fed offset sets the standard by which other processes are measured. Nowadays digital printing methods are keeping up to speed.

On the following pages we will describe the different printing processes, what distinguishes them, and when they are used. We will also take a closer look at the history of print products and their typical features, plus the different printing forms used.

Letterpress

Letterpress is one of the very oldest printing methods. For centuries, rigid printing forms made of metal produced mainly books. The printing elements are raised higher on the form than the non-printing elements. The first letterpress printer worked in the previously mentioned flat-flat method. At this point we have to mention

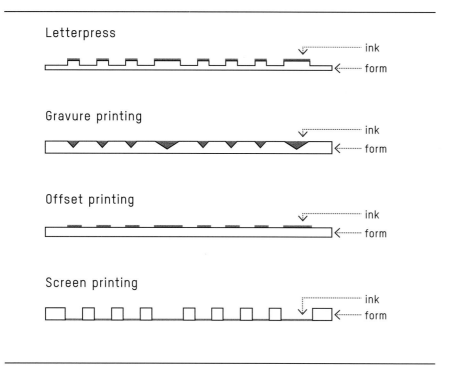

Letterpress
ink
form

Gravure printing
ink
form

Offset printing
ink
form

Screen printing
ink
form

Johannes Gutenberg once again. He was responsible for the spread of book printing around 1450. The first rotary letterpress printing machine was only introduced in 1865. In the early 1970s letterpress printing was largely superseded by offset printing. Letterpress is used very little today, for art prints or simple business or family stationery, for instance. One of the very oldest printing machines—known as the Heidelberg Platen—is still used to this day, albeit only for specific details in the later stages of processing. Some printing houses still keep one ready for scoring or perforating.

Letterpress book printing has one or two features that distinguish it from other methods: due to the high pressure during the process, a shadow of the print image is visible on the reverse side. Plus all the printed edges have a marked dark halo, which is particularly noticeable with colored letters or halftone dots in highlight areas. In addition, the halftone dot is very sharp-edged, exclusively surface variable and is found even in very bright parts of the image.

There has been another representative of letterpress printing for the last few decades: flexo printing. The first flexo printing press was unveiled in 1914. The printing plates are made of flexible soft materials—rubber or photopolymers—whose hardness and thickness is customized for each kind of print material used. Like letterpress, the areas to be printed are

raised on the form. Because of the flexible form, many more print materials can be used. Hence materials with a rough surface and even fabric may be printed.

Flexo printing was once used to produce newspapers, but it is now chiefly used in the packaging industry. Flexo printing allows up to 10 colors to be superimposed in one process, which is especially significant for package printing, where the use of special colors is important. After printing, the paper is either processed immediately or rolled up again and processed externally.

The relatively broad spectrum of printable stock is a special feature of flexo printing. It can be used to print paper, paperboard, or card, but also plastic, composite, and aluminum foil. This means that alongside packaging of all sorts, bottle labels and plastic bags can be printed. Flexo printed products also have a halo on the printed edges that can be even more noticeable than in book printing, although there is no shadow of the print image on the reverse.

Gravure printing

Etching is a gravure printing method that was already in use in the early fifteenth century. In gravure printing the printing elements are recessed in a copper-laminated printing cylinder that is then chromed. The printing cylinder is dipped in ink. A squeegee then removes the excess ink so that it is only in the recesses. These are called cells. These used to be etched onto the material, but later they were engraved on the cylinder using a diamond stylus. Today they are lasered into the form.

Because of this cell structure, full surfaces such as type are always halftone, giving the edges a sawtooth effect. However, the computer-guided lasers used today create very fine cells in comparison, so this effect is considerably reduced.

Letterpress print enlargement

halo

Flexo print enlargement

halo

Both book printing and flexo printing are easily recognizable by their halo.

Gravure print enlargement (diagram)

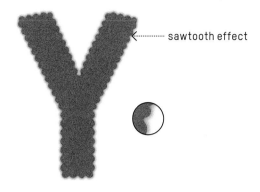

sawtooth effect

Gravure printing is recognizable by its sawtooth effect on the edges.

A distinction is generally made between illustration and packaging gravure printing, most of which is produced with rotogravure and only rarely sheet-fed gravure. In principle everything with a high print run from around 100,000 to 300,000 or with a very large page count can be produced. This is largely due to the printing forms, which are elaborate and expensive in comparison. Some typical products are glossy magazines, catalogs, advertising material, and weekly publications with a high circulation. As opposed to newspaper printing, gravure printing has the distinct advantage of consistency in quality during the entire print run, without any color fluctuations. Gravure printing is also used for wallpaper, gift wrapping paper, shopping bags, and flexible packaging made of plastic or paper.

Gravure printing is responsible for the biggest printing presses used today. Web widths of up to 4.3 meters are used for magazine printing, and up to 2 meters for packages. In package printing it is practical to use 10 to 12 colors, sometimes even more. Its chief distinguishing feature is its previously mentioned screened edges. Gradated transitions and slightly cloudy shadow areas are also common.

One subdivision of gravure printing is pad printing, otherwise known as tampo printing, with which all kinds of different-shaped objects may be printed. As usual, the ink is only in the engraved recesses of the form. However, it is drawn out of the recesses using a silicone pad and so carried onto the printable object.

All kinds of objects can be printed in pad printing. These include ballpoint pens, lighters, caps, remote controls, and stereos. As a rule, line elements and unscreened text are normally only printed in one color in pad printing.

Planographic printing

In planographic printing the printing and non-printing elements are on the same level. It can be subdivided into lithographic printing, also called stone printing; offset printing, collotype printing, and dilitho. In principle lithographic printing is the predecessor of offset printing, the most extensively used printing method today. Screenless collotype printing, also called phototype, is mostly used for reproductions of art prints and high-quality facsimiles in very small print runs. The dilitho process was only temporarily important for newspaper production. It was used for producing offset-printed newspapers on letterpress web machines, in which the print units were completed with a damping unit. This method was superseded over the years by web offset presses.

The playwright Alois Senefelder invented lithographic printing around 1796 in order to make copying texts and sheet music for actors easier and faster than it was with letterpress. In 1797 he built the first lever press, with the form made of limestone. Lithographic

Lithograph

Lithograph by Ulrich lithographic printers, Esslingen, Germany

Offset positive printing plate

ink
emulsion

plate

Offset negative printing plate

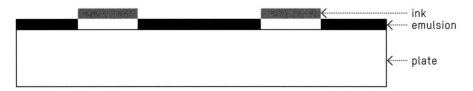

ink
emulsion

plate

On positive plates the lightfast areas are ink-bearing. On negative plates this is in the areas where light shows through.

printing takes advantage of the properties of water and oil. First the form is drawn onto the stone plate with a litho crayon. After laboriously stabilizing the drawing, the stone is dampened. Because of the crayon, only the undrawn areas become moist. Since water and oil repel each other, oily ink will not stick to the stone where it is damp.

This method was called lithography in 1803 in France. In 1826 Senefelder refined his technique and started printing with several colors. In the mid-nineteenth century the first lithographic high-speed printing press was built in France. At the time the method was considered good for advertising because posters could be reproduced relatively quickly. Even in the early twentieth century posters, advertising material, and picture postcards were still being produced using lithographic printing. However, seeing as the process was rather laborious, it was better suited to artists for reproducing sheet music, maps, graphics, and illustrations. Thus letterpress remained the dominant printing method for over 400 years. Today lithographic printing is hardly used anymore.

The breakthrough in photography at the start of the twentieth century made offset printing possible. In 1904 two Americans developed indirect offset printing independently of one another. After some initial setbacks, George Mann & Co. opened the first offset printing press factory in London shortly thereafter. In Germany, Faber & Schleicher AG in Offenbach built their first sheet-fed offset press in 1910, calling it Roland. In 1912 in Leipzig, the world's first web offset press started printing, developed by VOMAG. It was called Universal, and was commissioned by the Felix Böttcher Company. The famous printing press manufacturers Heidelberger Druckmaschinen AG and MAN Roland Druckmaschinen AG were both founded in the mid-nineteenth century.

For a few decades both letterpress and offset printing ruled the market, until letterpress started losing ground in the 1960s. The conversion to the four-color Euroscale was the decisive blow in favor of offset printing, which remains the leading printing method to this day. The patent for the first Heidelberger Druckmaschinen AG offset press was registered in Germany in 1962. In the early 1970s special newspaper offset presses replaced letterpress machines. The introduction of phototypesetting together with the use of compact repro cameras saw sheet-fed offset printing gain in popularity, due to its more economical form of production compared to letterpress.

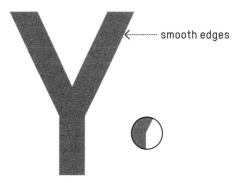

Offset enlargement

smooth edges

There is no halo or sawtooth effect in offset printing.

Offset printing exclusively uses the round-round process. Like lithographic printing, conventional offset printing utilizes the properties of water and oil. The oil-containing ink will only stick to the dry parts of the dampened printing plate. A light-sensitive emulsion is applied to the plate, which is usually made of aluminum. The light exposure and processing partially destroys this emulsion before it is rinsed off. The printing elements are ink-bearing, and the non-printing elements ink-repellent, and either positive or negative plates are employed. On the positive plates the residual emulsion forms the ink-bearing printing form, so that the oily ink will only stay on the areas where the emulsion has not been rinsed off. On the negative plates the residual emulsion is water-bearing, so that the oily ink only stays on the areas where the emulsion has been rinsed off after exposure. Since the 1980s waterless offset printing has also been possible, in which an ink-repellent silicone emulsion in combination with special inks replaces the use of water.

Nowadays offset printing uses 1- to 10-color machines, although 10-color machines are used comparatively rarely. A 5-color machine can print the four process colors plus a special color, without having to clean the inking unit in between. Some printing presses also have an additional special varnishing unit, which can give the print a protective or decorative coat of varnish while it is still inside the machine. Unlike inking units, it works like flexo printing. (See "Letterpress," p. 63.)

Computer-to-plate technology (CTP) is also used in offset printing. Here the plate is produced with a laser without the use of chemicals. That way misregisters that arise when the print is carried from film to plate can be ruled out, although these may still occur during the printing process.

Offset printing is generally divided into sheet-fed and web offset. In sheet-fed offset a sheet of paper is stretched over the printing cylinder, while in web offset the paper is fed onto webs from the reel. In sheet-fed offset, the sheet has to be turned after printing the front side in order to also print the reverse side. In web offset the ink is applied to both sides at the same time.

In sheet-fed offset, nearly everything with a print run of around 1,000 to 50,000 copies can be printed. Gravure printing is often used for larger print runs for economical reasons. Typical sheet-fed products include business stationery, books, brochures, and flyers, but packaging may also be produced.

Web offset is used mostly for media with large print runs and page counts, such as daily newspapers and magazines for which sheet-fed offset is too slow (whereas the print run of a daily newspaper is too small for gravure printing). By using paper reels, web offset can print at speeds that sheet-fed offset cannot attain. As opposed to gravure printing, in web offset the prints are directly processed to the end product, in other words they are cut and folded.

A distinction is generally made between illustration and commercial web offset (heatset web offset), and newspaper printing (coldset web offset). Because heatset web offset prints onto coated paper that is less absorbent, these printing presses have a built-in drier to speed up the ink drying time with hot air, hence the name "heatset". After the drier, the web runs straight into the folder, where the publication is processed into the end product. This may entail saddle stitching or adhesive binding. Sewing is out of the question due to the high speed.

Heatset products are recognizable by their slight gloss and smell of solvents, and the printer's ink does not rub off on one's fingers. The fact that print does not show through on the other side is a particularly relevant advantage over coldset when it comes to low grammage. Typical heatset products include magazines, catalogs, leaflets, and sometimes note paper in very large quantities.

Offset printing is typically distinguished by its lack of inconsistencies. Thus the lack of halos and shadows on the reverse side could be seen as an indication of offset. For a long time it was the case that bright highlight areas would break off and dark shadow areas would fill in. However, with FM screening this does not necessarily happen anymore.

Another offset method that is hardly used anymore is collotype, in which halftones may be printed without screening. It was developed in the mid-nineteenth century. The form consists of a light-sensitive gelatine emulsion on a glass carrier. The exposure, developing, and dampening create a kind of relief, which hardens in different ways during further processing. The ink settles depending on the degree of hardness of the gelatine emulsion, which is made possible by screenless reproduction.

Collotype prints almost look like photographs, and are recognizable by their distinct collotype grain. By using many colors—up to 20—works of art can be reproduced very realistically. As well as being good for reproducing art in small print runs, it is an art form in its own right in the form of collotype original graphic art.

Screen printing
Screen printing, or serigraphy, is perhaps the oldest printing method. Its name stems from the fact that the ink is always carried onto the print material through a screen. Since all screen printing methods use a stencil to border the print image, it is also sometimes referred to as stencil printing. The printing form is carried onto the material with the help of a stencil, while the ink is applied with a brush or paintbrush, a squeegee, or an airbrush. The famous cave paintings featuring handprints in southern France, which were made around 10,000 BC, are basically stencil prints.

The most well-known screen printing method is silkscreen printing. In ancient China, Japan, the Middle East, and in some European cloisters in the Middle Ages, the first textile prints were made using a woven mesh made from human hair and paper stencils. This technique was later rediscovered in the United States and developed further. The first screen printing machine was built in the United States in 1924. Starting in 1950 it was also used in Germany, albeit using a nylon cloth. Today either synthetic fabric made of polyester or polyamides, metallic fabric made of bronze or stainless steel wires, or sometimes even silk fabric is used.

Screen printing is subdivided into industrial screen printing, which is mostly used for printing packaging such as bottles or tubes; commercial screen printing for different kinds of advertising, art screen

Silkscreen printing

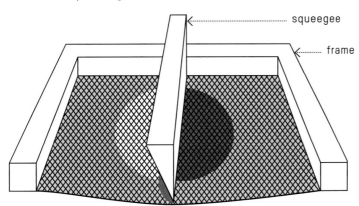

squeegee

frame

In screen printing the ink is pressed through a screen onto the printing surface using a squeegee.

printing, and screen printing for special processes such as textile printing. Digital technology has embraced screen printing, so that printing films no longer need to be produced. This is called computer-to-screen, or CTS for short.

In screen printing the ink is pressed through a screen onto the printable surface. The screen is only open in the areas that are to be printed; the other holes are closed by means of a coating. After being used the coating is washed off so that the screen may be used again.

The flat-flat method is normally used. If the screen stencil and the print material are both flat, it is called flat-bed screen printing. Flat-round and round-round methods have their uses too. If a flat screen form is used with a flexible print material that is pressed against a round, rotating cylinder, it is called flat-bed cylinder screen printing. On the other hand, in rotary screen printing both the printing form and the impression cylinder are round. The print material is stretched flat between the form and the cylinder. Rotary screen printing is often used for fabric, paper or plastic webs, textiles, wallpaper, and labels, but also for wall and floor tiles. Then there is also cylinder screen printing, in which round or other non-flat objects can be printed. Here flat forms or forms to fit the print material, such as semi-round forms, can be used. Plastic containers, glasses, and bottles are often printed using this method.

Of course, screen printing may also be multicolor, including process colors from the Euroscale. The screen may be relatively widely spaced, which does not look noticeably worse on products such as displays or flags when viewed from a distance. Opaque or translucent screen printing colors are used depending on the print material. However, the former make mixing the colors more difficult, so special colors may have to be used where needed.

Compared to other printing processes, many different types of materials may be printed using screen printing. These include paper, textiles, glass, ceramics, plastics, and metals. Textile items, such as T-shirts or caps, are printed using screen printing, as well as objects like mugs or glasses. Glasses are preferably printed using screen printing because the inks can also be opaque. Other typical products include CDs and DVDs, ballpoint pens, balls, toys, posters, displays and works of art in small print runs, signs and signage systems, vehicle dashboards, wallpaper, ceramics, and stickers made from metal or plastic.

The distinguishing features of screen printing are its thick, strong ink application, which is at least eight times stronger than offset printing; its often shiny colors due to the frequent use of special colors, its opaque inks, and the screen texture which is visible on the edges, making the outlines of the type or the halftone dots appear blurry. A disadvantage of screen printing is the high risk of moiré due to screen texture, plus the relatively long time the thick ink coverage takes to dry.

Digital printing

In the course of ongoing digitalization, digital printing established itself in the 1990s as a new, independent printing process.

The origins of digital printing, however, go back much further: the American Chester Carlson invented the copying process based on electrophotography in 1938.

Flat-bed screen printing

screen stencil
print material

Rotary screen printing

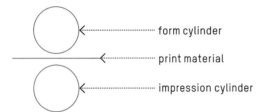

form cylinder
print material
impression cylinder

Flat-bed cylinder screen printing

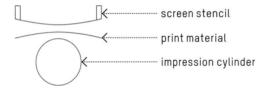

screen stencil
print material
impression cylinder

Cylinder screen printing

screen stencil
print object

Screen print enlargement (diagram)

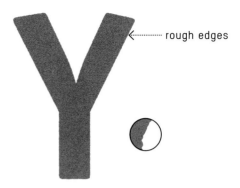

rough edges

When screen prints are enlarged, the texture of the screen becomes visible around the edges.

He created an electrostatic charge on a metal plate coated in sulfur by rubbing the surface. He installed a glass slide in front of this, onto which he had written some lettering. After exposing the metal plate to light, he sprinkled it with lycopodium, which made the lettering visible on the metal plate, thus enabling it to be carried onto paper. In the early 1950s the Haloid Company, now famous as Xerox, introduced the first photocopiers onto the market. The first color photocopiers were sold around 1990, until the first digital color printers became commonplace in the mid-1990s. The continuous development of this technology directly controlled by computer led to a new and independent printing process.

In principle, it is digital printing if there are no printing plates. Instead, the data is sent directly from the computer to the printing system, leaving out all intermediate stages, such as film or printing plate production. Hence it is called computer-to-print, or Ct-Print for short. This means that if a printing form is required, it is dynamic compared to conventional printing processes, as the form of a digital printer may be reused constantly because the data is erased from the form after each printing session.

The digital methods are: electrophotography, also called xerography; ionography, magnetography, thermography, and inkjet. The dominant methods today are electrophotography and inkjet, which we will look at in closer detail. Computer-to-print very often uses electrophotography, in which light-sensitive drums carry the image onto the print material instead of conventional plates. A slightly different digital process is called computer-to-paper, where the ink is carried directly onto paper. Inkjet belongs to this category.

Digital printing processes are also classed as non-impact printing (NIP), as opposed to impact printers, such as needle and type wheel printers, which require a more or less loud impact. In non-impact printing the print image is either transferred directly onto paper, or first with a laser onto an intermediate carrier, the drum. Special ink called toner is applied to the latently stored image. The image is transferred onto paper from the drum.

Digital printers are used in various different fields. They are available in all sorts of sizes, starting with portable models and tabletop units right through to entire production lines. Digital printing is especially frequently used when conventional printing is too expensive. This is the case with very small colored editions, proof prints, variable-data printing (VDP), or printing on demand (POD).

In printing on demand only as many copies are printed as are actually needed. In principle it applies to very small print runs. In variable-data printing, variable data within the edition is processed. These might be pure text elements such as addresses or whole letters, but also variable images aimed at the target subject. This way, products may be personalized or printed in different versions. VDP can also be combined with conventional printing methods such as offset printing, for instance if personal, variable data needs to be added to conventionally printed letters or flyers for mailing lists or competitions.

From a financial point of view, the difference between digital and analog printing methods is that digital printing is charged per sheet or page rather than per hour. Therefore costs for digital printing are less economical when it comes to large print runs, whereas with analog printing the larger the print run, the cheaper each copy is. Also, digital printing is still relatively slow, and the toner or ink is more expensive than conventional inks, so analog printing is used for large print runs.

Spot colors are seldom used for digital printing. Instead, the process colors cyan, magenta, yellow, and black are almost exclusively used. In theory, every color can be produced as liquid printing ink or as dry toner, but since it is laborious to do so and a certain minimum amount has to be purchased, it is not usually worthwhile for digital printing. However, there are digital printing systems that can print a fifth or sixth color.

Electrophotography

Electrophotography is a digital printing technique that is used for many photocopiers, printers, and fax machines that use normal paper. A light-sensitive material placed on a drum is given a uniform electrostatic charge. The print image on the drum is exposed to light from lasers or LEDs. The drum charge is dissipated in the exposed areas, so that the toner can be stored there. After this the image is carried onto paper. The toner is fixed onto the paper using heat and pressure, often with the addition of silicone oil. Then the drum is electrically neutralized, and the remaining toner is cleaned off with a brush.

Electrophotographic products are recognizable by the fact that the toner is usually very shiny and cracks when folded. In terms of color accuracy, some of these machines can still keep up to the standard of offset printing.

Inkjet

There are different inkjet systems, which are divided into continuous inkjet and drop-on-demand inkjet. In the continuous flow system fine droplets of ink are sprayed from a nozzle onto the print material. Before these droplets reach to the material, they are led through an electromagnetic field where they are given an electrostatic charge. The superfluous droplets are directed away from the material into a storage tank.

Inkjet printers cannot reproduce conventional halftone dots of different sizes, with the exception of piezo printers. Instead, they generally always produce the same-sized dots, which are distributed at random. This is called error diffusion.

Drop-on-demand inkjet includes the bubble jet system, in which the ink is heated in a special container by a heating element on demand only, so that an air bubble is formed which spreads out toward the nozzle. This forces out the ink. Once the heating element cools, enough ink flows back for the next use.

In a third, similar process there is no bubble to squeeze the ink from its container. Instead, what is called a piezo element spreads out on demand by using electric tension. The properties of piezoceramic materials are exploited to achieve the mechanical squeeze, as they alter their shape or volume in the electrical field.

The quality of an inkjet print depends on the ink employed. The products are often neither lightfast nor waterproof. On the other hand, the color range for inkjet printers is much wider than for electrophotography up to now.

Digital proofing

Today visually and metrologically high-quality proofs can also be produced using digital printing, meaning that analog proofing systems are losing their importance. Inkjet printers are normally used for digital proofs, due to the wide color range of the ink used. A proofing system has to cover the entire color range of the intended printing process. This color space is kept in an ICC profile with the help of a color management system and special software. That way digital proofing systems are able to simulate the various output conditions in combination with special proofing papers. In order to guarantee the color accuracy of the proofs, these must include a Ugra / Fogra media wedge CMYK whose chromatic values have to comply with the specified values of the reference print. The media wedge also counts as an independent and trustworthy means of control in legal disputes. **(See the section "Ugra / Fogra media wedge" in this chapter, pp. 93–94)**

Plotter A plotter is a special digital printer. Plotters are basically divided into pen, cutting, and laser plotters. They were originally intended for technical drawings or similar curve graphics. Pen plotters have ink pens that draw lines or letters of various widths onto paper. Here text is exclusively employed for labeling, for example in technical drawings. Pen plotters are rarely used nowadays.

Cutting plotters have special knives instead of pens, with which lettering or other line graphics may be cut out of adhesive film without damaging the carrier material.

Laser plotters replace knives with lasers. The letters or graphics are pulled from the film and may be used for company signs, construction signs, or vehicles. The films are available in many colors. ORACAL PVC film is very frequently used. Materials such as wood or leather may also be engraved using a laser plotter.

Large format printing Nowadays large format inkjet or laser printers are sold as large format printers. They can print relatively wide and long paper webs, which are sometimes several meters wide. In this case it is often referred to as wide format printing, or WFP for short. Large format printing, or LFP, applies to the longer sizes, although the boundaries between LFP and WFP are fuzzy.

Large format printers are well suited for the production of construction signs, shop window stickers, art prints and posters in small quantities, but also for proofs. Large format printers are sometimes also used for stage design. In principle, they can be used wherever particularly large formats need to be produced in very small quantities.

Computer-to technology Different "computer-to" technologies were able to establish themselves within the production chain during the course of digitalization. One refers to digital printing only when data is transferred to a dynamic printing form by a computer. This category includes computer-to-print and computer-to-paper, but there are other computer-to technologies that merely complete and simplify conventional printing processes, such as offset printing. These include computer-to-film, computer-to-plate, and computer-to-press.

Computer-to-film One of the first digital techniques was computer-to-film, or CTF for short. The films needed for analog printing plate manufacture are produced using a digital imagesetter. Imagesetters are controlled like printers. The films are exposed to light using a laser before being developed in the developing machine. CTF had its heyday in the 1980s. The introduction and spread of computer-to-plate technology and other digital techniques meant that it became limited to film manufacture.

Computer-to-plate Like CTF, computer-to-plate, or CTP for short, is not a digital printing method. CTP only produces printing plates, which are then used in conventional analog printing processes. Plates are produced with a laser and without using chemicals. Data is exposed directly onto the plate. This saves time and work, but also chemicals and materials. Thus for example, films that are required for analog plate manufacture do not need to be produced.

Computer-to-screen Here screens for screen printing are produced digitally, so that films are no longer required.

Computer-to-press Computer-to-press, or CTPs for short, is sometimes considered a method of digital printing. CTPs is a development of CTP, in which the digital platesetters are built into the printing machines. This technology was never able to break through because the printing machines stand still while the plates are exposed to light. Therefore this technology was too expensive.

Computer-to-print Computer-to-print is the first true digital printing process. Here printing plates are superseded, not just films. Electrophotography is principally used, in which a light-sensitive drum transfers the image in place of a plate, as previously described.

Computer-to-paper This also counts as a digital printing process. Computer-to-paper includes the previously described inkjet process, in which neither a plate nor a drum is needed. Liquid ink is carried directly onto paper.

Raster image processing When a computer is used in connection with a color management system a raster image processor, or RIP for short, is required for the printout. A computer is installed in front of the printer and changes the incoming digital data into the electric impulses that the printer requires. The RIP interprets the digital data and changes it to the raster image. Colors may also be reinterpreted by RIP if necessary using the color management system, as can the calculations for page imposition on a print sheet, or the processing of variable data. At the same time RIP acts as an interface between the user and the printer, enabling the user to check the state of the printer or to calibrate it.

<u>2.2 Color reproduction</u> In the chapter titled "Color" (p. 178 ff.) we will explain the theoretical foundations of color, functionality of color management, practical approach to color conversion, and different color modes. It is important to understand the technical requirements for color reproduction in this context. The following section explains the fundamental basics of print colors, screening, screen ruling, dot gain, and total area coverage. All of these points are significant when it comes to color management.

The aim for any reproduction is to be as true to the original as possible. This includes certain colors and grayscales. The quality of a reproduction depends on many factors, especially when it is color. For instance, the print colors used in the various printing processes play a pivotal role because their color spaces are not all the same size. The print material used is another factor because not every kind of paper is able to reproduce colors with sufficient brilliance, contrast, and ink density. In this context the kind of screen and its definition also influence the result, while the definition itself depends on the printing process used. Thus finer screen ruling is possible in offset printing than in silk-screen or flexo printing, for

Spot black

Small type (this is 6 pt) is still easy to read in black. Fine lines are in focus.

⟵ 0.5 pt
⟵ 0.15 pt

Process color (60% black)

Small type (this is 6 pt) looks screened and out of focus. Fine lines look as though they are dotted.

⟵ 0.5 pt
⟵ 0.15 pt

Process color (90% magenta and 100% yellow)

Small type (this is 6 pt) looks screened and out of focus. Fine lines look as though they are dotted.

⟵ 0.5 pt
⟵ 0.15 pt

Small or fine objects should not be screened if possible because it makes them look out of focus.

example, whereby offset printing also has a higher detail resolution. Another significant factor is the procedure for color separation because it has to be coordinated with the colors, paper, and printing process employed.

<u>Print colors</u> The principle print colors available for use are the spot colors cyan, magenta, and yellow. Along with black, these colors are described as Euroscale or process colors. The well-known term "Euroscale" is actually incorrect. In America this term is used for European offset printing. Strictly speaking, cyan, magenta, and yellow alone should be called Euroscale. Their properties are defined in the DIN standard ISO 2846.

In theory all colors, including black and gray, can be mixed from the base colors cyan, magenta, and yellow, with the exception of special colors such as silver or gold. The three print colors form the cornerstone of the color space that includes all the colors that can be mixed from process colors. Although it is theoretically possible to produce everything from these three

spot colors, in practice black is added. "K" stands for key black, hence "CMYK." Incidentally, the order in which the three colors are printed over one another is usually KCMY.

The addition of black has several advantages. For example, it is much easier that way to produce gray tones, pure black, and all other neutral tones. Adding black means that the proportion of chromatic colors can be reduced. This helps lower the expense and stabilizes the printing procedure, making it less sensitive to color fluctuations. Also, overprinting the three spot colors cyan, magenta, and yellow does not really produce a pure, rich black. This is partly due to the fact that the print colors do not correspond exactly to the theoretical spot colors cyan, magenta, and yellow, but are slightly dirtied. In other words, print colors behave very differently when printed over one another than they do in theory, which is why the sequence for overprinting colors also affects the outcome. This is why black is used to reinforce contrast.

If a certain color, for instance the house color of a company, cannot satisfactorily be reproduced using the four process colors, a further color will have to be used. These additional colors are called special, decorative, or spot colors. Spot colors can be printed with a 100 percent chromatic component, whereas in the Euroscale spot colors are partly screened, i.e., they are printed in different color gradations in order to simulate all kinds of colors in combination printing. Simulation can become a problem if a particular color cannot be reproduced well using these base colors, or if a printing process is used in which screening is not possible or would not work for other reasons. An example would be when the screen is comparatively widely spaced and visible to the naked eye, or when very fine lines or very small type is composed of several screened colors.

Print colors are composed of several ingredients. The colorants are color pigments and dyes. Binding agents (varnish), additives, and carriers are also required. Color pigments are solid organic or inorganic substances that float in a fluid carrier. Dyes are organic compounds that are dissolved in a liquid (solvent). Dyes have a higher color range than color pigments. They are very intense, but fade over time; therefore , printing colors contain a high percentage of pigments. While the organic pigments give color its tone, the inorganic pigments produce special effects. These include metallic effect pigments for gold and silver colors, and pearl luster and fluorescent pigments. Pigments need a binding agent in order to stick to the print material, whereas dyes often stick directly to the surface. Binding agents are usually made of resins dissolved in mineral oil. The use of additives depends on the printing method used. They influence the drying process, flow properties, and rub resistance of the ink. The carriers for the colorants may be thinners, such as mineral oil or solvents. In digital printing, one refers to toner rather than ink. Toner may be liquid or dry, depending on the method used.

The precise composition of any given ink is determined by the printing method. The ink's consistency may range from thin fluid and semi-fluid through to dry powder, depending on how the ink is applied, dried and fixed. In gravure printing, for example, thin fluid inks are required, whereas in offset printing viscous, semi-fluid, pasty inks are used. Moreover, offset inks are subdivided into several classes for different kinds of use. In addition to the standard and universal kinds of ink there is gloss and high-gloss ink for glossy coated paper, highly rub-proof ink, low-odor ink, highly pigmented ink, UV ink, film ink, and waterless offset ink, heatset ink for web offset, and coldset ink for newspaper printing.

In order to create an even greater color space in multicolor printing, more than four spot colors may be used for special applications. By adding the chromatic colors red, green, and blue, one can create a color space that suits our visual perception better than the more limited color space composed of cyan, magenta, and yellow. This is referred to as HiFi color printing. This means that seven colors are used, although black is still used mainly for type.

Pantone, Inc. developed the Hexachrome system, which extends the color space with the addition of the spot colors orange and green. The Hexachrome system is printed using five colors plus black, which also considerably extends the color space. Here each mixed color is only composed of three of the six colors. According to Pantone, over 80 percent of Pantone colors and nearly all RGB colors can be produced this way.

The Hexachrome and HiFi color systems are relatively seldom used because they require more time and effort than conventional four-color printing. Using two or three extra colors naturally makes printing more costly, and is only worthwhile for projects that require exact color reproduction for several special colors, or where a particularly extensive color space is deemed absolutely necessary for reproducing photos. In that case a special plug-in is required that offers a Hexachrome color palette for Illustrator, and enables the separation of relevant images in Photoshop.

Color separation A color is separated for process color reproduction into the spot colors cyan, magenta, yellow, and black. As previously described in "Print colors," all possible kinds of colors can be mixed from the three spot colors cyan, magenta, and yellow. In theory, with the addition of the fourth print color black, all of the 16.7 million RGB colors that are representable on a monitor can be displayed. In order to realize this, however, the colors have to be screened. This means that alongside the solid area of 100 percent color, halftones of a color are also printed, so that a color might only cover 25 percent of the area, for example. This is how different spot color mix ratios are created, from which the corresponding visual perceptions arise.

In conventional screening the dots more or less overlap one another and some are on their own next to each other. This creates a color perception on the one

Hexachrome color space

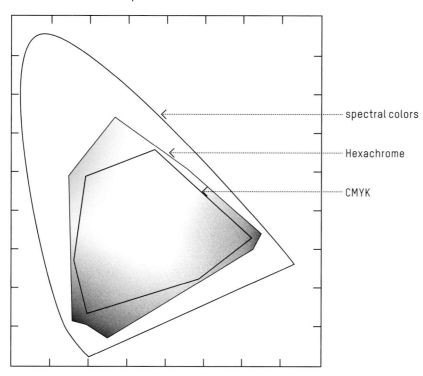

spectral colors

Hexachrome

CMYK

The Hexachrome color space is greater than the CMYK color space.

hand from the subtractive color mix due to the over-printing of the overlapping dots, and on the other hand from the additive color mix of the dots on their own that only merge into a color in the eye of the beholder. This is known as autotypical color synthesis. The additive color mix may only be perceived when the individual dots are so small that they cannot be seen from a normal viewing distance, while subtractive color mixing can only occur when the colors are transparent. Otherwise the overlapping color would totally cover the color underneath it instead of mixing with it. Therefore in subtractive color mixing, the thicker the ink coverage, the darker the color becomes.

The fact that the screened reproduction process is a combination of additive and subtractive color mixing shows how complicated this process is, all the more so because the dots that are next to each other in additive color mixing do not create the same color impression as in the subtractive color mixing of overlapping dots. Furthermore, colors used in reality are not optimal colors. In other words,

they do not correspond exactly to the colorimetric ideal of cyan, magenta, and yellow, which are mixed from the spectral colors red, green, and blue in a theoretical color triangle. For this reason the theoretically possible color range cannot be printed.

This is made trickier by the fact that print colors do not behave perfectly colorimetrically in practice or in the reproduction process. If, for example, one mixes red, green, and blue in equal measures in additive color mixing, the resulting color will always be neutral, i.e., white, black, or gray. However, these neutral colors cannot be reproduced with cyan, magenta, and yellow by simply inverting the RGB parts. Instead, standardized offset printing has demonstrated how a neutral gray can only be produced in practice by mixing the spot colors cyan, magenta, and yellow in unequal measures. Thus a neutral gray tone in four-color printing is always produced by using a higher cyan component compared to magenta and yellow. (See the "Light colors and body colors" section in the "Color" chapter, and in particular the illustration of a color triangle, pp. 181–182.)

Black composition
As previously explained in "Print colors" (pp. 75–76), the spot colors cyan, magenta, and yellow are complemented by black for practical reasons. There are several methods for determining the black component of a color. There is chromatic composition, chromatic composition with under color removal (UCR), gray component replacement (GCR), and under color addition (UCA). In under color removal all color tones are exclusively generated from cyan, magenta, and yellow,

Color mixing in screened multicolor printing (enlargement)

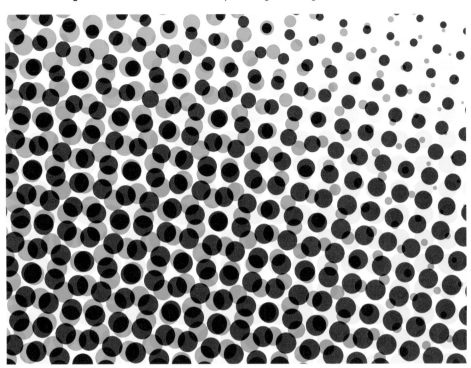

The color impression is created by separate and overlapping dots, which are depicted as circles here for the sake of simplicity.

without the addition of black. Black is only needed to give support to the image shadows and to improve outlines. Pure chromatic composition has the disadvantage that the color balance of a printing machine is hard to maintain. Chromatic composition without black is also more expensive because more ink is required.

In chromatic composition with under color removal (UCR) a part of the achromatic component of a color or image is replaced with black. In under color removal, colors are only replaced with black in the dark and neutral areas. The achromatic component of a color is limited by the spot color with the lowest component. In the case of the color brown, the achromatic component is determined by cyan, which has a 60 percent component. In under color removal of, say, 30 percent, 30 percent black is mixed in with the color. That way chromatic colors may each be reduced by 30 percent. The total area coverage is thus reduced from 210 to 150 percent without the colors looking noticeably different. Reduced total

Neutral gray

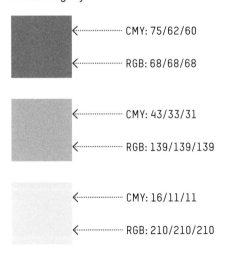

CMY: 75/62/60

RGB: 68/68/68

CMY: 43/33/31

RGB: 139/139/139

CMY: 16/11/11

RGB: 210/210/210

A neutral-looking gray process color is not composed of equal measures of cyan, magenta, and yellow.

Chromatic composition

60% 80% 70% 0% 210%

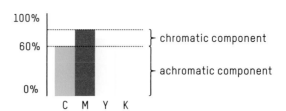 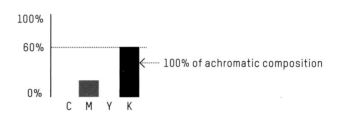

100%
60%
0%
C M Y K

chromatic component

achromatic component

Achromatic composition

0% 20% 10% 60% 90%

100%
60%
0%
C M Y K

100% of achromatic composition

30 percent achromatic composition

42% 62% 52% 18% 174%

100%
60%
0%
C M Y K

30% of achromatic composition

Chromatic composition

80/85/40/0 60/80/70/0 50/35/35/0

Chromatic composition + 30% UCR

50/55/10/30 30/50/40/30 20/5/5/30

Achromatic composition

40/45/0/40 0/20/10/60 15/0/0/35

Achromatic composition + 25% UCA

65/70/25/15 25/45/35/35 40/25/25/10

30 percent achromatic composition

68/73/28/12 42/62/52/18 40/25/25/10

area coverage has several advantages for the printer. The color balance is easier to maintain, plus the ink dries faster.

In gray component replacement (GCR) the entire achromatic component is replaced with black. In the case of brown, cyan is completely replaced with 60 percent black. As opposed to chromatic composition, where the addition of a complementary color darkens the color tone of the ink, in GCR the ink is only made darker by adding black. All that remains of magenta and yellow is the 20 or 10 percent chromatic component. Thus the total area coverage can be reduced even further than in chromatic composition, to 90 percent in the case of brown. The higher black component makes the printing process accordingly more stable. In GCR black is distributed over the whole tonal value range, and not just in the shadows or neutral tones as in UCR. However, less black is applied to the highlight areas than to the shadows, so that the black component does not rise continuously.

In gray component replacement with chromatic color addition, part of the chromatic colors is reintroduced to give support to the neutral shadows, thus reducing some of the black component. This raises the total area coverage again, to 140 percent in the case of our brown. This is particularly useful for dark colors and shadow areas if the black ink is not sufficiently dense. (See the "Bit depth" section in the "Image Editing" chapter, pp. 249–250) Adding chromatic colors makes shadows appear less flat. Thirty percent GCR is a variety of maximum GCR in which only 30 percent of the achromatic component is replaced with black. This means that the colors do not lose so much saturation and depth.

The type of black composition is given in the color profile. Since profiles are a matter of print standards, black composition cannot be altered on purpose. In the chapter titled "Color" (p. 178ff.) we will explain how black composition may be influenced in the sections "Separation options" and "Rendering intent." (p. 218ff. and p. 214ff.)

Total area coverage
The total area coverage indicates the maximum possible area coverage of the ink application in overprinting. The ink application influences the drying time and ink adhesion. The maximum permissible total area coverage should not exceed certain print standards, in order to guarantee a smooth printing procedure, but nor should it fall short of them, so as to use the full possible color range.

Separation and maximum total area coverage are automatically taken into account in a color profile. In the section "The most important color profiles" in the chapter on color, there is a list of current color profiles (p. 205ff.), divided into the different printing processes: commercial offset, coldset newspaper printing, and gravure printing. Looking at the list one can see that the maximum total area coverage fluctuates between 240 and 375 percent: in gravure printing between 360 and 375; in newspaper printing at 240; and in commercial offset printing between 260 and 350 percent. In commercial offset printing the low ink application maximum of 260 percent is recommended for heatset web offset on newsprint, and 270 percent for commercial offset on SC paper. On the other hand, gloss or matte coated art paper has a maximum of 330 or 300 percent for example, and matte coated art paper for continuous printing may be up to 350 percent. (Detailed information about types of paper are to be found in the chapter titled "Paper," for example in the list of paper grades, p. 13ff.)

Screening
Screening is used so that a print color may be printed in tonal gradations. This was not possible until Georg Meisenbach invented autotypical screening in 1881, which is still used today in a reworked form. Halftones can be simulated by screening an area into individual dots. Each individual dot may be recognizable as a spot, but because they are usually so small that they cannot be perceived as being individual spots, they merge into one tonal value in the eye of the beholder. When several print colors are used, the spot colors create a new mixed color.

The tonal value of a print color, and with it the color tone of a mixed color, is created by the size of the printed area. If for example, the tonal value is 50 percent, the halftone dots only cover 50 percent of an area. The printed area appears to merge with the unprinted, mostly white surface of the print material, creating the gradated impression of the print colors.

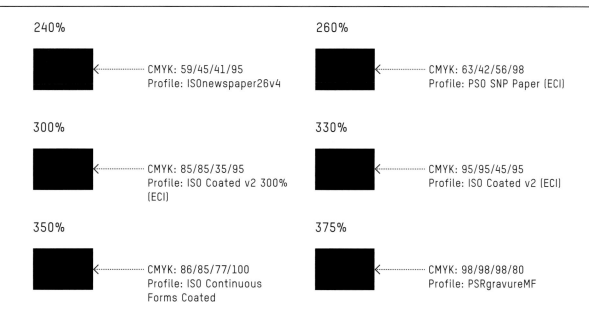

240%
CMYK: 59/45/41/95
Profile: ISOnewspaper26v4

260%
CMYK: 63/42/56/98
Profile: PSO SNP Paper (ECI)

300%
CMYK: 85/85/35/95
Profile: ISO Coated v2 300% (ECI)

330%
CMYK: 95/95/45/95
Profile: ISO Coated v2 (ECI)

350%
CMYK: 86/85/77/100
Profile: ISO Continuous Forms Coated

375%
CMYK: 98/98/98/80
Profile: PSRgravureMF

The maximum permissible total area coverage depends on the printing process and type of paper used.

AM screening

Conventional, periodic screening is called amplitude modulated screening, or AM screening for short. This is periodic screening because the individual halftone dots are always equally spaced. This spacing is defined by the type of screen ruling used, which is also called screen frequency. The respective light or dark impression is created by evenly spaced, differently sized dots. The previously explained autotypical color mixing process, in which some individual dots overlap and some are on their own, is what creates the color perception. (See "Color separation," pp. 76–77)

In multicolor printing, the screen angles of the separated colors are normally at 30 degrees to each other for round and square dots, although in four-color printing yellow is only turned by 15 degrees from magenta or cyan. The classic screen angles are: yellow 0 degrees; magenta 15 degrees; cyan 75 degrees; and black 45 degrees. Because a screen angle of 45 degrees is perceived as the least disruptive to the eye, this is given to the darkest color, which in four-color printing is black. The lightest color receives the most awkward angle of 0 degrees, which is the most likely to be perceived as a texture.

In two-color printing, the brighter color is printed at a 75-degree angle, and the darker at 45 degrees. In three-color printing, yellow, being the lightest color, is printed at a 15-degree angle, magenta at 75 degrees, and cyan at 45 degrees. In chain dot screening there are 60 degrees each between cyan, magenta, and black, while yellow has to lie at a 15-degree angle to one of these colors. The darkest color ought to lie at a 45- or 135-degree angle.

A noticeable moiré effect can be pretty much avoided by adhering to certain angles, although visible patterns may sometimes arise. A moiré pattern is a periodic texture. One pattern that regularly crops up is what is known as offset rosette. The finer the screen ruling, the less chance there is of producing a moiré effect. Thus a rosette is not perceivable from an 80-line (200 lpi) screen upwards, depending on color tone.

Another thing that can occur in the reproduction of fine patterns is texture moiré, for instance in certain textiles or metal surfaces with grooves. This can more or less be avoided by changing the screen angle where necessary.

Halftone dot shapes

Individual halftone dots do not always have to be round. There are different shapes such as round, square, chain, and elliptical. The shapes may vary within a screen between the light, middle, and dark areas. A fine screen has fewer possibilities for designing dot shapes.

20%   50%

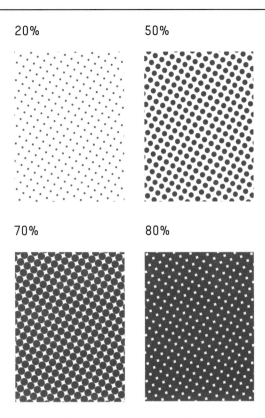

70%   80%

In conventional screening tonal values are produced with halftone dots of different sizes.

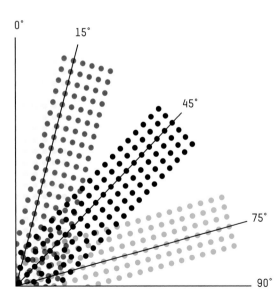

Classic screen angles of the process colors cyan, magenta, yellow, and black.

Rosettes in AM screening

Rosettes are a special kind of moiré pattern in conventional multicolor printing.

The basic rule is that the circumference ought to be as short as possible, because dot gain increases with the length of the circumference.

If they are big enough, all halftone dots will touch, which drastically alters the tonal value. When non-round dots touch each other, they can be divided into two different tonal values, which is called dot touch. Thus the jump in tonal value can be shifted from 50 to 60 percent area coverage, for example.

In offset printing, the recommended shape is the smooth elliptical dot. This screen starts in the highlight areas with nearly round dots, and then becomes diamond shaped in the midtones, then elliptical and nearly round again in the shadows. Choosing the elliptical dots in the midtones limits dot touch, that is to say the moment that the dots become so big that they touch in two places. This has the advantage of moderating the jump in tonal value brought about by dot touch, and making it easier to control. That is why the elliptical shape is also recommended for letterpress and screen printing.

In flexo printing (letterpress) round dot shapes are used. The dots meet at a relatively late point in time, since they taper, so jumps in tonal value can be avoided to a large extent.

Frequency modulated screen (diagram)

In frequency-modulated screening, equal-sized dots can be produced with variable spacing, or different-sized dots with variable spacing.

Digital FM screen (diagram)

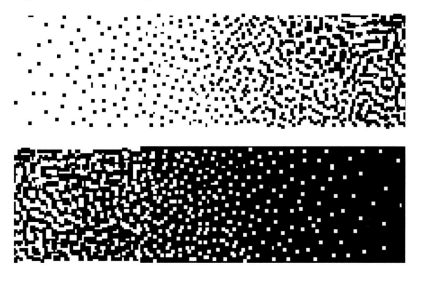

The digital FM screen starts in the highlight areas with small dots that grow into worm-like textures in the midtones. In the shadow areas all that remains are little holes.

FM screening

Another kind of screening is frequency-modulated screening, or FM screening for short. Here the individual dots all have the same diameter but are spaced differently. Unlike a conventional screen, where dot size varies, here tonal values are produced by changing the screen frequency, also called screen ruling. The higher the tonal value, the more halftone dots there are. If the tonal value is high enough, the dots touch until they merge, leaving only small gaps in the shadows.

Detail reproduction is better in FM screening than in conventional AM screening. That is why it is especially good for reproducing pictures. It is capable of reproducing very fine details of photo-realistic images. Dot sizes vary between 10 and 40 µm (micrometers), depending on the system. It is also free of rosettes, screen moiré, and tonal value jumps. Rosettes are avoided due to the absence of screen angles, and moiré is avoided due to the more or less random distribution of the dots. FM screening is also less liable to color shifts caused by register fluctuations. However, sharpness of detail is only possible when in register. There are some disadvantages; gradations and spots are generally harder to print, particularly using older systems.

By now there are also systems with which both types of screen can be used on one printing plate. This is referred to as hybrid screening. Using this method, image data can be mapped exclusively on an FM screen, and color areas can be transferred to the plate on a conventional AM screen. Or the highlight areas and shadows are produced on an FM screen, and the midtones on an AM screen.

Digital halftone cells

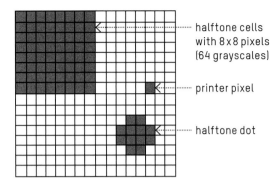

halftone cells with 8 x 8 pixels (64 grayscales)

printer pixel

halftone dot

The size of a halftone cell depends on the screen ruling of the printer. The higher this is set, the smaller the halftone cell is along with the amount of available pixels contained within it.

AM screening

FM screening

In FM screening the different tonal values are produced by random distribution of dots within the dot matrix.

Digital screening Nowadays printing plates or screen films are produced almost exclusively using a laser imagesetter. Laser imagesetters or printers can only process a certain dot size, also called a spot or pixel. In principle this unit is the smallest dot a laser beam can produce. In digital reproduction an individual halftone dot is composed of several of these laser spots or pixels. The available pixels are divided into several areas known as halftone cells. The size of a halftone cell depends on the selected screen ruling in relation to the printing resolution. The finer the screen ruling, the smaller each individual cell is and the fewer printer spots there are contained within them.

The higher the printer resolution, the smaller the individual laser spots are and the greater the amount of them that may be contained in a halftone cell is. In a printer resolution of, say, 2400 dpi, a halftone cell with a screen ruling of 150 lpi consists of 16 x 16 pixels, which allows 256 possible halftone dot sizes. In a printer resolution of 600 dpi and a screen ruling of 150 dpi, a halftone cell merely consists of 4 x 4 pixels, which only allows 8 different dot sizes. Within a halftone cell the individual laser spots form any kind of dot shape. This is the case with all computer-to methods and digital printing. (For more information on individual dot shapes see "AM screening," p. 82–83) The quality of halftone dot reproduction is directly connected to printer resolution.

The first kinds of digital screening were ordered dithering, which is pretty much insignificant nowadays, and error diffusion. The latter is still used for inkjet printers. FM screening has continued to gain importance as digital screening has developed.

In FM screening the printer or imager resolution determines the reproducible size of individual dots and the minimum space between them. The printable area is also divided into individual halftone cells in FM screening, although the size of each cell has no effect on the amount of tonal values that can be represented. However, there is always the danger of texturing in all kinds of digital screening. This is due to the even division of the printable surface into individual halftone cells, even if the dots are randomly distributed. By now digital screening has become so advanced that repeated textures are hardly recognizable.

Over the course of time different kinds of digital screens have been developed, with the aim of extremely high-detail resolution and photo-realistic reproduction. These advancements have also tried to overcome the disadvantages of FM screening that have already been mentioned, for example by only employing a conventional screen in the midtones that appear smooth at high screen widths.

Screen definition depends on the kind of paper used. It is determined by the smallest printable dot or smallest printable gap in the shadow areas. In many cases dots with a diameter of 20 or 30 μm can still be printed well, although in newspaper printing as a rule a dot diameter of at least 40 μm is recommended. Higher screen definition in conventional printing methods carries the danger of halftone dots breaking away in the highlight areas and of losing shadow detail.

Intensity modulation
In most cases, different tonal values in screening are simulated solely by different sizes or a different amount of same-sized halftone dots, in which the ink coverage thickness of the dots is more or less equal. In a few printing methods the tonal value of each individual dot may also be altered by changing the thickness of the ink coverage. Different tonal values of a print color are no longer produced merely by expanding the printed area but also by the height of the individual dots. In conventional printing methods this is possible in gravure printing because adjusting the cells can alter the density of dots. In digital printing processes this is also possible in electrophotography and inkjet printing. Inkjet printers and dye-sublimation printers are capable of creating halftones through different strength dots. Translucent pigments with different strengths are applied to the print material so that a single dot can have variable tonal values.

Thus each halftone dot may be printed with a different optical density, in which as a rule a dot can have five gradations from white to black. That way a much greater color space can be reproduced with the respective screening techniques. A relatively high-definition reproduction is possible in combination with FM screening. Known as halftone printing, this enables the reproduction of many tonal values even at a comparatively low printer resolution of 400 dpi, and so gives the impression of a much higher resolution.

Screen ruling
In conventional AM processes screen ruling indicates the screen frequency in which the individual dots are arranged. In other words, it defines how many are reproduced in a given space. Screen ruling is measured in lines per centimeter (l/cm) or lines per inch (lpi). Screen ruling definition depends on how precisely the dot texture can be reproduced. The finer the screen ruling, the closer together the dots are, the smaller the maximum dot diameter is and the less it catches the eye. The type of screen ruling used depends on the printing method

Halftone printing

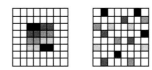

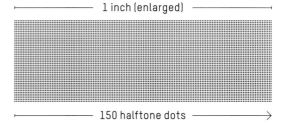

variable strength pixel

In three-dimensional screening, ink layers with different densities make halftone dots appear thicker or thinner.

150 lpi (enlarged) in AM screening

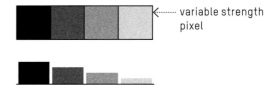

1 inch (enlarged)

150 halftone dots

Different screen widths in AM screening

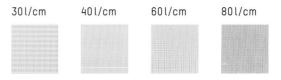

30 l/cm   40 l/cm   60 l/cm   80 l/cm

In a 1-inch section there are 150 halftone dots at a screen ruling of 150 lpi.

and the kind of paper. The individual dots and gaps in the shadows must not be too small, or else some of the detail in the light and shadow areas may be lost in print.

The human eye can barely see the individual dots at a normal reading distance at a screen frequency of 60 l/cm (150 lpi) on up. Therefore this screen is sufficient for simple image reproduction. There are up to 3600 halftone dots per cm^2. In high-quality print-

Maximum possible screen ruling

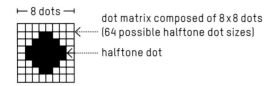

⊢ 8 dots ⊣

dot matrix composed of 8 x 8 dots (64 possible halftone dot sizes)

halftone dot

Printer resolution	Screen ruling
300 dpi	37 lpi
400 dpi	50 lpi
600 dpi	75 lpi
1200 dpi	150 lpi

Dot gain in print

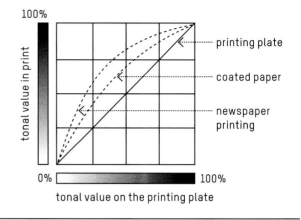

100%

tonal value in print

printing plate

coated paper

newspaper printing

0%   100%

tonal value on the printing plate

Expansion of dot diameters during printing

halftone dot printing plate

halftone dot print

ing the screen ruling is from 60 to 80 l/cm. A 70 to 80-line (175 lpi – 200 lpi) screen is normally employed today. High-quality art prints on coated paper should be printed with an 80-line screen at the very least, and preferably higher, because rosettes may be visible at that definition, depending on color tone. In newspaper printing the screen ruling is between 30 and 54 l/cm, and frequently at 40 l/cm. In gravure printing it is typically 70 l/cm, in continuous printing it is 52 to 60 l/cm, and in silkscreen printing 10 to 40 l/cm. These have an optimal appearance at a typical reading distance of around 25 to 30 cm, depending on the printing method. Large billboard posters, on the other hand, are viewed from a greater distance, so they are normally reproduced with a lower screen ruling.

In FM screening the screen ruling is only of secondary importance. The quality of the screen depends on the size of the halftone dots, which in turn depends on the printer resolution, hence it is determined more by its definition than its width, although the minimum dot or hole size also depends on the printing method and kind of paper used. On a high-resolution platesetter using halftone dots composed of 4 to 9 pixels, screen widths of, say, 300 lpi (120 l/cm) or 400 lpi (160 l/cm) can be produced.

The smallest size can be set at 2 x 2, 2 x 3, or 3 x 3 imagesetter pixels per halftone dot, which produces a halftone dot with a diameter of 20, 24, or 30 μm at an imagesetter resolution of 2,540 dpi (1,000 l/cm). These

fine dot sizes are particularly useful for high-quality art and commercial products. FM screening with larger dot sizes is also good for silkscreen printing, for example.

Continuous gradations A gradation normally consists of as many stages as possible between two colors or grayscales, so that there is a flowing transition where the individual stages cannot be recognized. A gradation may be used as a background. Photos have color gradations too, for example in images of the sky.

When high-resolution imagesetters, current programs, and PostScript versions are used, staged gradations are generally not a problem because more than 256 tonal gradations of a color can be reproduced. This means that gradations without jumps in tonal value can be created. However, sometimes gradations are printed with clearly visible staged outlines, particularly in laser printing, with its comparatively low resolution. This problem can be avoided by printing with a low screen ruling.

A certain amount of tonal gradations have to be reproduced in order to produce a continuous gradation. On a laser printer with a conventional screen, at least 64 different grayscales are required to print a continuous gradation from black to white. In other words, an individual halftone dot has to be able to assume 64 different sizes. In order to create halftone dots that can assume these 64 states using the available printer dots, at least 64 printer dots are needed per halftone dot, i.e., 8 x 8 dots per halftone dot.

The finer the screen ruling gets, the fewer spots there are available for depicting a halftone dot. This means that there are fewer possible states per halftone dot and thus fewer gradations per color. If, for example, there are only 6 x 6 dots per halftone dot, a mere 36 grayscales can be reproduced, which leads to stage gradations. Thus the number of possible halftone dot sizes depends on the screen ruling in connection to the printer resolution.

The printer resolution is divided by eight in order to calculate the maximum screen ruling that can be used to print a continuous gradation. Calculating the screen ruling in this manner guarantees that a halftone dot will have 8 x 8 dots, or 64 possible states. For instance, a laser printer with an output resolution of 600 dpi has a maximum screen ruling of 75 lpi (600 dpi / 8 dots = 75 lpi). The standard screen ruling of a 600 dpi laser printer is, however, 85 lpi, which is too high for a continuous gradation. An imagesetter with a resolution of 1200 dpi enables a screen ruling of 150 lpi, which corresponds to a classic 60-line screen. Most imagesetters have a resolution at least twice as high, enabling screen widths of 175 lpi.

Dot gain

An important criterion for preparing colors and images is knowing how much dot gain to expect. This is also known as tonal value increase. It is called dot gain because the diameter of a halftone dot is expanded. The tonal value of a screened color increases in comparison to the copy in print.

The more absorbent the paper is and the more fluid the ink, the larger the printed halftone dot area becomes in relation to the copy. Also, the halftone dot stretches during the manual printing that carries the image onto paper. The print image becomes darker, depending on the circumstances.

Dot gain has to be taken into account so that the ink is not darker than expected in print. In standardized offset printing dot gain is already taken into account during the printing plate production by carrying the halftone dots at a slightly smaller size onto the plate, so that the desired tonal value is only produced once they expand during printing. Nevertheless a certain amount of dot gain has to be taken into consideration. The printer setup ensures that the tonal value increase does not exceed acceptable levels. Dot gain is given as a percentage. As a rule, the indicated value is to be taken as an absolute measurement. At a dot gain of 20 percent, for instance, a color tone of 50 percent increases to 70 percent. The highest dot gain is usually in the midtones. At 0 or 100 percent, it is 0. In other words, from 0 to 50 percent it increases, and from 50 to 100 percent it decreases once again.

Allowable dot gain curves in color profiles

ISO Coated v2	A (CMY) and B (K)
ISO Coated v2 300%	A (CMY) and B (K)
ISO Web Coated	C (CMY) and D (K)
ISO Uncoated Yellowish	C (CMY) and D (K)
SC Paper	B (CMY) and C (K)
PSO MFC Paper	B (CMY) and C (K)
PSO SNP Paper	C (CMY) and D (K)
PSO Coated NPScreen ISO12647	F (CMYK)
PSO Coated 300% NPScreen ISO12647	F (CMYK)
PSO Uncoated NPScreen ISO12647	F (CMYK)

Dot gain curves: curve A: 13%; curve B: 16%; curve C: 19%; curve D: 22%; and curve F: 28%.

Dot gain becomes higher in conventional screening when the paper is more absorbent. Paper with an uncoated surface, such as newsprint, has a greater dot gain than coated art paper. There are five main dot gain curves for commercial offset print color profiles measured in a 40 percent control swatch: curve A: 13 percent; curve B: 16 percent; curve C: 19 percent; curve D: 22 percent; and curve F: 28 percent. In frequency-modulated, non-periodic screening, the kind of paper has no noteworthy influence on dot gain. However, it has a higher dot gain in general than a conventional screen, so it also corresponds to curve F. Since there is no shortage of possible dot gain curves in relation to printing and screening processes plus the kind of paper used, it is hardly possible to predict results without a color management system. If the correct color profile is used, however, dot gain is accounted for, so the colors and images on screen ought to correspond to the printed outcome—at least on a calibrated monitor.

This makes it possible for the user to produce predictable colors that are adapted to suit the printing process and type of paper. They make sure that the print does not deviate from the respective print standards at the printing press. The characteristic printing curve of the printing machine is necessary for creating the color profile. This measures dot gain. Frequent calibration and appropriate use of the printing machine is important for maintaining this print standard, which regulates dot gain in relation to the printing requirements. Certain norms are established for standardizing the printing requirements, which precisely define how high the dot gain is. Color profiles are based on these norms.

Notes

<u>2.3 Quality control</u> The quality of a print product is influenced by various factors including the printing method, ink quality, type of paper, and technology used.

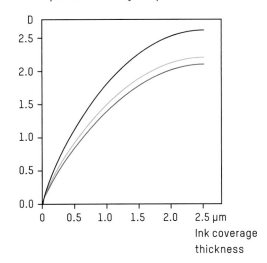

Optical density of print colors

The optical density of print colors increases with the thickness of the ink coverage.

To ensure that the print results meet the requirements of a high-quality product throughout the entire print run, the printing processes have to be constantly monitored both visually and by measuring. Certain minimum requirements for lighting and viewing conditions must be met in visual controls. Measurement checks allow the results to be absolutely objectively checked. These include color-measuring instruments and elements such as the print control strip with its various measuring fields.

Quality control includes checking color, resolution, register accuracy, and the surface of the print image. The optical density of the ink is measured, and halftone dot shapes, dot gain, ink trapping, and distribution of colors are checked. The print sheet must also be checked for any possible errors in transmission, such as slurring or doubling. Checking the resolution consists of making sure the focus and reproduction of fine textures are in order, plus controlling dot gain. Checking the register consists of making sure the halftone dots and print image are in the right place. The surface gloss, evenness of the ink application, and blushing of solid areas, also known as mottling, must all be checked too.

The measure of print quality is determined by customers, and also by certain industry standards and various guidelines. These include Process Standard

Offset printing (PSO). On the basis of ISO 12647-2 a printing house can obtain a bvdm/Fogra certificate for four-color printing. The ISO standard 12647 covers several areas: 12647-1 determines the basics, such as parameters and measuring techniques; 12647-2 is sheet and web offset printing; -3 is newspaper offset; -4 is gravure printing; -5 is silkscreen printing; -6 is flexo printing (not newspapers); and -7 covers digital printing and proofing.

In addition there is also the Media Standard Print, which contains the technical guidelines for data, proofs, and films, and which is published by the German Printing and Media Industries Federation (bvdm). These guidelines help improve cooperation between customers, prepress service providers, and printers.

Color measurement

Ink density is very important in relation to quality control and color measurement. It is the measure of the perceived brightness of a color or D. The thicker the ink coverage, the less light it reflects. Mathematically speaking, the ink density is the logarithm of the radiance factor, that is to say, the logarithm of the opacity of a body.

The formula is $D = \log(1/\text{radiance})$. The logarithm was chosen because the pure radiance factor does not correspond to human brightness perception, which is also nonlinear. The radiance factor in turn indicates the amount of light that is reflected back off a body, "b" for short. It is measured by dividing the amount of reflected light by the amount of emitted light.

The optical density of the colors is continuously measured with a densitometer. It is used to check different areas on the print sheet and on the color control strip. The density must not exceed or fall short of certain set values. Density depends on the ink application, the amount of which is controlled and corrected by the printer. Therefore ink density is also a measure of the ink coverage and dye concentration. In addition to optical density, a densitometer also measures dot gain and relative print contrast. These measurements are taken during the printing process by constantly checking the print sheet and the control strip. The control strips are printed along the entire print sheets. The individual swatches are positioned so that they can be allocated to specific areas of the ink duct in the printing machine inking unit. That way the relevant color areas of the printing machine can be targeted and controlled. In addition to spot checks using a hand densitometer, fully automatic checks are carried out with densitometric scanning units. These were developed mainly for offset printing. If irregularities occur, the printing machine has to be adjusted accordingly and monitored throughout the entire print run to ensure consistency.

<u>Print control strip</u> Print control strips are printed across the entire sheet width to check the print result. Each strip contains various color measurement swatches and control swatches. A densitometer can check both the print image and the halftone and solid areas of the control strip for optical density and gray balance. The control strip allows the colors to be judged neutrally, seeing as other colors on the print sheet sometimes outshine the measuring signal. Control swatches are special line swatches next to the color measuring swatches that can determine printing transmission errors.

Ink density and dot gain may be measured in the halftone swatches of the control strip. A change in the halftone dot diameters leads to a change in the tonal value, which in turn leads to color shift. The printer ensures that dot gain stays within acceptable boundaries by measuring the optically effective area coverage of these halftone swatches. There is a difference between the optically effective area coverage and the actual area coverage, because the halftone dots trap some of the reflected light beams. This is due to the fact that light does not reflect back at the same angle it hits the paper. This makes the halftone dots appear bigger than they really are.

The density of base colors and spot colors may be measured both individually and in overprinting in the spot color swatches. A densitometer checks for coloration. The three-color overprinting swatch is next to 100% black, and is for monitoring ink application.

The gray balance swatches make sure that there is no unwanted color cast in print. A particular combination of uneven spot colors must produce a neutral gray when printed over one another. That is why there are one or several screened grayscale swatches on the color control strip that are composed either of all black, or the spot colors cyan, magenta, and yellow. The swatches ought to appear as evenly gray as possible.

Certain transmission errors may be identified using the control swatches. These include dot slur and doubling of the print image. Dot slur is when the shape of a halftone dot is changed during printing so that a circle becomes oval, for example. Doubling is when

Different swatches on a print control strip

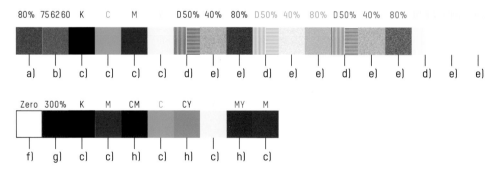

a) 80% true gray
b) gray balance swatch composed of 75% cyan, 62% magenta, and 60% yellow to monitor the color balance
c) spot color swatch to monitor coloration
d) dot slur and doubling swatches to monitor cylinder progression
e) halftone swatches to monitor dot gain
f) paper color
g) three-color overprint swatches to monitor trapping
h) two-color overprint swatches

Control fields for errors in transmission

correct

doubling

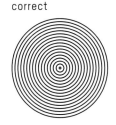 

dot slur

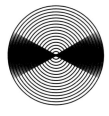

D-field

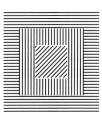

Halftone swatches

40% 80% 40% 80% 40% 80% 40% 80%

One-, two-, and three-color spot swatches

K   M   CM   C   CY   Y   MY   M   300%

Gray balance swatch next to 80% true gray

80% 75 62 60

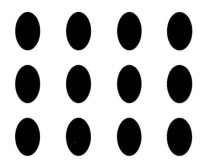

Transmission error: dot slur (diagram)

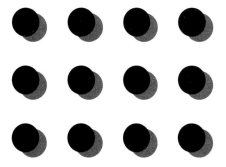

Transmission error: doubling (diagram)

Dot slur and doubling are typical printing transmission errors.

the print image is printed twice so that a halftone dot has a slightly offset and lighter shadow. The D-swatch must appear evenly bright in order to avoid dot slur or doubling.

Ugra/Fogra media wedge

The Ugra/Fogra media wedge is a proof control medium recognized worldwide. This control strip, which must be included on a proof, is for checking true-color proofs. It consists of a TIFF or EPS file. There are several color and grayscale swatches on the wedge that can be measured colorimetrically. This guarantees that the colors on the proof conform to the respective print standards.

There are 72 measuring swatches in total on the 3.0 version wedge from 2008. The vast majority are color swatches composed of spot colors and other colors that can be critical for printing. In addition the paper color and two gray wedges are also on the test strip, although the upper parts of the grayscales consist solely of black, while the lower parts are composed of cyan, magenta, and yellow.

Ugra/Fogra digital print scale

The Ugra/Fogra digital print scale is a process control tool for digital printing. The test image includes an information panel, type swatch, resolution panel, line panel, checkered panels, fine dot swatches, halftone wedge, and registration swatch.

Altona Test Suite[1]

The Altona Test Suite was released by the bvdm, the European Color Initiative, Empa/Ugra, and Fogra. It contains various PDF files, which, in combination with reference prints can test the color accuracy of different output devices, proof printers, and digital and conventional printing systems in particular. The reference prints have to be produced very carefully and comply with various requirements according to the ISO standard 12647-2.

The suite consists of Altona Measure, Altona Visual, and Altona Technical. Altona Measure is composed of several color swatches composed of single- or combination-printed Euroscale colors that can be measured colorimetrically. Altona Visual is for visually checking the PDF/X-3 compatibility and color accuracy of an output device. The test file contains CMYK and spot colors, as well as different device-independent colors, such as RGB or CIE Lab. These are recalculated in a color management system into the respective print colors. Altona Technical is for checking color overprinting. There are also several formats for fonts, such as TrueType or Type 1, 2, or 3.[2]

Media Standard Print

The Ugra/Fogra media wedge and the Altona Test Suite are part of the Media Standard Print, which is released by the German Printing and Media Industries Federation (bvdm). It defines the technical guidelines for files, proof prints, and films, and contains the international standards for print. These standards help enable the smooth exchange of files and proof prints between customers, prepress companies, and printers. They indicate what color formats or ICC profiles should be used, for example, and or how files and proofs should be delivered to the printing press, and describe how the contents of such files should be prepared. The Media Standard Print may be downloaded as a PDF file for free from the bvdm website at www.bvdm-online.de. The Ugra/Fogra media wedge and the Altona Test Suite are not free of charge, however.[3]

Endnotes for USreaders

1 – Altona Test Suite is also available in the United States.

2 – The Printing Industries Proof Comparator is a tool for evaluating the accuracy and consistency of proofs. One can calibrate and control device reproduction using the Proof Comparator. It can also be used on the print sheet to check that the proof matches the print result.

3 – The Printing Industries Plate Control Target is a test image for diagnosing, calibrating, and monitoring the platemaking process. It can also be used for digital proofing and digital printing systems. The target helps improve consistency and is used for measuring pixel resolution, directional effects, and the minimum/maximum number of dots. The target includes an information panel, star targets, line panels, checkered panels, fine dot swatches, and a halftone wedge.

Notes

3. Composition and Typography

As a design process, typography is an important means of communication that emphasizes the meaning of a printed work with its type, pictures, lines, and backgrounds. Words give books meaning but professional typesetting makes them respectable. Typography helps define the tone and statement of the written word. It helps visualize the purpose of a sentence before the words have been read.

Elucidation, seduction, and punishment, for example, are three totally distinct intentions that have to be set differently to each other. The consumer reacts to that, whether consciously or not, and either reads on or not. He either believes or has doubts. When typography corresponds to content and aims for optimal readability, then the path is cleared for successful communication.

Composition and typography are important tools for graphic, media, and layout designers. They include calculating the type area; constructing the grid layout; selecting the typeface; determining the type size, line and letter spacing, type of composition, and alignment; optimizing hyphenation, adhering to typographic rules, and designing fine typographical subtleties. There are a few important basic rules for typography and composition; they are described on the following pages.

3.1 Grid layout A grid is one of the fundamental elements of layout design. The choice of type area, column width, or vertical alignment is not arbitrary. They are aligned around a grid divided by vertical and horizontal lines. This opens up the possibility of placing the design elements within a flexible yet fixed framework with clear rules.

Double-page grid

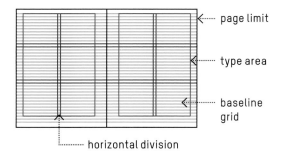

page limit

type area

baseline grid

horizontal division

Grid colors indicate the different sections.

A grid gives a layout order and geometric clarity. It makes work stages simpler, because the division of the layout into various sections means that the arrangement of the design elements is more or less predetermined. For example, in multipage documents everything can be positioned relatively easily and quickly according to a set plan. Pictures are only placed in certain positions and in recurring sizes. This structure gives the layout harmony. All that needs to be done is to work out a sensible sequence for the elements and to create some excitement where needed.

The grid layout defines the type area. This is also true for the baseline grid and the type, which can be structured with additional horizontal and vertical reference lines. The vertical division of the type area generally consists of a fixed number of baselines. Page width is an important factor in horizontal grid division and its division into one or more columns, taking body text size into consideration.

Type area The type area defines the position of the text within a format. The positioning of all other objects is usually in relation to the type area, although individual elements such as pictures or lines can break through the type area up to the page margin. Also, there are elements that are never arranged inside the type area. These include side notes and page numbers. The latter should only be in the type area if they are in what is known as a running page header or head, which contains additional information, such as chapter titles or table of contents. A header is described as running if its content changes during publication. If the content stays the same it is simply called a page header or head, and is outside of the type area.

A type area can be defined in different ways. Usually the inner, top, outer, and bottom margins have a fixed ratio, where the bottom margin is always somewhat wider than the top, and the outer margin is twice as wide as the inner margin. The latter only applies to double-page documents. In single-page documents the left and right margins have the same width.

Throughout the years various methods have been developed to calculate the page margins. These ratios guarantee balance in both the printed and unprinted areas of the page.

Traditionally, in double page publications there are three ratios to choose from for inner, top, outer, and bottom margins: $2:3:4:5$; $2:3:4:6$ for page formats with the ratio $2:3$; and $3:4:6:8$ for page formats with the ratio $3:4$. When the margins are constructed in this way, the type area corresponds roughly to the page format ratio. In DIN formats the page lengths have the ratio $5:7$.[1]

In order to calculate the page margins and the size of the type area in this way, one needs a certain reference size. The size of this depends on the available space, which is the size of the page plus the extent of the design. So if there is a lot of text or many objects to fit into the available format, the basic reference unit must not be too generous. If, however, the design allows for a lot of free space, the basic unit may be accordingly larger.

In single-page documents the margins are often the same size on the sides and at the top, but slightly larger at the bottom. This makes the type area appear calm and balanced. The ratio of the type area corresponds roughly to that of the page. The margin ought to be slightly larger at the bottom compared to the top because the elements on a page tend to appear bottom-heavy. If an object were placed right in the middle, it would appear as though there were more space at the top than at the bottom.

Should the designer be free to choose the format in addition to the type area construction, a different size ratio other than the DIN format would be recommendable. The golden section has a ratio of 5:8, which is often more elegant than the DIN format, for example. A slimmer ratio is recommendable for slim formats such as a 100 x 210 mm flyer. As a rule of thumb, the type area height should roughly accord with the page width, if the format is not particularly narrow.

Type area

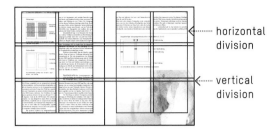

The elements are both inside and outside of the type area.

Page margins

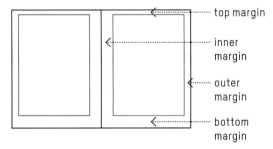

The page margins are divided into inner, top, outer, and bottom margins.

Another method of type area construction is the classic division into ninths. Here the page is divided into 9 x 9 horizontal and vertical areas. The inner and top margins comprise one part, while the outer and bottom margins comprise two parts. The type area becomes relatively small in this method. There are a lot of these classic ratios. Another one was by Jan Tschichold (1902–1974), the typographer and graphic designer, who designed the Sabon typeface, among others.

Basically, it is up to the designer to decide which method to choose for calculating the type area, or how large a unit should be within the ratio of a type area construction. Rules do not have to be followed rigidly; they are more of a reference point. There are always exceptions that justify breaking classic regulations. However, when determining the type area height, the line spacing of the body text must always be taken into consideration.

More than anything, what is important is that the content is placed in the available space in a pleas-

ing manner. If, for example, the type area of a DIN long flyer has to be determined and there are a lot of graphics and text in relation to page size, it is a good idea to set relatively narrow margins. That way the type and line spacing will not be too small, and there will be sufficient space for tables, if required.

Column width A grid also defines the widths of the individual text columns. The type area consists of one or several text columns, depending on page width. It consists of only one text column in narrow formats, such as DIN long flyers or advertisements that contain little text. Wider formats, such as magazines or this very book page, have around two to four columns, depending on page width. Even wider formats such as daily newspapers have around seven columns.

The principle reason for having several text columns is to improve readability. Very long lines of text can make reading difficult. If the lines are too long, it becomes hard to find where the next line begins. On the other hand, if the lines are too short there are too many word breaks and very irregular and large spaces between words, particularly in justified text. A line length of six to ten words is recommended for good reading flow. This is between 50 and 75 characters per line including spaces and punctuation marks.

If very narrow text columns cannot be avoided, where using a normal type size would produce a line with fewer than 35 characters, readability should be improved by using a smaller type size and more condensed weight or flush left composition. However, a smaller point size or a condensed weight can lead to the exact opposite outcome. Here it is often a case of choosing the lesser of two evils.

In the end, a layout ought to be designed in such a way that the column widths guarantee optimal reading fluency. A design incorporates the right format in relation to the type area, type size, line spacing, and column width.

Gutter The individual columns need a small space between them that is called a gutter. Normally this should be no narrower than the width of the two letters *mi*. In case the columns need to be divided by an additional vertical line, the space should be no narrower than the width of the letters *mii*. This ensures that the gutter is clearly wider than the word spacing and cannot be confused with it. A word space is roughly the width of an *i*, including the letter space on either side.

The white space appears slightly larger in flush left composition than in justified composition because not all lines run to the end of the column. Therefore the gutter can be slightly narrower. In principle, there is nothing wrong with setting gutters for flush left multicolumn

Double-page type area construction with the ratio 2:3:4:5

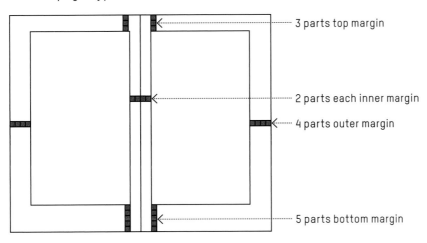

3 parts top margin

2 parts each inner margin

4 parts outer margin

5 parts bottom margin

The page margins have a set ratio to one another.

Single-page type area construction with the ratio 5:8 and 5:7

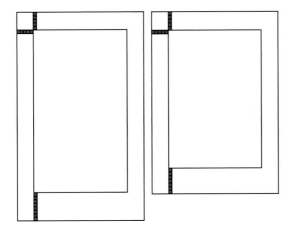

The page margins have the same ratio as the page format.

Division by ninths

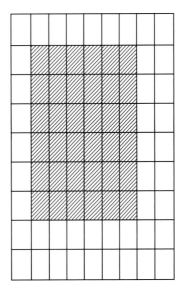

Type area construction divided by ninths of the page lengths.

Optimal column width with 45 to 65 characters

I am a dummy text. I was born this way. It took me a long time to figure out that I make no sense whatsoever. Nobody takes me seriously and they usually don't even

Column width is too wide, with over 75 characters

I am a dummy text. I was born this way. It took me a long time to figure out that I make no sense whatsoever. Nobody takes me seriously and they usually don't even bother to read me properly. Is it my fault? More than anything I'd love to be revered as a true classic of modern literature, but instead everyone just ignores me. Sometimes I feel like I'm just talking to myself, like a great big dummy.

Column width is too narrow, with fewer than 35 characters

I am a dummy text. I was born this way. It took me

composition by eye rather than mathematically, so that they look as though they are more or less the same. However, in practice this would create far too much work. Justified composition is more suitable in such a case for maintaining an even gray value. **(See next section, "Line spacing.")**

If the line spacing is comparatively wide, the gutter should be too. The latter should be roughly the height of a blank line. The height of a blank line is calculated by the type size plus the space to the next line. The type size consists of the entire height of a letter: ascender, x-height, and descender.

Line spacing
Line spacing is the vertical distance between each line. As a rule it is measured from one baseline to another. The distance between lines is called leading. This is measured from the bottom edge of the first line to the top edge of the next. Thus line spacing consists of the leading plus the cap height.

In typographical specifications, point size and line space are indicated separately with a forward slash. For instance, 10/12 pt means that the point size is

Page ratios

5:7	1:√2	1:1.414	DIN series
2:3	1:1.5	1:1.538	Tschichold
5:8	3:5	1:1.618	Golden section
3:5	1:√3	1:1.732	
5:11	1:√5	1:2.236	For slim formats

Ratios between inner, top, bottom, and outer margin

Origin	Page format	Type area ratio
Middle Ages	2:3	2:3:4:6
Middle Ages	3:4	3:4:6:8
Renaissance	2:3	2:3:4:5

Column width without dividing rule

I am a dummy text. I was born this way. It took me a long time to figure out that I make no sense whatsoever. Nobody takes me seriously and they usually don't even bother to read me properly. Is it my fault? More than anything I'd love to be revered as a true classic of modern literature, but instead everyone just ignores me. Sometimes I feel like I'm just talking to myself, like a great big dummy. I am a dummy text. I was born this way. It took me a long time to figure out that I make no sense whatsoever. Nobody takes me seriously and they usually don't even bother to read me properly. Is it my fault? More than

mi

↑ ┈┈┈┈┈ column width

Column width with dividing rule

I am a dummy text. I was born this way. It took me a long time to figure out that I make no sense whatsoever. Nobody takes me seriously and they usually don't even bother to read me properly. Is it my fault? More than anything I'd love to be revered as a true classic of modern literature, but instead everyone just ignores me. Sometimes I feel like I'm just talking to myself, like a great big dummy. I am a dummy text. I was born this way. It took me a long time to figure out that I make no sense whatsoever. Nobody takes me seriously and they usually don't even bother to read me properly. Is it my fault? More than

mii

↑ ┈┈┈┈┈ column width

Column width in justified text

I am a dummy text. I was born this way. It took me a long time to figure out that I make no sense whatsoever. Nobody takes me seriously and they usually don't even bother to read me properly. Is it my fault? More than anything I'd love to be revered as a true classic of modern literature, but instead everyone just ignores me. Sometimes I feel like I'm just talking to myself, like a great big dummy.

↑ ┈┈┈┈┈ column width: 3.5 mm

Column width in ragged text

I am a dummy text. I was born this way. It took me a long time to figure out that I make no sense whatsoever. Nobody takes me seriously and they usually don't even bother to read me properly. Is it my fault? More than anything I'd love to be revered as a true classic of modern literature, but instead everyone just ignores me. Sometimes I feel like I'm just talking to myself.

↑ ┈┈┈┈┈ column width: 2.5 mm

The column width appears wider in ragged text than in justified text, and can therefore be set narrower.

10 point and the line spacing 12 point. This is spoken as "10 on 12" or "10 over 12."

The choice of line spacing depends on several factors. In general the desired gray value determines the line spacing. When one looks at a page from a greater distance the design elements merge into gray, known as gray value. An ideal gray value improves readability. It is achieved by balancing the typeface, line width, word spacing, line spacing, and sometimes line weight with each other. If the line spacing is too tight, it makes the type appear too dark. If the line spacing is too wide, it looks too bright. Both are harder to read than optimally adjusted type.

As a rule of thumb, the x-height ought to correspond to the optical line spacing in a line of around 45 characters. The x-height varies depending on the typeface. It is best measured using the letters *mir*. The optimal line spacing is in direct relation to word spacing, since this too is influenced by the gray value of the text. The word spacing increases in justified text as the lines get shorter because there are fewer possibilities for separating words. This makes the line spacing appear wider, as the lines seem to fall apart a little. Therefore the line spacing in justified text may be wider in longer lines and tighter in shorter lines in order to achieve a particular gray value.

In bold type the line spacing may be set tighter than in light type to achieve a particular gray value. This is due to the fact that at the same column widths the word spacing is often wider using bold fonts, making the lines appear to fall apart a little.

If all the lines of a text have to be in register, i.e., they all have to be on one baseline, different weights cannot be set with different line spacing. In this case, increasing the letter spacing in the bold type can produce the optimal gray value.

There are different rules when it comes to headlines or subheadings. Multi-line headings often produce the impression that the line spacing is too wide. This is because in larger type sizes the ascenders and descenders of a font are more noticeable, especially if the lowercase letters are relatively small. In order for a heading to appear self-contained, its line spacing has to be reduced, as long as the ascenders and descenders do not touch.

In uppercase headings the problem of touching ascenders and descenders does not apply. Here the optical line spacing should be set roughly as wide as the word spacing. This in turn should be as wide as the inner space of the letter *U*. As this space is narrower in

a bold typeface than it is in a light one, the line spacing has to be narrower for bold fonts than for light ones.

The adjustable automatic line spacing is measured in percentage to the type size. The standard value is 120 percent. This setting is not always optimal, for the reasons listed above.

Baseline grid

When one holds a book or brochure up to the light, all the baselines should be at exactly the same height on the front and back. The lines are said to be in register when this is the case. A set baseline grid guarantees that the layout has a certain degree of clarity and order. It also prevents lines on the back from showing through and disturbing the foreground grid, thus influencing the desired gray value.

If the headlines and subheadings are set in the same size and with the same line spacing as the body text, they will have no problem being in register. On the other hand, choosing a different type size and line spacing for headings can accentuate the hierarchy between headings and body text, which increases the readability and understanding of the text.

The distance between the subheading and the text that follows should be smaller than it is from the preceding paragraph. This helps make it clear that the subheading belongs to the paragraph that follows it. When subheadings and body text are set in the same size, two blank lines are set before the subheading and one blank line after it. Alternatively, one blank line can be set before the subheading, and none after it. Much of the time subheadings are simply thrown in to loosen up the layout, with the same spacing on either side.

A subheading that is set in a bigger size and that has wider line spacing than the body text can have one blank line of the body text above it and half a blank line below it, for example. Although the subheading is not aligned with the baseline grid, it is clear that it belongs to the paragraph that follows it.

It becomes trickier when subheadings are sometimes one line and sometimes two. In order for the body text to stay in register, the space between the heading and the following text is always the same, while the space between the subheading and the preceding text varies. A headline or subheading with more than two lines ought to be avoided in general. Headings should be kept as short as possible. As a rule, they are set without a period at the end.

Column width is too narrow with wide line spacing

I am a dummy text. I was born this way. It took me a long time to figure out that I make no sense whatsoever. Nobody takes me seriously and they usually don't even bother to read me properly. Is it my fault? More than anything I'd love to be revered as a true classic of modern literature, but instead everyone just ignores

column width: 3.5 mm

Correct column width with wide line spacing

I am a dummy text. I was born this way. It took me a long time to figure out that I make no sense whatsoever. Nobody takes me seriously and they usually don't even bother to read me properly. Is it my fault? More than anything I'd love to be revered as a true classic of modern literature, but instead everyone just ignores me.

height of a blank line

column width: 6 mm

The column width with wide line spacing corresponds roughly to the height of a blank line.

Line spacing

I am a dummy text. I was born this way. It took me a long time to figure out that I make no sense whatsoever. Nobody takes me seriously and they usually don't even bother to read me properly. Is it my fault? More than anything I'd love to be revered as a true classic of modern literature, but instead everyone just ignores me.

line spacing

Optical line spacing

Optical
Line spacing   mir

Line spacing is measured from baseline to baseline. The optical line spacing consists of the distance between the lines, and should be the same as the x-height.

Line spacing ratio to line width

I am a dummy text. I was born $\longleftarrow$ 9/9.5 pt
this way. It took me a long
time to figure out that I make
no sense whatsoever. Nobody
takes me seriously and they
usually don't even bother to
read me properly. Is it my fault?

I am a dummy text. I was born this way. It $\longleftarrow$ 9/10 pt
took me a long time to figure out that I make
no sense whatsoever. Nobody takes me seriously and they usually don't even bother to
read me properly. Is it my fault? More than
anything I'd love to be revered as a true classic of modern literature, but instead every

I am a dummy text. I was born this way. It took me a long time to fig-$\longleftarrow$ 9/10.5 pt
ure out that I make no sense whatsoever. Nobody takes me seriously
and they usually don't even bother to read me properly. Is it my fault?
More than anything I'd love to be revered as a true classic of modern
literature, but instead everyone just ignores me. Sometimes I feel
like I'm just talking to myself, like a great big dummy. I am a dummy
text. I was born this way. It took me a long time to figure out that I

The wider the column, the wider the line spacing should be.

9/10 pt

I am a dummy text. I was born this way. It took me a long time to figure out that I make no sense whatsoever. Nobody takes me seriously and they usually don't even

bother to read me properly. Is it my fault? More than anything I'd love to be revered as a true classic of modern literature, but instead everyone just ignores me. Some

9/10.5 pt

I am a dummy text. I was born this way. It took me a long time to figure out that I make no sense whatsoever. Nobody takes me seriously and they usually don't even

bother to read me properly. Is it my fault? More than anything I'd love to be revered as a true classic of modern literature, but instead everyone just ignores me. Some

9/11 pt

I am a dummy text. I was born this way. It took me a long time to figure out that I make no sense whatsoever. Nobody takes me seriously and they usually don't even

bother to read me properly. Is it my fault? More than anything I'd love to be revered as a true classic of modern literature, but instead everyone just ignores me. Some

In bold type the line spacing may be reduced in order to achieve the same gray effect as regular type.

Reduced line spacing in headings

Reduced distance without descenders
←······ 30/28 pt

Ascenders go close to the descenders
←······ 30/28 pt

Not touching the descenders
←······ 30/30 pt

The line spacing should be reduced in headings, but the ascenders and descenders must not touch.

Word spacing in regular type: 65 percent

THE INNER SPACE OF THE *U* SAME AS WORD SPACING
←······ 30/30 pt

Word spacing in bold type: 55 percent

THE INNER SPACE OF THE *U* IS SMALLER HERE
←······ 30/30 pt

AND THAT MAKES THE LINE SPACING TIGHTER
←······ 30/28 pt

The word spacing and line spacing should be tighter in bold type than in regular.

Setting baseline grid in InDesign

--- InDesign

↓

Preferences

↓

Grids...

↓

Preferences

⌁

Baseline Grid

Start: 26.5 mm
Increment Every: 19 pt

Aligning text to baseline grid

Paragraph ·······> ≡ Align to baseline grid

Larger headings with variable spaces.

Larger headings out of register.

Headings in register with the same size as the body text.

The baseline grid in InDesign is set up in the document pre-sets. The important thing here is the size of the division. If the body text has a 14-point line spacing, one selects "14 pt" under "Increment Every". Another thing that is relevant is the start of the baseline grid, which might be indicated in relation to the upper page margin, for example. By changing this value the baseline grid may be moved so that the text is in the best place in the type area.

The baseline grid may be blended in or out in the InDesign menu under View > Grids and Guides. Grids in Back should be deactivated in the preferences so that it remains visible when there is a colored part of the page, for example.

To align the text automatically to the baseline grid, the corresponding icon has to be activated in the Paragraph palette or Control palette. This setting normally applies to a whole paragraph. However, there is the possibility of only aligning the first line to the baseline grid.

One example in this context is side notes, which are often smaller than the body text and therefore have tighter line spacing. This means only the first line has to be aligned to the baseline grid.

Endnotes for USreaders

1 – The page lengths of the ANSI paper size series alternate between the ratios 1:1.30 and 1:1.55.

<u>3.2 Text hierarchy</u> There are various text hierarchies for arranging a text. If it is substantial, up to four or five different arrangements can be represented—any more is too many to guarantee that they can be distinguished from one another.

Headline

Subheadline

Subheading

Text

Color subheading
Headings should be clearly distinguishable from the body text. This can be easily done using a different weight or color. Headings should be clearly distinguishable from the body text. This can be easily done using a different weight or color. Headings should be clearly distinguishable from the body text. This can be easily done using a different weight or color.

Different weights and sizes should make the text hierarchies clearly recognizable. No more than five hierarchies should be used if possible.

There is a distinction between headlines, subheadlines, and subheadings. Finally there is the body text. There is a further hierarchy for captions. The type looks clearer and calmer if captions are set in the same size as body text.

Distinguishing features
The different text hierarchies can be made clear by various means. The simplest way is by selecting different type sizes. As a rule, the heading is always bigger than the text that follows it. Different type sizes should be easily distinguishable so that the text hierarchies are recognizable at a glance.

The starting point for the choice of type size is always the body text. Usually there is a difference of at least two to three point sizes between the hierarchies. In commercial printing the size of the headline has no limit. A headline can be oversized if it fits the desired design effect. A subheading may also be set in the same size as the body text, but it should be set in a different weight in order to distinguish it. This would normally be a bold or semi-bold weight. The use of different weights within a text can disturb the type. Using a different color is another way of differentiating headings.

Style sheets
Style sheets are very useful for large works. The text can be formatted easily and quickly into the various text hierarchies. Different formats can be applied to whole paragraphs or individual characters with a single click or by using keyboard shortcuts.

Style sheets are principally used for whole paragraphs. This is also known as paragraph formatting. One can only apply one paragraph format to a paragraph. However, additional character formats may be applied to single characters or sections within a paragraph. Character formats are used for such things as color or italic emphasis within a body text.

Mixing typefaces
Different typefaces may be used to help differentiate text hierarchies. There are two rules that are useful to bear in mind when selecting different typefaces to be mixed together. The first rule is: different typefaces from different type families in the same style should never be used together. For instance, a sans serif typeface should never be mixed with another sans serif, or a transitional with another transitional typeface. If one needs a different typeface for a heading, one should either choose one from the same type family or in a different style.

Setting paragraph formats

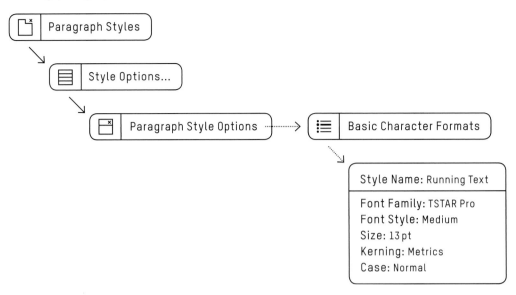

Aesthetic emphasis

The use of *italics* is unobtrusive when used in the body text.

Since not every font has proper SMALL CAPS, designers will often use CAPITALS to emphasize text. They are spaced a little and set in a smaller size so that they do not disturb the type.

A method of emphasis that is less unobtrusive and slightly jolty is when some of the body text is t r a c k e d , because the spaced type does not match the gray image of the body text.

If one wishes to underline part of the text, one has to make sure that the underlining fits the character of the type. One should also take care not to underline the spaces between words or any descenders.

Optical emphasis

An optical accentuation should clearly distinguish itself from the body text. Here the use of **bold** type can be very useful.

Even more conspicuous is the use of **color**. This is very good for making technical literature easier to follow.

Another good way of emphasizing text is to indent entire passages of text.

A line can also emphasize this indent, making important passages in the text easier to find.

Optical emphasis should be seen quickly, whereas aesthetic emphasis should be discreet.

Mixed typefaces from the same family

Heading ←···· TSTAR Bold
Copy text ←···· TSTAR Regular

Heading ←···· Palatino Bold
Copy text ←···· Palatino Roman

Unsuccessfully mixed typefaces in the same style

Heading ←···· TSTAR Bold
Copy text ←···· Univers Roman

Heading ←···· Baskerville Bold
Copy text ←···· Bonesana Regular

Mixing typefaces from different families

Heading ←···· TSTAR Bold
Copy text ←···· Bonesana Regular

Heading ←···· Bonesana Regular
Copy text ←···· Univers Roman

Features of successfully mixed typefaces

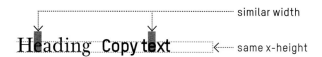

···· similar width
←···· same x-height

Typefaces have a similar structure when they are successfully mixed together.

The second rule states that if different type styles are mixed together, those typefaces should have a similar structure. They should have a similar character, i.e., a similar line weight and width, and also the same x-height.

<u>Emphasis</u> Individual words in a body text can be given special emphasis. Normally a different weight is applied to them rather than a different typeface. Using different weights from the same family is relatively unproblematic, as the different weights are sure to fit together.

Emphasis ought to be used sparingly because overuse makes its function pointless. There is a distinction between aesthetic and optical emphasis. Aesthetic emphasis should be unobtrusive, whereas optical emphasis is supposed to be conspicuous. Optical emphasis is easier to find and is used in technical texts, for example.

The most discreet way to emphasize individual words is by italicizing them. Italic fonts blend perfectly into the gray image of the body text and are therefore inconspicuous. Italics are typically used to emphasize new or foreign words that have not yet been adopted into English.

The use of small caps or capitals is also relatively unobtrusive. They are often used for such things as company names. Both should be spaced a little. Capitals stand out less in large texts when they are set one to two points smaller than the body text. An emphasis may also be set in a smaller point size and spaced a little.

Another way to emphasize words is by underlining them. Care must be taken to ensure that the line weight of the underlines fits the type character, so as not to influence the gray effect of the text. Descenders and spaces between words should not be underlined.

When emphasized words are clearly letter spaced compared to the body text, it carries the disadvantage of affecting the gray value of the text. This is why words ought to be spaced as discreetly as possible, and only applied where necessary.

When a clear optical emphasis is required, bold or semi-bold weights can be very effective. These too should be slightly spaced compared to the body text in order not to disturb the gray image of the text.

3.3 Types of composition

A text may be set in different ways. There is a basic difference between left or right ragged composition, symmetrical composition, and left or right justified composition. Furthermore, there is shape composition, which can assume a particular shape, such as filling in a circle or snaking along a line.

There are several things to consider when selecting a particular type of composition. Left or right ragged composition looks more relaxed as a rule than justified type. On the other hand, justified type looks neater than ragged composition. The best reason to avoid using justified type is if the column width is narrow, with fewer than 35 characters per line, as previously mentioned in "Column width" (p. 100). In this case flush left type is more suitable.

In both symmetrical and ragged composition attention should be paid to a certain dynamic in the line arrangement. It is more effective if the lines have noticeably different lengths. Rhythm gives the composition a pleasing order. Symmetrical composition is only really useful for comparatively short texts, such as the title page of a book or the subheaders in a large text, because it is quite hard to read after a while.

Flush right type is only ever used if there is a good reason for it, for example, picture captions to the left of a picture, or side notes to the left of the body text. Side notes are aligned to the body text. They are set flush right when they are to the left of the body text*, and flush left if they are to the right of the body text.

*I am lush right side note

Shape composition

I am a dummy text. I was born this way. It took me a long time to figure out that I make no sense whatsoever. Nobody takes me seriously and they usually don't even bother to read me properly. Is it my fault? More than anything I'd love to be revered as a true classic of modern literature, but instead everyone just ignores me. Sometimes I feel like I'm just talking to myself, like a great big dummy. I am a dummy text. I was born this way. It took me a long time to figure out that I make no sense whatsoever. Nobody takes me seriously and they usually don't even bother to read me properly. Is it my fault? More than anything I'd love to be revered as a true classic of modern literature, but instead everyone just ignores me. Sometimes I feel like I'm just talking to myself, like a great big dummy. I am a dummy text. I was born this way. It took me a long time to figure out that I make no sense whatsoever. Nobody takes me seriously and they usually don't even bother to read me properly. Is it my fault? More than anything I'd love to be revered as a true classic of modern literature, but instead everyone just ignores me. Sometimes I feel like I'm just talking to myself, like a great big dummy. I am a dummy text. I was born this way. It took me a long time to figure out that I make no sense whatsoever. Nobody takes me seriously and they usually don't even bother to read me properly. Is it my fault? More than anything I'd love to be revered as a true classic of modern

I am a dummy text. I was born this way. It took me a long time to...

Ragged composition

Ragged composition is fairly laborious compared to justified type because it has a dynamic line arrangement that cannot be achieved automatically. A dynamic line arrangement is distinguished by the fact that the lines have noticeably different lengths. This can only be achieved by manually correcting the automatic line arrangement. One can create a particular rhythm as desired. For example, two long lines can always alternate with one short line.

In ragged type one must be careful that the hyphenation and line breaks are simple ones that do not disturb the copy flow. Unfortunate splits that leave only two letters at the start or end of a line ought to be avoided. Step-like patterns or similar shapes at the end of lines should also be avoided. Sometimes a single manual line break is enough to produce a more attractive line arrangement.

Justified composition

Justified type is different from ragged type because all the lines run to their full width. One normally does this by increasing or reducing the word spacing. However, the spaces must not be too big or too small. In addition, the letter spacing may be altered slightly. The settings for changing the word and character spacing of lines in InDesign are under Justification in the pop-up menu of the Paragraph or Control palette.

The minimum, desired, and maximum value is defined under word spacing and letter spacing. Desired value defines the spaces that are normally used, for instance in flush left text. The ideal space between words is roughly the width of the i plus the natural space between letters.

For headers, the word spacing should be the same as the inner space of the n plus the natural space between letters. For bold or particularly narrow fonts a reduced space of maybe 55 to 75 percent is better suited because the inner space of the n is accordingly narrower. Added to this is the fact that the space between bold fonts appears bigger than it does between light fonts.

In justified composition the spaces vary between the minimum and maximum value. They can never be smaller than the minimum value or greater than the maximum value needed to push a line to its full width. The greater the range, the more possibilities there are for changing the line breaks and hyphenation

Boring rough composition

I am a dummy text. I was born this way. It took me a long time to figure out that I make no sense whatsoever. Nobody takes me seriously and they usually don't even bother to read me properly. Is it my fault? More than anything I'd love to be revered as a true classic of modern literature, but instead everyone just ignores me. Sometimes I feel like I'm just talking to myself, like a great big dummy.

Dynamic line arrangement

I am a dummy text. I was born this way. It took me a long time to figure out that I make no sense whatsoever. Nobody takes me seriously and they usually don't even bother to read me properly. Is it my fault? More than anything I'd love to be revered as a true classic of modern literature, but instead everyone just ignores me. Sometimes I feel like I'm just talking to myself, like a great big dummy.

Lines arranged according to meaning

I am a dummy text. I was born this way. It took me a long time to figure out that I make no sense whatsoever. Nobody takes me seriously and they usually don't even bother to read me properly. Is it my fault? More than anything I'd love to be revered as a true classic of modern literature, but instead everyone just ignores me.

Step patterns

I am a dummy text. I was born this way. It took me a long time to figure out that I make no sense whatsoever. Nobody takes me seriously and they usually don't even bother to read me properly. Is it my fault? More than anything I'd love to be revered as a true classic of modern literature, but instead everyone just ignores me. Sometimes I feel like I'm just talking to myself, like a great big dummy.

A dynamic line arrangement makes the text livelier.

InDesign Paragraph Spacing

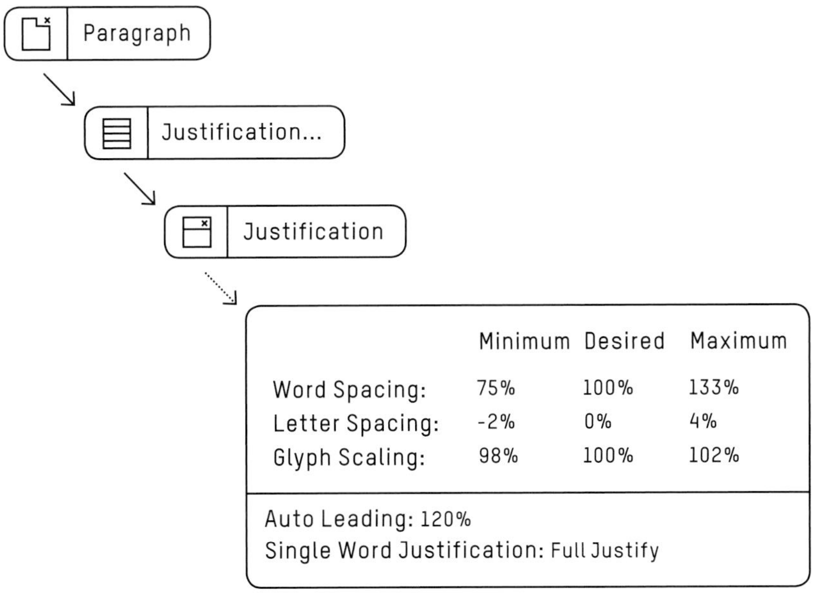

```
┌──┬──────────────┐
│ ☐ │ Paragraph    │
└──┴──────────────┘
      ↘
    ┌──┬──────────────────┐
    │ ☰ │ Justification... │
    └──┴──────────────────┘
          ↘
        ┌──┬────────────────┐
        │ ☐ │ Justification  │
        └──┴────────────────┘
              ↘
```

	Minimum	Desired	Maximum
Word Spacing:	75%	100%	133%
Letter Spacing:	-2%	0%	4%
Glyph Scaling:	98%	100%	102%

Auto Leading: 120%
Single Word Justification: Full Justify

Optimum word spacing in continuous text

Theispaceibetweeniwordsiinicontinuousitextishouldibeiroughly theiwidthiofiailowercaseii.

Optimum word spacing in a headline

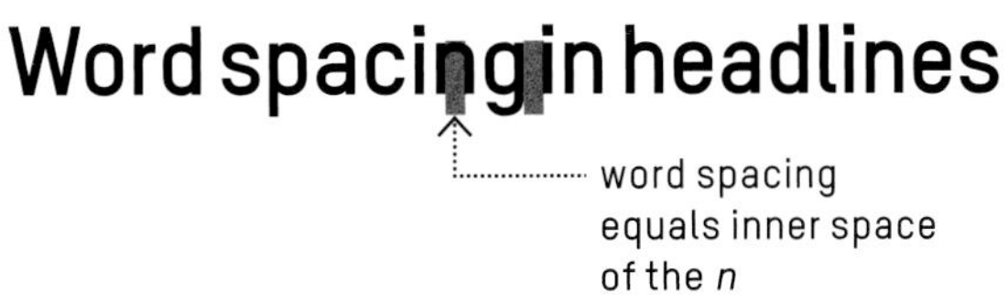

Word spacing in headlines

⌐
|····· word spacing
      equals inner space
      of the *n*

---

manually. If the range is set too large, there is a risk of spaces becoming too big or too small.

The minimum value for word spacing should be set at around 75 percent, and the maximum around 130 percent. Justified type looks more harmonious the less difference there is between the minimum and maximum value. These values can be changed further in exceptional cases, for instance when the line width is comparatively narrow. In such a case a more generous spacing setting might reduce the word breaks. However, it would be better to expand the line width to at least 35 characters per line, or to use flush left composition.

In letter spacing the difference between the minimum and maximum values should equally be kept as slight as possible. It is recommendable to set everything to 0 percent, so as not to alter the spacing. However, if the line width is very narrow, these values may be changed to avoid word spaces that are too big or too small. The minimum value may be changed to -2 percent and the maximum value to +2 percent, for example.

Hyphenation in InDesign

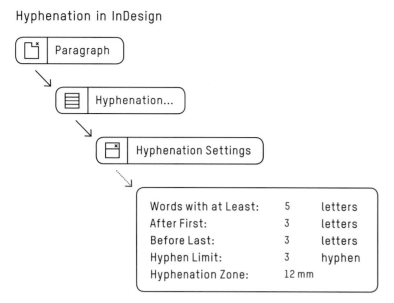

Words with at Least:	5	letters
After First:	3	letters
Before Last:	3	letters
Hyphen Limit:	3	hyphen
Hyphenation Zone:	12 mm	

I am a dummy text. I was born this way. It took me a long time to figure out that I make no sense whatsoever. Nobody takes me seriously and they usually don't even bother to read me properly. Is it my fault? More than anything I'd love to be revered as a true classic of modern literature, but

I am a dummy text. I was born this way. It took me a long time to figure out that I make no sense whatsoever. Nobody takes me seriously and they usually don't even bother to read me properly. Is it my fault? More than anything I'd love to be revered as a true classic of modern literature, but instead everyone

The hyphenation settings affect the quality of justified type.

Glyph scaling relates to the horizontal widths of the individual letters. This value should be set at 100 percent for everything because otherwise the horizontal and vertical line weights do not change in proportion to one another during scaling, and the counters, i.e., the spaces inside letters, are modified. The type can become distorted. There are exceptions, such as when there is a narrow column width where scaling at 98 percent minimum or 102 percent maximum makes sense. This sort of scaling cannot normally be noticed by the naked eye.

After glyph scaling, automatic line width can be set. This is in relation to type size. Automatic line width of 120 percent is 12 point if the type size is 10 point. Altering the automatic line width can be useful when all the line widths of different type sizes are to be set at a ratio other than the preset 120 percent.

Single word alignment occurs when columns are narrowed down to just one word because of an object in the type area, such as an illustration. In justified composition this word can be aligned symmetrically on either side. Finally one selects which composer to use. The Adobe Paragraph Composer sets the spaces and hyphenation with regard to all the lines in a paragraph. The Single-line Composer sets the spaces and hyphenation of each line independently of the other lines in the paragraph. The Adobe Paragraph Composer allows for relatively few manual changes.

Hyphenation By setting hyphenation one can control how often and in which cases words have to be separated. Good composition should not gener-

Hyphenation zone: 24 millimeters

I am a dummy text. I was born this way. It took me a long time to figure out that I make no sense whatsoever. Nobody takes me seriously and they usually don't even bother to read me properly. Is it my fault? More than anything I'd love to be revered as a true classic.

Hyphenation zone: 6 millimeters

I am a dummy text. I was born this way. It took me a long time to figure out that I make no sense whatsoever. Nobody takes me seriously and they usually don't even bother to read me properly. Is it my fault? More than anything I'd love to be revered as a true classic.

The hyphenation zone determines at what point hyphenation is necessary. It can only be set using Adobe Single-line Composer.

Separate last word

I am a dummy text. I was born this way. It took me a long time to figure out that I make no sense whatsoever. Nobody takes me seriously.

Sometimes I feel like I'm just talking to myself, like a great big dummy.

Do not separate last word

I am a dummy text. I was born this way. It took me a long time to figure out that I make no sense whatsoever. Nobody takes me seriously.

Sometimes I feel like I'm just talking to myself, like a great big dummy.

The last word in particular should not be separated when the next paragraph starts with an indent.

Paragraph palette in InDesign

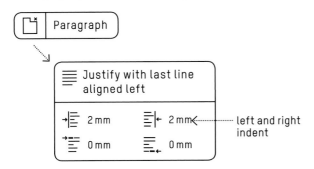

Paragraph — Justify with last line aligned left — 2 mm, 0 mm, 2 mm, 0 mm — left and right indent

Paragraph — Justify with last line aligned left — 2 mm, 2 mm, 2 mm, 2 mm — first and last line indent

I am a dummy text. I was born this way. It took me a long time to figure out that I make no sense whatsoever. Nobody takes me seriously and they usually don't even bother to read me properly. Is it my fault?

I am a dummy text. I was born this way. It took me a long time to figure out that I make no sense whatsoever. Nobody takes me seriously and they usually don't even bother to read me properly. Is it my fault?

ally have more than three divisions in a row. The settings in InDesign are in the Paragraph or Control palette pop-up menu under Hyphenation. They may also be set in the paragraph formats. The settings only apply to whole paragraphs.

First, hyphenation is either activated or deactivated. In justified composition it should always be activated. In ragged composition it occasionally makes sense to deactivate it. Headlines should ideally be set without splits. After that, one has to decide how many letters a word needs to have to be hyphenated. A setting of at least five letters means that a word with only four letters can never be separated. Four-letter words should not be separated anyway, because two letter syllables at the start or end of a line are ugly and not easy to read. However, if the type is set extremely narrow it can make sense to separate four letter words. A minimum of six letters should be set if one wishes to disable two-letter separated syllables. If one wants to disable two-letter separated syllables at either the start or end of lines alone, then one specifies that only words with five letters minimum can be separated. Then at least one of the separated syllables will have three letters.

Setting the maximum amount of hyphens determines how many lines in a row may be hyphenated. Both in justified and ragged type one must take care not to include too much hyphenation in a paragraph. The Hyphenation Zone only affects ragged type with Adobe Single-line Composer instead of Adobe Paragraph Composer. It does not work at all for justified type. Setting the Hyphenation Zone defines the margins that words have to enter in order to be hyphenated. The larger the zone is set, the earlier in the line hyphenation is to occur. To keep the line arrangement dynamic, the hyphenation zone should not be too small in relation to line width. A hyphenation zone set to zero allows InDesign to hyphenate whenever possible.

One sets the priority for justified and ragged type using a slider. More value is either given to regular word and letter spacing—which might mean having more hyphenation—or to having the fewest possible word breaks. Sometimes perfect spacing is sacrificed to achieve this.

One can deactivate hyphenation for uppercase words, to prevent proper names from being hyphenated, for example.

Subsequently one can deactivate so that a word at the end of a paragraph cannot be separated, to prevent a lone syllable from ending a paragraph. These create an unnecessary gap, particularly when the next paragraph starts with an indent.

After all the automatic settings have been adjusted, it can still be worthwhile to optimize the hyphenation or line arrangement manually. Line arrangement can be fine-tuned both aesthetically and according to meaning by hand. This should not be to the detriment of the copy flow in justified type. However, automatic hyphenation programs are sometimes defective or not up to date on spelling.

Manual hyphenation should not merely consist of a hyphen followed by the next line, because both the hyphen and the line change remain in the text even if they move to another place due to any corrections. A discretionary hyphen, however, disappears automatically if the spot where the line changes moves. To insert a discretionary hyphen, press Ctrl + Shift + - (Windows) or Command + Shift + - (Mac OS). In InDesign it is in the menu under Insert Glyphs or Special Characters > Discretionary Hyphen. If hyphenation is not possible, it may be because it is outside of the set hyphenation zone, or because other settings for hyphenation or word and letter spacing have been affected.

Indents and spacing

Type may be formatted yet further by using indents and spaces.

Various indents in a paragraph, or spaces between the preceding or following paragraph can be set in the Paragraph or Control palette.

Paragraphs can have an indent on the left and right side in order to stand out. Thus they are set in a box no wider than the text column. The space on the left and right of the box should be roughly as wide as a lowercase m. The space above the text should be the same width as the space to the edge of the box. The space below the text should be slightly bigger: between one-quarter and one-third of the body text size. If the boxed text is inside a text with several columns, the space above and below the text should be the same as the column width. The line weight of the box should match the typeface. Its line weight can be a little heavier if the box border is colored, because color lines always look a little thinner than black ones. Thin lines should be avoided if the ink is screened. The thinner a line is, the rougher its outline. The same goes for color type, which is best not screened when it is small or fine. Entire blank lines should not be used to mark paragraphs apart from each other because it affects the gray value of the type too much. A blank line is only used to help clarify a transition to a completely new

Hanging indent

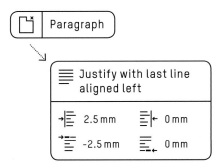

I am a dummy text. I was born this way. It took me a long time to figure out that I make no sense whatsoever. Nobody takes me seriously and they usually don't even bother to read me properly. Is it my fault? More than anything I'd

– I am a dummy text.
– I was born this way.
– It took me a long time to figure out.
– That I make no sense whatsoever.
– Nobody takes me seriously.

Left indent and first line negative indent

A negative indent can set the first line back to zero, which is used for lists.

Space between paragraphs

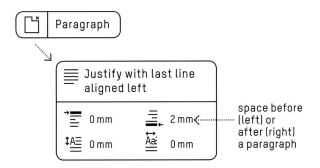

space before (left) or after (right) a paragraph

I am a dummy text. I was born this way. It took me a long time to figure out that I make no sense whatsoever.

Nobody takes me seriously and they usually don't even bother to read me properly. Is it my fault? More than anything I'd love.

One can separate paragraphs from each other by defining a space before or after each paragraph.

context. It can also be used to emphasize a particular paragraph or point, or to break up a very long text so that it is easier to read.

An indent can only be defined for the first or for the last line of a paragraph in justified type. In ragged type the first line should not have an indent because it disturbs the type image too much. The last line of the preceding paragraph should also be no shorter than the indent of the new paragraph, as this would look like a blank line. The indent of the first line should be set small enough to prevent this from occurring. In the classic sense an indent is equal to the length of an em space of the body text, plus spacing if necessary. An

em—also called mutton—defines a square space with the height and width of the type size.

An indent in the last line of a paragraph only affects lines that are so long that they would otherwise fill the column, making it less separate from the following paragraph. To prevent this from occurring one should set at least one blank space the size of half an em of the body text in the last line. This is known as en space because in most typefaces this corresponds to the width of an *n*.

A hanging indent is another option. All lines except for the first one are given a left indent. This kind of paragraph design is used a lot for itemization and

Automatic bullets

Paragraph

Bullets and Numbering...

Bullets and Numbering

List Type: Bullets

Add... → Add Bullets

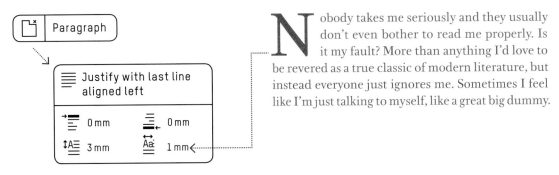

	!	"	#	$	%	&	'	(	)	*
/	0	1	2	3	4	5	6	7	8	...

Font Family: TSTAR Pro
Font Style: Medium

Automatic initials

Paragraph

Justify with last line aligned left

0 mm   0 mm

3 mm   1 mm

Nobody takes me seriously and they usually don't even bother to read me properly. Is it my fault? More than anything I'd love to be revered as a true classic of modern literature, but instead everyone just ignores me. Sometimes I feel like I'm just talking to myself, like a great big dummy.

Initials placed manually

Nobody takes me seriously and they usually don't even bother to read me properly. Is it my fault? More than anything I'd love to be revered as a true classic of modern literature, but instead everyone just ig-

Nobody takes me seriously and they usually don't even bother to read me properly. Is it my fault? More than anything I'd love to be revered as a true classic of modern litera-ture, but instead everyone just ignores lists. The individual items are marked using a dash or sometimes a middle dot, called a bullet. The space after the character should be half an em space, or one en space. The text in the first line after the bullet should be aligned with the following lines. One can do this by setting a tab with the same width as an indent for the bullet, which keeps its position.

In InDesign there is an automatic solution for list composition. In the Paragraph palette menu under Bullets and Numbering one can define which bullets are automatically used, how wide an indent is, and where the tab position is.

The next two settings in the Paragraph palette define the distance to the preceding and following paragraphs. This extra spacing between lines also helps separate paragraphs. This sort of spacing cannot be used if the lines are supposed to be in register. It can be useful in advertisements for arranging individual sections.

Next an initial can be defined in the Paragraph palette. The left setting defines the height of the initial. The height is given in lines. The right setting defines how many lines the initial contains. Initials should always be used sparingly and never in each paragraph. As a rule, paragraphs are only used at the start of a text.

A different typeface can be used for an initial. It should be set on the body text baseline. If, for example a script font is used for an initial, it will have to be set a little lower.

An initial should also be aligned at the left margin so that it looks like it is in the left-hand type area. Sometimes that means the initial has to start slightly outside of the type area. This happens a lot when the left outline of the initial is uneven. One can do this by creating an initial manually with the Paragraph palette. One can also make an initial start at the left column margin by activating the Optical Margin Alignment option in the Story palette. This applies to the whole text section rather than merely for one paragraph. The optical margin alignment should correspond to the body text size. That is why one has to set the most-used type size in the Story palette.

The horizontal distance from an initial to the text should be around the same as the vertical distance, which is determined by the line spacing. This produces an evenly balanced appearance. The text after the initial should fit snugly along the shape of the initial where possible.

<u>3.4 Fine typography</u> Small but fine differences in type and typography can refine a print product. Aligning a closing margin to optical features or changing individual letter spaces manually are some of the things that help create a harmonious type image.

Finetypography or microtypography is an area that is neglected for practical reasons at the layout stage. It would be a waste of time to perfect every last detail of a composition when it can still change. On the other hand, the final artwork can be fine-tuned here if the customer or editorial office has given the go-ahead to finish the final details.

Optical margin alignment The side outlines of the composition should be as even as possible. However, even if the lines start or finish at the same mathematical position, the margins do not always look perfectly aligned. There can be many reasons for this unevenness but it can be straightened where necessary.

The importance of optical margin alignment is especially plain to see in headlines. Many headlines have an optical indentation on the left compared to body text. Although this can happen with any kind of typeface, it is very common with italics and sans serif Roman fonts.

The simplest method is to use the automatic Optical Margin Alignment setting, which is activated in the Story palette in InDesign (Window/Type and Tables/Story). The type size of the body text has to be set in the palette. In individual cases it can work out better to choose the type size of the bigger headline. This is the case when the text box consists of very few lines, such as a title headline and a subheadline. If this automatic margin alignment fails to satisfy, the margin can be aligned manually. There are different ways to do this, which will be explained using the following examples.

The technical realization depends on what the intention is. If a headline sits inside its own text frame and its left margin is also straight for a two-line headline, it will be enough to simply let the text frame stick

Without margin alignment

Some text close
to the margin is flush left.

With margin alignment

Some text close
to the margin is flush left.

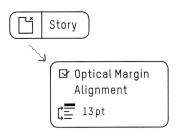

Headline

Some text close
to the margin is flush left.

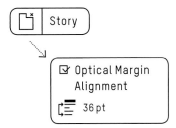

Automatic margin alignment in headlines

Wonderful Headlines

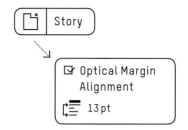

Wonderful Headlines

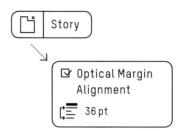

Manual margin alignment

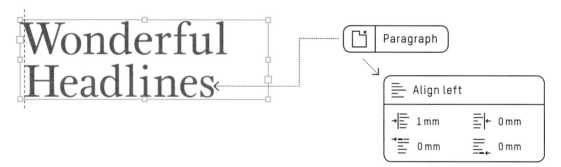

out a little on the left. A blended-in reference line helps to find the correct position. To really judge the result, the reference lines have to be blended out. Here it is a matter of the optical impression of perfect alignment rather than exact mathematical positioning.

The more inclined or round the left edge of the headline is, the more the start of it has to stick out of the type area. Sometimes each line has to be positioned for multi-line headlines. However, to avoid having to set every line in an individual text frame, a left indent in a line can align the margin. There is also the possibility of setting a blank space before the indented line so that it can be kerned to shift the line along to the desired spot in the type area.

Another common example of optical margin alignment is a headline that starts with punctuation marks, such as quotation marks. The type only looks horizontally even when punctuation marks start before the text margin. If not, then there is an optical gap at the start of the text. The use of hanging quotation marks does not always lead to the best results. For example, if one wants precise side margin alignment, it can look much nicer without hanging punctuation marks.

Headlines are not the only things to require margin alignment. In justified type there are optical gaps at the end of lines caused by punctuation marks. In ragged type one can more or less see when the sides are uneven, depending on the typeface. In a running text it would be disproportionately costly to do manual margin alignment. That is why the InDesign Optical Margin Alignment feature provides a good solution.

The punctuation marks are set slightly outside of the type area so that the beginning and end of the text produce a harmonious vertical line. This too is a case of hanging punctuation marks. At the same time words or characters that do not begin or end with a straight edge are nudged along to the sides so that there are no optical gaps.

Tracking

Tracking, or letter spacing, determines what size the spaces between letters are. In this context it is also character width, which is the width of a letter plus what are known as its side bearings. Normally the type designer specifies the course of a text, but a typographer can also change it by increasing or reducing the spaces between the let-

Hanging quotation marks

I am a dummy text. I was born this way. It took me a long time to figure out that I make no sense whatsoever. Nobody takes me seriously and they usually don't.

Non-hanging quotation marks as initials

❝❝ I am a dummy text. I was born this way. It took me a long time to figure out that I make no sense whatsoever. Nobody takes me seriously and they usually don't even bother to read me properly. Is it my fault? More than anything I'd love to be revered as a true classic of modern literature, but instead ❞❞

Hanging punctuation marks begin outside of the type area. It can sometimes look better though when they are inside the type area.

ters individually. When the tracking is reduced it is called kerning.

It is not necessary to kern the natural character width of a bread-and-butter typeface with a size between 6 and 14 point. The tracking should be reduced in large sizes upwards of 18 point. This is because the side bearings of a typeface increase in proportion too. After a certain size the type starts to look spaced.

The bigger the type is, the more its natural letter spacing should be reduced. Exactly by how much depends on the kind of font used. The tracking must not be reduced until letters actually touch.

Tracking must never be changed without a reason. There are few reasons to space type. Capitals and small caps may generally have a little spacing. If one wants to use very wide spacing, one only does it with capitals and small caps as a rule. A few individual words can be spaced a little for emphasis, as can bright text on a dark background, or bold accentuation to maintain the gray value of the body text. Other than that, spacing body text or headlines is unnecessary. It is important to note that many fonts have different tracking on Mac and PC, which can lead to line breaks and the like.

Optical kerning

Apart from general kerning that alters the natural spacing of type, certain pairs of letters may have to be kerned. Some characters have a lot of beard, or white space, on either one or both sides. When these letters are next to characters that are smaller than they are, optical gaps occur that have to be corrected.

Kerning changes the natural character widths of the letters so that the respective pairs of letters sit closer together.

Letters should not be kerned too obviously. It is perfectly natural that some pairs of letters sit further apart from each other than most. The natural text image should not be totally destroyed. Sometimes spaces might even have to be enlarged to produce a consistent type image.

High quality typefaces include kerning tables that show the degree of kerning for the most important letter combinations. For PostScript fonts, these combinations are not in the font data file, but separately in AFM files (Adobe Font Metric).

In this context, InDesign differentiates between metric and optical kerning. Metric kerning is the default setting in InDesign. It uses the letter spacing given in

Character palette in InDesign

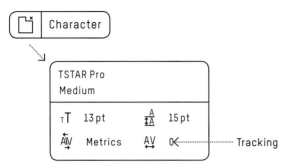

Control palette in InDesign

One can set the tracking in InDesign in both the Character palette
and the Control palette.

Adjusting tracking

Headline
Tracking 0

Headline
Tracking 0

Headline
Tracking 0

Headline
Tracking -20

Headline
Tracking -10

Headline
Tracking -15

Spacing capitals

HEADLINE
Tracking 0

HEADLINE
Tracking 10

The kind of font and type size affects how much spacing has to be reduced in bigger
type. On the other hand, capitals and small caps should always be spaced a little.

Without kerning

SENSUAL SEDUCTION

With manual kerning

SENSUAL SEDUCTION

−19 +11 −30 +10 −123 +43   −9 +16 −55 −54 +29 +36 −37 −41

Exaggerated kerning

SENSUAL SEDUCTION

−99 −69 −110 −70 −203 −37   −89 −64 −135 −134 −51 −44 −117 −121

Letters should not be kerned too tightly or else they will squash together.

Control palette in InDesign

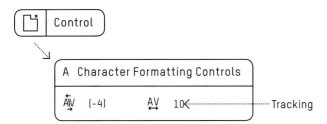

A value in parentheses indicates the automatic kerning.

Typical combinations for kerning

AT AV AW TA LT LV LY
AG DT LO LW UA L* "A"
Te Wa Xo 10 11 41 1−0

the font and automatically kerns the spaces between certain pairs of letters, such as Wa and Tm, if this is specified in the typeface's kerning table.

In optical kerning the letter spaces between individual pairs of letters is reduced or enlarged according to letter shape. This makes sense when the font does not have any, or has very few, kerned letter combinations. Optical kerning is used for all kinds of texts. It can be used for headlines as well as body text.

However, because the letter spaces are distributed differently, the tracking can change so much when it is switched from automatic to optical that the line breaks change on longer texts. One- or two-liners such as headlines can normally have optical kerning applied without too much trouble. Automatic kerning can also be deactivated. To do this one must select Zero instead of Optical or Metric.

With automatic optical and metric kerning, letters only rarely need to be balanced manually. It is only usual for capitals and small caps to have their letter spacing corrected. This would be too much trouble to go to for long body texts. However, it can be worthwhile for a large headline or logo. By turning the letters upside down, it is easier to tell whether the characters are evenly distributed and whether the character widths need to be altered.

In order to balance capitals or small caps, it might be necessary to reduce some letter spaces and increase others. This is done in the following sequence: First, the pairs of letters that are still compar-

atively widely spaced after kerning are kerned. These then form the reference for the other pairs to copy. Their spaces are adjusted to match those of the reference.

First, one must reduce to a minimum the spaces between pairs of letters where both letters have a lot of beard or white space. These include TA, for example, and LA. The spaces between these letters are reduced as much as necessary. It may be that a word or line does not include any letter combinations with a lot of white space. In that case, other letter combinations are used as a reference for tracking, for instance a pair of letters where only one letter has a lot of white space, such as TM. In addition to letters with a lot of white space, letters with curves also have to be kerned. Therefore if there are no letter combinations where either letter has much white space, then combinations such as RO or RM may be used as the standard by which to set the tracking for all the other letters.

Some letter combinations can be kerned too much for them to be useful as a reference. These include LT and AW, for example. Despite their ample white space they can move so close to one another that other combinations such as PT or AF ought to be used instead for reference.

In kerning, one has to be careful not to reduce the tracking so much that letters touch. The only exception being serif Roman fonts where certain pairs of letters intertwine harmoniously; WE and AR are examples.

Automatic metric kerning

SENSUAL SEDUCTION

0   0   0   0   0   0   0   0   0   0   0   0   0

Automatic optical kerning

SENSUAL SEDUCTION

−9   +11 −20   0 −63 +23   −9   +6   −35 −34 +9 +16 −37 −31

Notes

3.5 Typographic rules

Typographic rules do not cover how to spell or use punctuation. They cover aspects of writing such as how to arrange various rows of numbers or the use of different dashes and quotation marks. When the rules are applied properly, they improve the readability of a text.

It is important to apply typographic rules consistently because they make the text easier to read and more uniform. Typographic rules are particularly useful when it comes to different kinds of dashes. Using the wrong dash can lead to misinterpretation of the text.

Different spaces

One uses a quarter space (one quarter of an em) or a nonbreaking space for abbreviations or terms that belong together, such as Dr. Frankenstein, 2%, 2 in, or vol. 2. Since the point in abbreviations makes the quarter space look bigger than one word space, one can use a sixth space or a thin space, which is one eighth of an em, or eight-per-em.

One important typographic rule shows how to break down rows of numbers in order to make a series of digits easier to read. When digits are arranged together in groups, the space between them should be noticeably smaller than a word space, which is one third (also called a thick space) or one quarter of an em. A thin space is used instead for numbers.

Dr. Frankenstein, 2 mm, 2 in⟵····· quarter space
fl. oz, vol. 2, p. 12⟵····· sixth space
123 456 789⟵····· thin space (eight-per-em)

Abbreviations Abbreviations are spaced with a quarter space (four-per-em). Some have a point and some do not. If the point makes the space look bigger, a six-per-em can be used. Abbreviations should not be used at the start of a sentence; they should be written out instead.

Some abbreviations with a space:
H. P. Lovecraft
fl. oz, p. 400

Abbreviations without a space:
a.m., §4m

Abbreviated units Abbreviated units are separated from the number with a quarter space.
4 m, 4 kg, 4 s
4 Hz, 4 W

In the context of computing there is no space between the unit and number.
4MB, 2.4GHz, 4kB

Apostrophes Apostrophes are set without spaces in the middle of words. At the start or end of a word they are preceded by one blank space.
Let's go. 'Scuse me. Groovin' down.

Asterisks An asterisk should be set in the same font and size as the text it is used in. It may have to be raised a little.
F*** off
The asterisk* is below.

Dashes The ability to tell the different kinds of dashes apart makes understanding the text easier.
Hyphen: -
En dash: –
Em dash: —
2-em dash: ——

Dates Years are separated with a comma when they have five figures or more.
10,000 BC

In the United States all-numeral dates are normally set using slashes rather than points, in the order month, day and year.
12/24/05

The ISO system is year, month and day, with a hyphen to separate.
2005-12-24

When the name of the month is written out, one sets an empty space, and separates the year with a comma. The date should not be separated unless necessary.
December 24, 2005

One must not use an apostrophe when referring to a period.
In the 80s, 1960s

BC and AD should be set in small caps. BC follows the date, while AD precedes it.
250 BC; AD 250

Degree symbol The degree symbol stands alone after the number without space—one word space from the number if the unit of measurement is included, and without any space to the unit.
30°, 30° West or 30° W
30 °C, 30 °F

Different white space in InDesign

The thin space character is used for a series of numbers.

Quotation marks

Double	Single	Double	Single
„German″	‚German'	»German«	›German‹
„Danish″	‚Danish'	»Danish«	›Danish‹
"English"	'English'		
″Finnish″	'Finnish'	»Finnish»	›Finnish›
"French"*	'French'*	«French»	‹French›
"Italian„*	'Italian„*	«Italian»	‹Italian›
„Dutch″	‚Dutch'		
„Norwegian″*	‚Norwegian'*	«Norwegian»	‹Norwegian›
„Polish″	‚Polish'	»Polish«	›Polish‹
"Portuguese"*	'Portuguese'*	«Portuguese»	‹Portuguese›
„Russian″	‚Russian'	«Russian»	‹Russian›
″Swedish″	'Swedish'	»Swedish»	›Swedish›
«Swiss»	‹Swiss›	„Swiss″	‚Swiss'
„Slovenian″	‚Slovenian'	«Slovenian»	‹Slovenian›
"Spanish"	'Spanish'	«Spanish»	‹Spanish›
"Turkish„*	'Turkish,*	«Turkish»	‹Turkish›

*The quotation marks with an asterisk may only be used for headlines.
Single quotation marks are used inside quoted speech, for example.

”A” „A” “A„ «A» »A»

“A” „A“   »A«

Ellipses Ellipses are three dots, often used to end a sentence. They are set with one word space. However, if they are used for words that break off, or are next to punctuation, parentheses, or quotation marks, then they are set closed. When they are at the end of a sentence the period disappears.

The rest is history …⟵┈ normal word space
These f…ing dots⟵┈ closed
Your … plants have withered⟵┈ normal word space
What was that …?⟵┈ normal word space and thin space to punctuation mark (See "Punctuation marks," p. 136)

Em dash An em dash is twice as long as an en dash and is used to separate explanatory passages and other interpolations, although some prefer to use an en dash. It is usually set closed. It is used as a parenthetical dash or to convey a distinction in sense, where it stands for "and" or "to." A parenthetical dash is closed or with a hair space.

A thought—or maybe not.
Busy going—dashing—nowhere.

It can be used to indicate speech that breaks off abruptly.
"I want—. Nothing."

One can use a 2-em dash with one word space to indicate an omitted or repeated word.
We are waiting for ——.

Set closed, a 2-em dash indicates an omitted part of a word.
We are waiting for A—— .

En dash An en dash is slightly longer than a hyphen. An en dash between words is set closed.
Roman–italic, 1984–85
London–Glasgow train

One can use a hyphen in compound adjectives.
Punk-influenced

An en dash may also be used between groups of numbers.
May 3rd–September 4th

Spaced en dashes may also be used to indicate missing letters.
Elvis P - - - - ey

Figures with plus/minus sign If a number includes a plus or minus sign, it should not have a space. However, if a unit of measurement follows the number, then the space from the plus or minus sign should be the same as it is from the number to the unit, i.e., a quarter space.
+4, -10

Formulas and measurements Formulas and measurements are separated from the number with a quarter space or a thin space.
4 x 4 = 16⟵┈ quarter space
4 : 4⟵┈ thin space
4 / (4 x 4)⟵┈ thin space and quarter space

Forward slash A forward slash is either set closed or with very little space. If it seems too low, the baseline can be adjusted.
Roman/italic, 1984/5
One can also set a quarter space before and after the slash if it is helpful, for instance when the descriptions are more than one word.
New York / New Jersey

From/to An en dash is used between the from/to letters or numbers with only a hair space of 24-per-em, if at all.
8–12 p.m.

Hyphens Hyphens are set closed. They usually connect two words. They can also be used to separate words.
Word-connecting

Hyphens are also used to separate prefixes and suffixes in telephone numbers and the like.
1-900-1234-567

Ligatures Ligatures connect two letters. Their origins go back to hot metal setting. They were used to make the type look more attractive. They were very useful because the top arc of *f* would break off when it was followed by an *f, i, l,* or *t*.

Nowadays ligatures are only used for aesthetic purposes, especially in headlines, although not in all typefaces. In general ligatures are not used to connect two word roots, so not in "rooflighting," for example. One should also make sure that they can be substituted for two single letters if they are split. This is why they are not used much in long body texts.
fi instead of fi, fl instead of fl

Minus sign The minus sign is an en dash, the same width as the plus sign. Sharing the same width is useful for tables.

-20 °C, 7 – 4 = 3

Parentheses Parentheses often look too low and can also be raised a little. Round and square parentheses are set closed.

(normal), (slightly higher)

PO Box numbers Post office box numbers are arranged like telephone numbers in pairs from the back.

PO Box 12 34

Postcodes Postcodes or ZIP codes are set without spaces or hyphens.

Town 50109, BR5 1LZ

In the United States the optional further code is set with an en dash without a space.

11208–1010

Punctuation marks Exclamation marks, question marks, colons, and semi-colons are all set with a space no bigger than eight-per-em (thin space).

I'm here! Where are you? Colon: Semi-colon;

Quotation marks Quotation marks identify speech. There is a difference between single and double quotation marks. In the United States single quotation marks are used within a quote or for certain terms.

"Are there any 'flotation marks'?" he asked. "I think you mean 'quotation' marks," she replied, "but don't 'quote' me on it."

In British usage this is the opposite—double quotation marks are used for quotes within quotes:

'Are "inverted commas" quotes?'

Relation signs Relation signs, such as – (minus), + (plus), = (equals), and > (larger than), vary from country to country.

British: + 4, > 4⟵⋯⋯ quarter space or thin space
US: + 4, > 4, ± 4⟵⋯⋯ closed up or hair space

Rows of numbers As a rule the last three digits are separated by a comma in series of four numbers and over.

1,000; 10,000
100,000; 1,000,000

In numbers of one thousand or more, commas are used between groups of three digits, counting from the right.

1,234
12,345
1,234,567,890

Symbols Abstract and purely typographical symbols follow similar rules. Some symbols are set without a space to the number:

4%, 4‰, 4°, 4″, 4′
£4, $4, €4

Some symbols are set with a quarter space to separate the number:

4 Ω, 3 : 8

Telephone and fax numbers Telephone and fax numbers are arranged differently throughout the world according to national preference and custom. In Europe, telephone and fax numbers that consist of more than three digits are set in pairs starting from the back. This is not the case in the United States. One should set a space smaller than a whole blank space: a thin space (eight-per-em), for example. Extension numbers are set with an en dash without a space, and arranged from left to right.

British: 12 34 56 78-00 1
American: 12 34 56 78-001

Word formation Word formations are set closed. Some formations can be written in various ways.

The 20th century, the twentieth century
20% or 20 percent
16th, sixteenth, 32nd, 4-piece
10-fold, tenfold
6-pound, 11-cylinder
4-page, four-page, one-line

Notes

<u>3.6 Corrections</u> Almost all print products go through several stages of correction. Somebody who has not worked on the document should always proofread the layout after composition because experience shows that one often misses one's own mistakes.

Proofreading is the process of checking hyphenation and typographic rules as well as spelling and grammar. A proofreader also checks that there are no mistakes in tables or illustrations, often optimizes the wording of a text, and makes sure that certain formulations and terms are employed consistently throughout.

The customer should reread the document before signing its release. This is to safeguard against any subsequent claims for compensation. Because despite all the best efforts, it can happen that a product is printed with mistakes, thus incurring high costs to rectify it. There are standardized DIN correction marks to make the typesetter's corrections quicker and clearer. These are handwritten in the text and in the margins so that they are not missed. There is more room in the margin for explanations and changes in longer texts. If the margin space is not enough, for example, if a whole sentence has to be rewritten, extra corrections can be written at the head or foot of the page. Corrections should also be identified by color. Naturally, they have to be unambiguous and easily legible. When there are several corrections in a single line, they should be separated by slashes.

Important correction marks

US: (wf)
TSTAR Reg.
└┘ US: (ital)
~~~~~ US: (bf)

If a different font is to be used for emphasizing text, the relevant words are underlined or circled. The circle is repeated in the margin with "wf" (wrong font) circled and the name of the new font. If italics are required, one writes "ital"; if a bold face is required, one writes "bf."

r/ and/

Incorrect letters or words are struck through in the text and replaced with the correct letter or word in the margin.

t/
i/

Missing letters and punctuation marks are marked in the text by inserting a / in the previous or next letter, and writing the missing letter in the margin.

∧ are

Missing words∧marked in the text with a caret and written in the margin. When longer text passages are missing, the relevant parts of the manuscript are marked with a side note.

ℐ US: ℓ

ℐ US: ℓ

Superfluous letters and words are marked using the hook-like delete symbol in the margin. The close-up symbol should be added when a letter or letters are deleted from within a word.

US: #

↑/ Y/

⌒/

Missing word spaces are marked using a hash symbol. Word spaces that are too big↑are marked using a ↑. Too little space is marked using a Y, and extra space with two arcs.

ℐ ℐ US: ℓ

/ni

* 2 breaks !

Incorrect end-of-line word breaks are marked at both the beginning and ends of lines and corrected in the margin. If there are too many end-of-line hyphenations in a paragraph, they are marked in the margin with a side note.

*

ron /

⌐┘/

⌐┘/

446/

Letters that are in the wonrg order are marked and written in the correct order in the margin. Words that swap position are |by|marked|the transpose symbol. When[4] it[5] affects[6] many[7] words[8] they[1] are[2] numbered[3].[9] Displaced figures such as 644 are always struck through and written out correctly in the margin.

When a word or a group of words has to be transposed to a certain position, the area in question can circled be with an arrow pointing to the right position.

When there is not enough leading (space between the lines) it is marked using a line and an opening parenthesis. When there is too much space it is marked using a line with a closing parenthesis. Where a new paragraph should begin is marked using this or this ¶ symbol .

Text that should be joined to the previous paragraph is marked using a reverse S-shaped line.

Displaced lines ———————————————————————————————— 1
using horizontal lines ———————————————————————————— 4
are numbered in the correct order —————————————————— 2
in the margin ——————————————————————————————————— 3

A wrong indent is marked in the left and right margins using the appropriate correction marks.

A missing indent should be marked as precisely as possible so that one can see how far the line has to move back.

When the same letter is repeatedly set bodly one correction mork is added in the mrgin for each letter.

When mistakes frequently reoccur, the correction mark in the margin can be written once with a note about its frequency.

One can also strike through a woleh word and write it correctly in the margin. /whole

If there are mistaken corrections, one circles a check mark or the word "stet" in the margin and writes dots under the erroneous correction marks in the text.

US: stet

3.7 Standard dimensions

One of the important aspects of print that this book would not be complete without is the size of standard letters, envelopes, and postcards. The standard letter shows the position of the window and the fold and hole marks. Envelopes and postcards are divided into printing and non-printing areas, since mail is sorted by machine at the post office.

Standard letter ISO A4

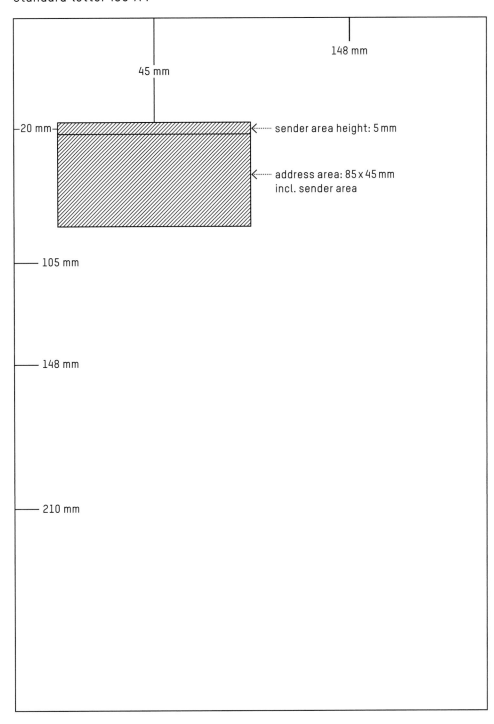

Standard envelope DIN C4 (162 x 114 mm)

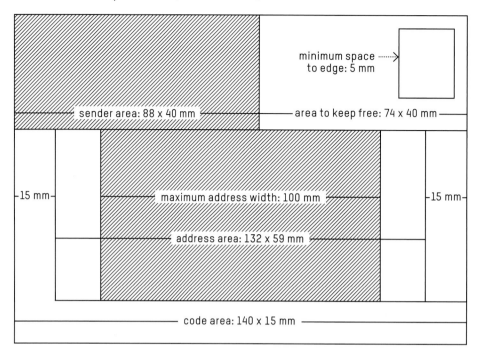

The printable areas are gray in the illustration above. The code area at the bottom guarantees machine sorting, which is more economical.

Standard postcard DIN A6 (148 x 105 mm)

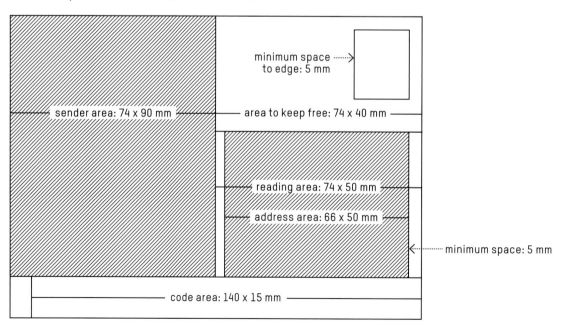

Standard business envelope, US

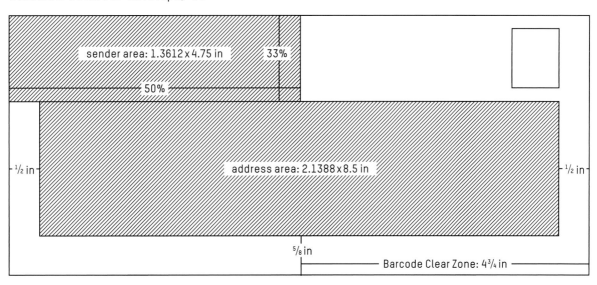

sender area: 1.3612 x 4.75 in

33%

50%

address area: 2.1388 x 8.5 in

½ in

½ in

⅝ in

Barcode Clear Zone: 4¾ in

Standard postcard, US

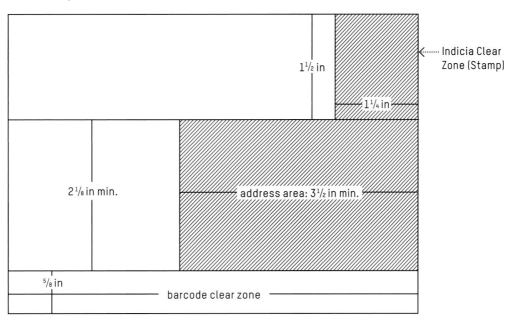

1½ in

Indicia Clear Zone (Stamp)

1¼ in

2⅛ in min.

address area: 3½ in min.

⅝ in

barcode clear zone

4. Trapping

A printing machine has to meet extremely high demands for speed and precision. However, it is impossible to print colors perfectly in register over each other onto flexible print material, such as paper or film. The degree of precision required is very high at one tenth of a millimeter, but in the end the odd register or rotation error has to be tolerated even under optimal conditions. White gaps can occur where two colors meet. To prevent this from happening, the colors have to overlap slightly. This is what trapping is.

In many cases, trapping is done directly at the printing house. However, there are exceptions, such as artwork that is sent to a publisher. Trapping is hardly ever done at the newspaper printing house. That is why it can make sense to make a PDF with trapping.

This chapter explains exactly what traps are, when they are needed, and how they should be applied in a document. We will look at the basics first, in regard to different kinds of printing methods, before explaining the trap presets in Adobe InDesign and Illustrator. The illustrated examples have had their trap width exaggerated so that one can see the traps with the naked eye. Normally, they ought to be so discreet that they are not noticed.

<u>4.1 Basics</u> First, it is important to know whether trapping is at all necessary, how big the traps have to be, and what they ought to look like. The shape and width of the traps depend on the printing method used. These parameters are specified in the trapping programs. The next pages look at the theoretical basics. After that, the program-specific settings will be explained.

Colors with enough components in common

magenta

magenta and yellow

magenta and cyan

cyan

Colors without enough components in common

magenta

cyan

magenta and cyan

yellow

Colors with enough components in common do not need trapping.

Trapping sequence

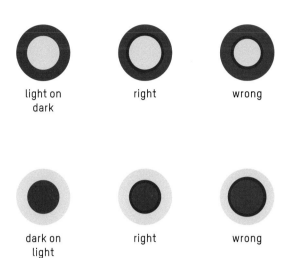

light on dark

right

wrong

dark on light

right

wrong

For the upper circle to keep its shape the brighter color has to trap the dark color.

Misregister can cause white gaps in multicolor printing. Colors are displaced so much that visible gaps occur between two color areas that should fit together tightly. Trapping—also called spreading and choking—prevents gaps from occurring by making one of the colors overlap the other. The degree of trapping depends on the registration tolerance value of each printing method in respect to the kind of paper used. This means that the degree of overlapping has to be slightly higher than the register accuracy.

Overprinting is when a color completely covers the color underneath. In many cases black objects can simply print over their background, thereby preventing white gaps from occurring like trapping does. However, black should only print over a background as long as there is no coloration of the black itself. (See "Automatic black overprint," p. 156.)

Trapping can be generated during the printing of the document using the built-in printer trap settings or with a special trapping program in the RIP (raster image processor). A composite PDF does not normally contain traps—apart from black. In many cases the data is only trapped at the printing house using a special program in the RIP.

There are exceptions, such as advertisements, where the trapping already has to be included in the artwork. A lot of newspaper and magazine advertisements do not have the trapping done at the printing house and should already include trapping. The specifications are often found in the publisher's advertising information. If not, one should ask the publisher or printer.

Trap threshold

The trap threshold determines at what point trapping is required. The most important value is the difference in color between the background and the object. This value ensures that colors are only trapped if they have insufficient components in common. Mixed inks, such as the process colors of the Euroscale, have enough components and do not need to be trapped. Colors such as red and magenta or blue and cyan have enough components in common. Trapping is not necessary to prevent white gaps. When, for example, four process colors meet four or three other process colors, they do not need trapping because even if the colors shift slightly there is always a sufficient amount of the remaining color to prevent misregister from being noticed. Spot colors do not normally have any components in common with other colors.

Register accuracy without trapping

Register accuracy with trapping

White gaps only occur when colors do not have enough common components.

Light colors without traps

When colors are very light, white gaps may be less noticeable than traps.

Trapping sequence The trapping sequence defines which object or color to trap. The sequence depends on the brightness ratio between the object and the background. One normally wants to maintain the shape of the object on top. One does this by increasing the shape of the brighter color.

When the object is brighter than the background, the object traps the background and becomes bigger. When the object is darker than the background, the shape of the background changes. In this case the background traps the object.

To select whether or not an object needs to trap or be trapped, programs such as InDesign compare the neutral density of the colors. If trapping needs to be done manually and it is not clear which color is lightest, then the colors in question can be transformed in Lab mode in Photoshop or Illustrator. Photoshop also has the grayscale mode. This way one can easily check which color is brighter. In the grayscale mode, the color with the least amount of black is the lightest, while in the lab mode it is the color with the highest value in the luminance channel (L).

Trapping has to be done manually for a logo or advertisement if they are EPS files that will not undergo trapping in the RIP, and if the trapping can be done using an overprinted line.

Trap color Trapping is affected by how light the object or background is. When very light objects meet very light backgrounds, trapping may not be needed at all. White gaps or color shifts are much less conspicuous in light colors than trapping, wich might be noticeably darker than the object and background.

In general, the trap color should not be darker than the object. One can influence it by trapping each color component of a mixed color to a different degree. A trap color is always darker than an object and background if it is mixed from the same components of object and background color. However, it looks lighter and less conspicuous when the proportion of spot colors is reduced slightly in relation to the object and background colors. If one takes a red that is composed of 100 percent magenta and 100 percent yellow, and traps it with 50 percent cyan, then the simple trap color would be 100 percent magenta, 100 percent yellow, and 50 percent cyan. The resulting trap would be very dark, almost brown. If, however, the trap color consists solely of components from the object and background color, it becomes much brighter. If the trapping is, say, 87 percent magenta, 81 percent yellow, and 41 percent cyan, it sticks out less. An inconspicuous and therefore optimal trap color always has the same brightness or luminance value as the darker of the two colors to be trapped.

Reducing the trap color

wrong

right

wrong

right

The luminance of the trap color is the same as the darker color when the individual color components are reduced.

Cyan is choked from magenta

cyan + magenta

Cyan prints over magenta

cyan + magenta

Overprinting black

black + magenta

When black prints over its background, it mixes with the background color and its tone becomes affected.

Trap width A trap should not merely have the same luminance as the darker object for trapping in order to work well. Its width also has to be adjusted so that it blocks white gaps without appearing too big. The trap always has to be slightly bigger than the registration tolerance value. This in turn is affected by the kind of paper and its weight and grain. One should request the trap widths from the printer or publisher if they are not included in the written production specifications.

The degree of trapping also depends on the size of the object, so that the trapping does not destroy its shape. If the lines are fine and the point sizes are very low, it is better not to trap. Overprinting may instead be better for eliminating white gaps. Relatively large objects should not necessarily have much trapping either because it can be easily visible and jarring to look at. The trap width can be different horizontally and vertically, depending on how the printing process affects the paper.

The most common trap widths are between 0.05 and 1.5 point. In sheet-fed offset printing, the default trap width is 0.15 to 0.4 point. In web offset, it is between 0.3 and 2 point. Gravure printing can require bigger trap widths than offset printing due to the high print speed. In silkscreen printing, the trap width depends on the print material. Because materials distort differently when drying, different trap

Unintended effects of overprinting black

uneven color

partial coloration

brown coloration

Various undesired effects can occur
when large black objects print over their
background.

Trapping black

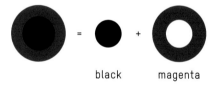

black   magenta

Trapping rich black

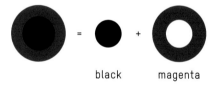

black   magenta   40% cyan

Overprinting

The simplest way to prevent white gaps in multicolor printing is by overprinting, where a color or an object completely covers the background. Normally an object would knock-out its background color in order for the color shape underneath to retain a negative imprint of it during color separation. However, when a color prints over its background, the background is not kept under the object. Because the object color is printed onto the background color, the colors mix and create a new mixed color. White gaps cannot occur because the paper is completely covered with ink.

Overprinting black

Black has a special position when it comes to trapping. Black can nearly always print over its background. However, the overlapping colors mix and make the black stand out a little more. This is hardly ever noticeable in small type or thin lines. When black is printed over large areas, it can be too conspicuous and trapping should be used instead.

Trapping black

When large black objects are trapped, their shape does not change, because the background traps the black object, seeing as black is the darker color.

Trapping rich black

Rich black is trapped like other colors in relation to the object color and the background, where all components except black change its shape. The color components in rich black must not go right up to the edge when a rich black object is on white. Otherwise, there is the risk of color gaps occurring if there is register inaccuracy. Therefore the shape of the color components is slightly smaller than the black shape, by the default trap size.

widths have to be applied accordingly. The individual color shapes on a T-shirt may need choking rather than trapping, because the material stretches and then tightens together.

Notes

<u>4.2 Trapping in InDesign</u> Like almost all other programs, InDesign includes its own trap settings that can be adapted as required. On the following pages we will explain all the different settings.

Attribute palette

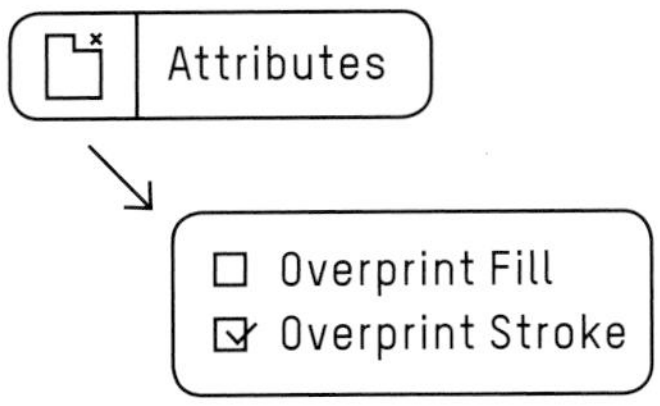

Attributes

☐ Overprint Fill
☑ Overprint Stroke

Separations palette

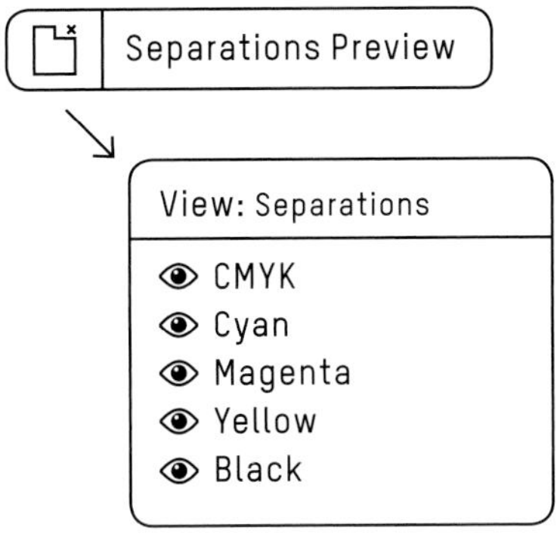

Separations Preview

View: Separations

👁 CMYK
👁 Cyan
👁 Magenta
👁 Yellow
👁 Black

Color palette with (black) and black

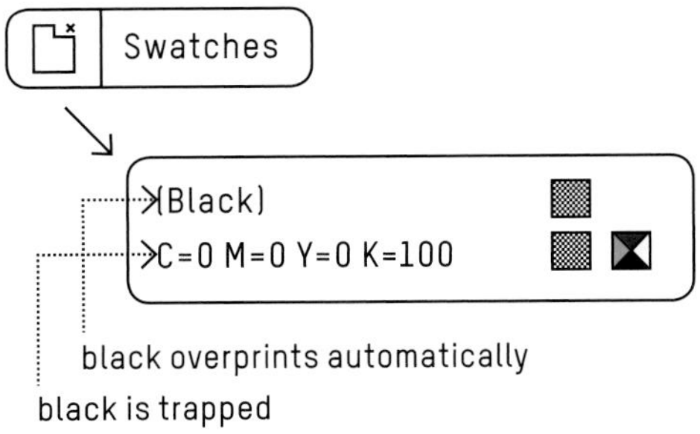

Swatches

(Black)
C=0 M=0 Y=0 K=100

black overprints automatically
black is trapped

One has to define a new black if one needs a
black that does not automatically overprint.

Checking black overprint

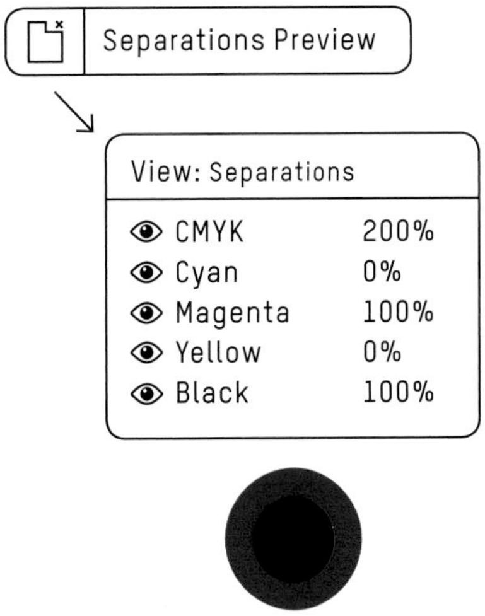

Separations Preview

View: Separations

👁 CMYK   200%
👁 Cyan   0%
👁 Magenta   100%
👁 Yellow   0%
👁 Black   100%

view with
black

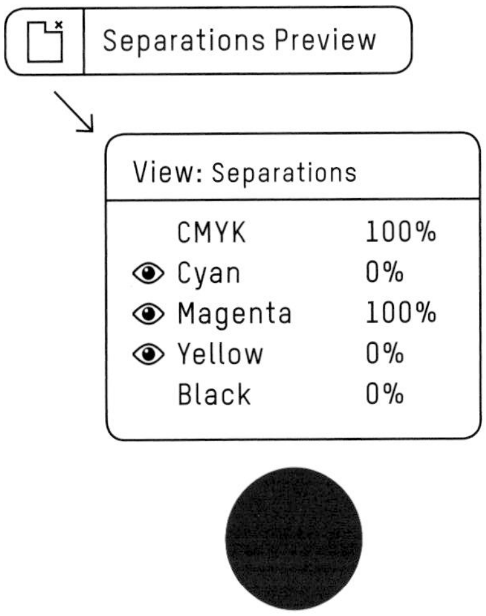

Separations Preview

View: Separations

CMYK   100%
👁 Cyan   0%
👁 Magenta   100%
👁 Yellow   0%
Black   0%

view without
black

The automatic traps in InDesign are all produced exclusively with printing ink. This means that automatic trapping cannot be displayed on a computer screen. It only happens during the output phase of production and has to be activated in the print dialog. Object-specific trap settings can only be created using overprint strokes, fills, or type in the Attribute palette. These manual traps are displayed onscreen when the overprint preview is activated in the View menu.

The monitor simulates the color result of the overprinting color areas or lines. It shows when the Overprint Preview (View > Overprint Preview) or the Separations Preview (Window > Output > Separations Preview) is activated. In either case, one can check before output that all the colors are correctly choked or printed over.

If one wants to check whether black objects are printing over their backgrounds using the Separations Preview, one clicks away black in the Preview palette.

Built-in trapping and EPS files

In built-in trapping nothing that needs trapping should touch the EPS image box because trapping will not work if it does.

When black overprints, there is no visible negative imprint of the black object.

Automatic black overprint
In the color palette along with the spot colors cyan, magenta, yellow, red, green, and blue, is black, although it is in parentheses. When one activates the option Overprint (Black) Swatch 100% in the program preferences under Appearance of Black, all objects that contain the black in parentheses automatically print over their background. However, if objects are not supposed to print over their backgrounds, an individual black has to be defined for them. This new black does not print over its background automatically, because only the black in parentheses in the color palette automatically prints over its background. The new black is instead trapped with the trap value for black.

Trapping text
All fonts can have trapping done with Adobe In-RIP. However, built-in trapping can lead to problems with TrueType fonts. If trapping really has to be done with In-RIP, Adobe recommends converting the text to paths.

Trapping imported vector graphics
Placed vector data in PDF files or Illustrator files can be trapped both using Adobe In-RIP and built-in trapping. Placed EPS files can only have trapping done in Adobe In-RIP. Built-in trapping cannot be used for EPS files. Built-in trapping does not even work for internally produced objects or type if they overlap EPS data. To prevent this problem from arising, the shape of one or both objects should be as small as possible so that they no longer overlap. (More information about Adobe In-RIP and built-in trapping to follow under "Creating traps," p. 166ff.)

Preferences for black overprint

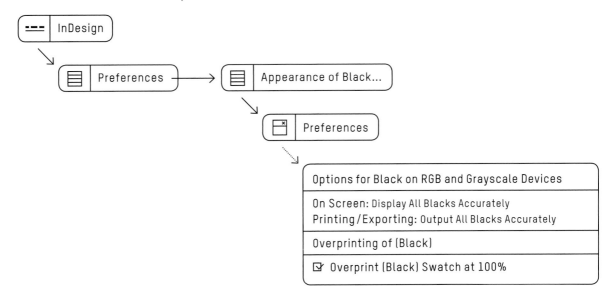

When the black in parentheses in the color palette is activated, it overprints automatically.

<u>4.3 Trap presets</u> The trap presets define what needs trapping, when, and how. "When" in this context means what value limits have to be exceeded, "what" tells us whether images are included, and "how" defines the strength and shape of traps.

The individual user can define various trap presets (Window > Output > Trap Presets) in addition to the default settings in InDesign.

<u>Trap width</u> The trap width can be adjusted individually. The maximum trap width in Adobe In-RIP is 8 point and in built-in trapping 4 point. (See "Creating traps," p. 166ff.) Trapping over 4 point is very rare. Usually trap widths are much smaller.

The trap width under Default affects all colors apart from black. The trap width should be entered here, bearing in mind all the requirements. As men-

tioned, one finds this out from the printing house, publishers, or from the relevant advertising information. The trap width under Black affects all colors with a 100% black component or whose density is over 1.6—the neutral density of black. Both of these values can be changed under Black Density Limit.

Black normally has 1.5 to 2 times the default trap width. The default setting is automatically bypassed for thin elements, such as fine black lines. The trap width of fine black objects is always equal to half the object value. The trap width for black also applies to rich black, in which all colors other than black are smaller by the trapping value, in order to prevent color gaps around the object's edges.

Trap presets palette

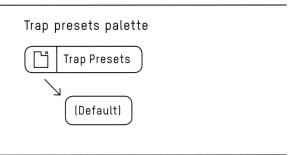

<u>Trap appearance</u> One can check how the trapping looks on corner points with trap appearance. This does not affect round objects without corners. Trap appearance has Join Style and End Style pop-up menus.

Join style defines how a trap is drawn on a corner when the colors of two objects meet; in this case both objects consist of object and background colors. There are three join styles: mitered, rounded, and beveled (see picture). The choice of style depends on the object. If it is not possible to trap it in InDesign, it is unlikely to work otherwise. However, this is fairly insignificant since the traps are so small that they are hard to spot with the naked eye anyway. Aside from this, Mitered yields the best results for normal corners, and Rounded works best for rounded corners.

Join style mitered

Join style rounded

Join style beveled

End style mitered

End style overlap

Trap placement in images

Without trapping

Centerline

Choke

Neutral density

Spread

End style defines how the trapping behaves if the corners of three objects meet. The options are Mitered and Overlap. Mitered should be used to avoid very dark overlaps. The corner traps are shaped so that they do not overlap.

Trap imported graphics Often trapping is not necessary when an object or type touches an image—at least not if the image and object are Euroscale colors. This is because a color photo normally contains all the colors, so that there are plenty of common scale color components to prevent any white gaps from occurring. One exception would be a colored object that touches a grayscale image. The object has to be trapped be-cause there are not enough common color components.

Trap placement This setting controls the position of a trap when a vector object traps an image. The options are Centerline, Choke and Spread. Neutral Density means that spreading or choking is required, depending on the pixel brightness of the abutting image. This can cause such uneven and shape-destroying traps that white gaps would be preferable.

Trap objects to images This option determines whether drawn vector objects, type, or placed Illustrator or PDF files with bitmap images are trapped in InDesign. This option should only be activated when there are insufficient color components in common.

Trap images to images This option determines whether traps are generated when bitmap images overlap. This option should only be activated when the overlapping pixel images have insufficient color components in common.

Trap images internally Here one makes sure that each pixel within an image traps the next pixel in accordance with the trap presets. This option has to be switched off for halftone images. Trapping may be suitable for images with large planes of color, such as screenshots that are separated so that the gray component only consists of black, or pixel graphics with strong color contrasts and few common components.

Trap 1-bit images This option creates a trap when a black and white image touches graphics or type. Trap placement cannot be changed for black and white images.

Default trap presets

Trap Presets

Preset Options...

Modify Trap Preset Options

Name: (Default)

Trap Width

Default: 0.088 mm
Black: 0.176 mm

Images

Trap Placement: Center
☑ Trap Objects to Images
☑ Trap Images to Images
☐ Trap Images Internally
☑ Trap 1-bit Images

Trap Appearance

Join Style: Miter
End Style: Miter

Trap Thresholds

Step: 10%
Black Color: 100%
Black Density: 1.6
Sliding Trap: 70%
Trap Color Reduction: 100%

trapping when color
difference is 10 percent
or more

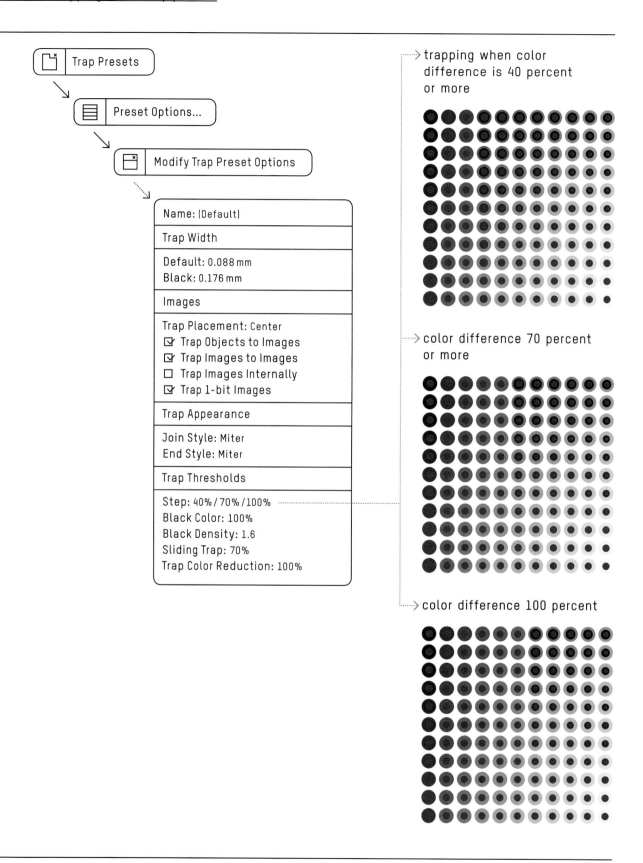

Trap Presets

Preset Options...

Modify Trap Preset Options

Name: (Default)

Trap Width

Default: 0.088 mm
Black: 0.176 mm

Images

Trap Placement: Center
☑ Trap Objects to Images
☑ Trap Images to Images
☐ Trap Images Internally
☑ Trap 1-bit Images

Trap Appearance

Join Style: Miter
End Style: Miter

Trap Thresholds

Step: 40% / 70% / 100%
Black Color: 100%
Black Density: 1.6
Sliding Trap: 70%
Trap Color Reduction: 100%

trapping when color difference is 40 percent or more

color difference 70 percent or more

color difference 100 percent

Optimized trap presets

[Trap Presets]

[Preset Options...]

[Modify Trap Preset Options]

Name: 2/100/100/1.6/100/0

Trap Width

Default: 2 mm
Black: 2 mm

Images

Trap Placement: Center
☐ Trap Objects to Images
☐ Trap Images to Images
☐ Trap Images Internally
☑ Trap 1-bit Images

Trap Appearance

Join Style: Miter
End Style: Miter

Trap Thresholds

Step: 100%
Black Color: 100%
Black Density: 1.6
Sliding Trap: 100%
Trap Color Reduction: 0%

Trap threshold The trap threshold determines when spreading or choking occurs. This depends on brightness and color composition and also on the object to be trapped.

Color difference The color difference value in percent defines how different colors have to be from each other for trapping. The lower the value, the more likely trapping is. The following illustrations show that trapping is done more than necessary at the default setting of 10 percent. Setting a higher value may be recommendable to prevent unnecessary traps. The best results are with a color difference of 100 percent. (See the following section "Optimized trap presets" below.)

Black color This value shows the minimum percentage of black a color has to contain in order to be trapped like black.

Black density This value shows the neutral density after which a color is treated like black. The values range between 0.001 and 10. The neutral density value of a color is measured using a densitometer. The standard default setting is to trap every color that has a density value higher than 1.6 with settings used for black.

Sliding trap This setting only works for objects that have different density values such as gradients. The value indicates in percent what difference in neutral density the bordering colors have to have for trapping to be moved step by step from the darker edge to the brighter edge. This setting is to prevent abrupt transitions between choking and spreading or vice versa along the trap edge in gradients. A continuous transition is created between the trap directions when the color brightness ratio changes in the traps.

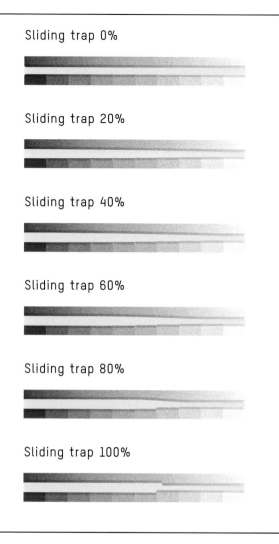

Sliding trap 0%

Sliding trap 20%

Sliding trap 40%

Sliding trap 60%

Sliding trap 80%

Sliding trap 100%

Trap color reduction This reduction prevents the trap color from becoming too dark. The trap color gets brighter in steps in values under 100 percent until it reaches 0 percent where it is exactly as bright or dark as the darker of the colors to be trapped. This is particularly important for very bright objects where traps can be more jarring than white gaps. It is not only bright objects that benefit from the default setting being changed from 100 to 0 percent, because the shape of an object never changes at 0 percent.

Optimized trap presets The default program presets are not always ideal in some circumstances. The illustrated setting could be an optimized preset—apart from the trap

Color trap reduction 0%

Color trap reduction 20%

Color trap reduction 40%

Color trap reduction 60%

Color trap reduction 80%

Color trap reduction 100%

Assign trap presets

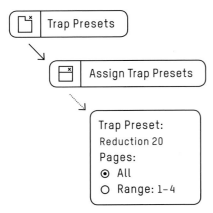

One must assign new trap presets when they are complete. The respective presets have to be assigned by the page to a document.

width, which may vary according to the printing method or preset.

Here is a summary of the reasons for the settings:

- The trap width should be adapted for the printing method used. The example here has been exaggerated for demonstration.
- The default trap appearance in Mitered is nearly always the optimum.
- Only the 1-bit image trap is activated in this case, since trapping imported graphics only makes sense in exceptional cases. If it is not possible in general to decide whether to choke or spread, one can choose Centerline for trap placement.
- When the color difference is set to 100 percent, there are no unnecessary traps, because the colors have enough common components.
- 100 percent may be set in Black Color. In doing so only colors with the same trap width as black are trapped if their black component is 100 percent.
- Black Density can also be set to 1.6. Colors that have reached a density of 1.6 are trapped with the same trapping width as black.
- The Sliding Trap should be set to 100 percent. That way the trapping is always created inside the darker of the two objects to be trapped. This ensures that the shape of the object does not change.
- When the Trap Color Reduction value is set to 0, the least noticeable trapping occurs because the trap color is just as dark as the darkest of the objects that need traps.

Assign trap presets All pages are assigned to the default trap settings. Custom trap presets have to be assigned in a document page by page. The dialog swatch is in the context menu of the Trap Presets palette. One can also specify that individual pages or whole page areas do not have traps by switching the preset to Off on those pages.

<u>4.4 Creating traps</u> In InDesign, the traps are only made during output, which is normally a color-separated print-out. However, in many cases the data is not sent as open InDesign files but instead to the printer's as composite PDF files. This composite PDF does not generally contain traps. Trapping is only done at the printer's using a trapping program in the raster image processor (RIP) during output. Sometimes the traps have to be included in the PDF, as is often the case for newspaper advertisements.

In-RIP separation

In-RIP separation has to be selected to create a PDF with traps. A composite PDF or composite PostScript file is created that is color-separated in the built-in printer RIP. For this, one needs a PostScript Level 2 or 3 printer that supports in-RIP separation, and a relevant PPD (PostScript Printer Description).

Built-in trapping

PDF or PostScript files can be created in InDesign using Built-in Trapping. The term "built-in" means that the trapping is already done in InDesign and not at the printing house with special trapping software.

Adobe In-RIP trapping

When using Adobe In-RIP Trapping the Adobe Trapping Engine calculates the traps in the RIP. InDesign only writes the trap settings in PostScript code. For in-RIP trapping, one needs a PostScript Level 2 or 3 printer. The Adobe Trapping Engine also has to be installed in the RIP. If not, the trap parameters may still be written into the PostScript file but they will not work, as they cannot be converted in the RIP without this engine.

Trapping in composite PDFs

When a composite PDF needs trapping, the PDF has to be created in the print dialog. One chooses Adobe PDF 9.0 as the printer. In the Output window under Color, one chooses In-RIP Separation, and under Trapping, Built-in.

One must be aware that in InDesign, embedded EPS or PDF files cannot have built-in trapping applied. If imported vector graphics have to have trapping done in InDesign, they should be imported as Illustrator files rather than EPS or PDF files. Otherwise EPS files have to have trapping done in the program they were created in (e.g.) Illustrator. Traps made manually, such as overprint strokes, fills or type, remain in the EPS files during output.

A PostScript file can also first be created with built-in trapping before being converted into a PDF using Adobe Distiller. A PostScript file can also be created in the print dialog, by choosin the hard disk

PostScript code

```
%!PS-Adobe-3.1
%ADO_DSC_Encoding: MacOS Roman
%%Title: Chucky.indd
%%Creator: Adobe InDesign CS4 (6.0)
%%For: Chucky
%%CreationDate: 01.07.2010, 21:58
%%BoundingBox: 0 -2 558 875
%%HiResBoundingBox: 0 -1.4999 557.2441
874.8071
%%CropBox: 23.5040 25.0040 533.7402
851.3031
%%LanguageLevel: 3
%%DocumentNeededResources: (atend)
%%DocumentSuppliedResources: (atend)
%%DocumentNeededFeatures: (atend)
%%DocumentSuppliedFeatures: (atend)
%%DocumentData: Binary
%%PageOrder: Special
%%TargetDevice: (Adobe PDF) (3018.101) 0
%%Pages: (atend)
%%DocumentProcessColors: (atend)
%%DocumentCustomColors: (atend)
%%EndComments
%%BeginDefaults
%%ViewingOrientation: 1 0 0 1
%%EndDefaults
%%BeginProlog
%%BeginResource: procset Adobe_AGM_
Utils 1.0 0
%%Version: 1.0 0
%%Copyright: Copyright(C)2000-2006 Adobe
Systems, Inc. All Rights Reserved.
systemdict/setpacking known
[currentpacking    true setpacking]if
userdict/Adobe_AGM_Utils 75 dict dup
begin put
/bdf
[bind def]bind def
/nd[null def]bdf
/xdf
...
```

instead of the printer. In principle, a PostScript file is created in every print dialog; it is either sent directly to the printer or only stored temporarily on the hard disk. This PostScript file contains the PostScript code, which is sent through the RIP to the printer so that it can make the print image out of it.

Creating traps

Step 1: General

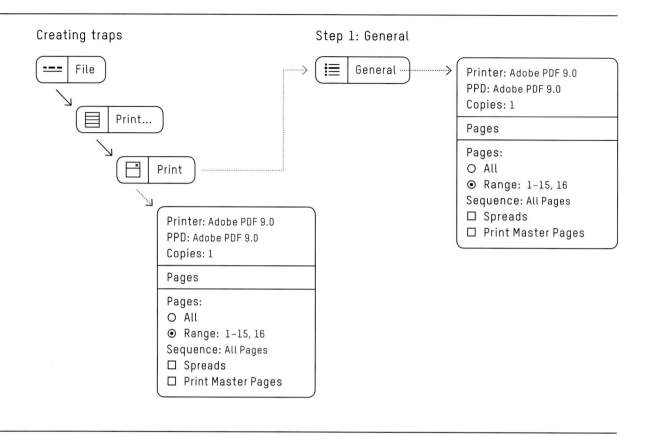

The illustration (p. 167) shows the start of a PostScript file. PostScript is a page description language that is understood by a PostScript printer. The printer is able to reproduce the pages with the help of this programming language.

Creating a composite PDF with traps

We will explain step by step the most direct way to create a PDF with traps in InDesign. After opening the print dialog, there are seven windows to make the necessary settings in.

Step 1: General First, the printer and the PPD have to be chosen. One chooses Adobe PDF 9.0 for a PDF with traps. The relevant PPD (PostScript Printer Description) is then activated automatically. Like in any other print dialog, the pages to print out are then chosen.

Step 2: Setup In the second step, the paper size is determined. It is normally slightly bigger than the document so that there is enough room for crop marks, register marks, and bleed if needed. Choosing Custom will automatically create the right paper size.

Step 3: Markers and bleed When the size of the file is not too small, all printer's marks apart from the bleed should be activated. This is excluded because it could get confused with the trim marks. If the size is very small, there is often not enough room for the color control strip and page information. The color control strip is usually printed out on the print sheet at the printing house anyway. Trim has to be activated if there is trim. The same goes for the system tray if it contains fold marks or a special color wedge, for example.

Step 4: Output One chooses In-RIP Separation under Color, and Built-in under Trapping to include the traps in the PDF. In-RIP Separation means that a composite PDF is created that is only separated in the printer RIP. Built-in means that the composite PDF contains all the traps that have been assigned to pages in InDesign. The settings under Flip only affect those who directly have to make a printing plate, so

Step 2: Setup

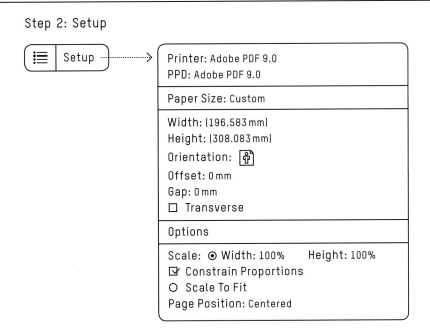

Setup ---------→

Printer: Adobe PDF 9.0
PPD: Adobe PDF 9.0

Paper Size: Custom

Width: (196.583 mm)
Height: (308.083 mm)
Orientation:
Offset: 0 mm
Gap: 0 mm
☐ Transverse

Options

Scale: ◉ Width: 100%   Height: 100%
☑ Constrain Proportions
○ Scale To Fit
Page Position: Centered

Step 3: Markers and Bleed

Marks and Bleed ---------→

Printer: Adobe PDF 9.0
PPD: Adobe PDF 9.0

Marks

☑ Crop Marks
☐ Bleed Marks
☑ Registration Marks
☑ Color Bars
☑ Page Information
Type: Default
Weight: 0.25 pt   Offset: 3 mm

Bleed and Slug

☑ Use Document Bleed Settings
☐ Include Slug Area

not normally designers or paste-up artists. The setting under Rasterize can also be ignored because the file was screened in the printer RIP with the settings for the printing method used.

Step 5: Graphics In this window, one makes sure that all images are displayed at full resolution. One chooses All under Send Data. It is worth placing all images in the correct resolution in InDesign—not too low nor too high—to avoid jumps in tonal value. The fonts should be embedded. Hence one must choose Full or Subgroup under Download.

Step 6: Color management In the color management one chooses Let InDesign Determine Color under Color Handling because otherwise colors are

Step 4: Output

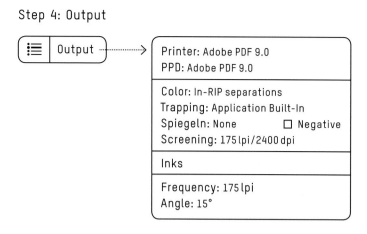

Step 5: Graphics

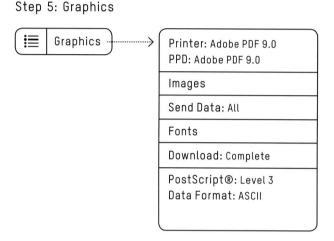

not predictable and the output color composition differs from the input. One must choose Document-CMYK here so that the selected Printer Profile matches the input profile. If not, the colors are converted in the destination profile, where pure black objects, such as type, may also be composed from all the process colors. One can activate the option Preserve CMYK Numbers so that only imported objects can be converted that have a color profile that does not match the chosen output profile—type and vector graphics created in InDesign, for instance. This affects all colors, not only black.

Step 7: Advanced This step affects documents in which transparencies have been used. One has to be sure to choose High Resolution under Transparency Flattener.

Step 8: Summary One checks the settings in this window. The command Print follows. The PDF file goes to the desktop and is called something like InDesign-file. The process can take longer depending on computer processing power, size of the file, and the time that the spooler takes to calculate the traps.

Creating a PostScript file Instead of directly creating a PDF in InDesign, one can also first create a PostScript file with which Acrobat Distiller can generate a PDF. However, the direct method is generally better because it is shorter and quicker. In the normal view of our example the version with the intent "Relative Colorimetric" looks most like the original.

Step 6: Color Management

☰	Color Management	┈┈┈>

| Printer: Adobe PDF 9.0 |
| PPD: Adobe PDF 9.0 |
| Print |
| ⦿ Document: (Profile: ISO Coated v2 (ECI)) |
| Options |
| Color Handling: Let InDesign Determine Colors
Printer Profile: Document-CMYK – ISO Coated |

Step 7: Advanced

☰	Advanced	┈┈┈>

| Printer: Adobe PDF 9.0 |
| PPD: Adobe PDF 9.0 |
| OPI |
| ☐ OPI Image Replacement |
| Transparency Flattener |
| Preset: (High Resolution)
☐ Ignore Spread Overrides |

Step 1: General In principle, one follows the same steps as previously described under "Creating a composite PDF with traps" but one must choose Post-Script File under Printer. It is best to choose Adobe PDF 9.0 under PPD.

Steps 2 to 8 These are the same as in "Creating a composite PDF with traps," with the only difference being that at the end one clicks on Save instead of Print. One is then prompted to name the PostScript file, which must have the file name extension .ps.

receives the settings that were last chosen in Distiller. To create a print PDF, the right setting has to be chosen. One cannot use the usual setting of PDF/X-3, because a PDF/X-3 cannot contain traps. (For more information about creating print PDFs, see the chapter "PDF," p. 268ff.)

Creating a PDF using Adobe Distiller

The PostScript file has to be opened by Distiller and converted into a PDF. One does this by dragging and dropping the PostScript file into the open Distiller window. The automatically created PDF

<u>4.5 Trapping in Illustrator</u> Illustrator also provides the possibility of creating traps. However, unlike InDesign, these are not produced during printing but manually, with the help of strokes or fills, and with the Pathfinder panel.

Type of trapping in InDesign

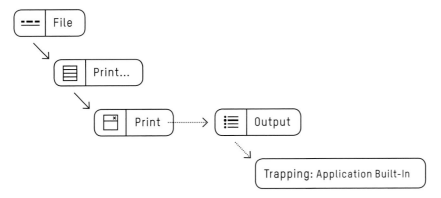

An Illustrator file placed in InDesign does not need to have traps if it has had built-in trapping done and is placed as an Illustrator or PDF file rather than as an EPS file.

Illustrator files are often placed in InDesign as EPS, PDF, or Illustrator files. The trap settings in InDesign also work for placed Illustrator files—albeit with the restriction that the InDesign built-in trapping only works for placed PDF and Illustrator files, and not for placed EPS files. Therefore, when InDesign files have to have built-in trapping, the traps in the Illustrator EPS files must be set directly in Illustrator using overprint strokes or fills. Adobe In-RIP Trapping, on the other hand, works for placed PDF and Illustrator files as well as EPS files.

Trapping with overprint strokes

Traps can be produced manually in Illustrator by placing lines or fills set to Overprint around the object or on certain edges. One activates Overprint Stroke or Overprint Fill in the Attribute palette (Window > Attributes).

In order to maintain the trap sequence, a trap that consists of an overprint stroke or fill should always be made of the brighter color. Illustrator draws strokes from the middle by default. The inner half of the stroke is inside the object and the outer half is on the background. The overprint stroke only works on the darker color when the overprint stroke is assigned the brighter color—whether the object on top that receives the stroke is brighter or darker. A trap is created automatically with regard to the neutral density; the object retains its shape and does not look thicker or thinner. The stroke has to be twice as thick as the desired trap

Stroke palette

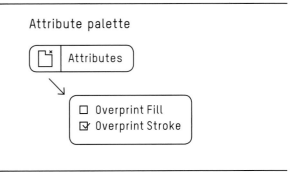

width because Illustrator files are drawn from the middle by default and only half of the stroke is trapped. Thus the actual trap is only half as wide as the stroke. One can check the result onscreen by activating Overprint Preview in the view menu.

The place where the stroke aligns to the object is important, in addition to the trap color, for maintaining the shape of the object. There are three options in the Stroke palette: the stroke can be aligned in the middle, inside, or outside. The shape and size of the object do not change when the stroke is aligned in the middle.

Trapping with the Pathfinder panel

Trapping with the Pathfinder panel is slightly more comfortable than trapping with overprint strokes, particularly when the trap objects are complicated. The basic requirement is that document color mode is CMYK and not RGB. Apart from that no trapping is done when the objects have color components in common.

One creates traps by producing a new object composed of two paths that is filled with the brighter color and overprints its background. A path is the original size and is increased or reduced by the trap width. The join style for this is Beveled.

Trapping is done with regard to the neutral density of the colors—their brightness. Traps are always over the darker color so that the shape of the object does not change. However, when the option Reverse Traps is activated, the trapping is applied to the brighter color, thereby changing the object's shape.

Trapping with CMYK When Trap with CMYK is activated in the Trap palette, the trap color becomes visible because the trap is already composed of the mixed color that would have arisen from overprinting the brighter color anyway. Apart from that, Overprint Preview has to be activated to view the trapping in Illustrator. This option makes no difference for process colors. On the other hand, spot colors are converted into CMYK using this option.

Trap sequence and stroke color

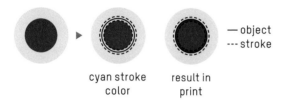

cyan stroke color / result in print
— object
--- stroke

— object
--- stroke

A trap from an overprint stroke or fill must consist of the brighter of the two colors.

Reverse traps

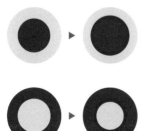

The Reverse Traps option alters the shape of the object. It appears bigger or smaller because the trap is on the brighter color.

Trapping with the Pathfinder panel

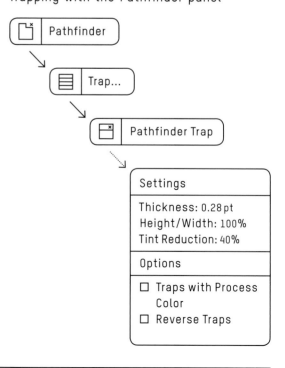

Tint reduced to 30 percent

CMYK: 50/0/0/0
CMYK: 15/100/0/0
CMYK: 0/100/0/0

Tint reduced to 60 percent

CMYK: 50/0/0/0
CMYK: 30/100/0/0
CMYK: 0/100/0/0

The Tint Reduction option brightens the bright color by the amount indicated.

Manually trapping strokes

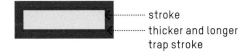

stroke

thicker and longer trap stroke

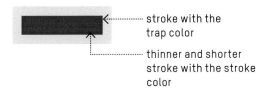

stroke with the trap color

thinner and shorter stroke with the stroke color

Manually trapping dotted lines

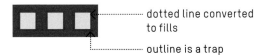

dotted line converted to fills

outline is a trap

Trapping as an effect

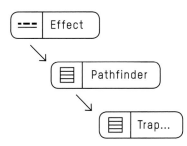

Reducing the trap color

One can automatically reduce the trap color in the Pathfinder trap dialog by entering a percent value lower than 100 under Tint Reduction. The trap color uses the indicated percentage of color instead of automatically becoming the same as the neutral density of the darker color.

When trapping has been done manually using outlines, for instance, and not using the Pathfinder panel, custom trap colors can be defined as an alternative to the Overprint Stroke option. These colors have all the components of the object and background colors. When the trap color is mixed, the individual color components can be reduced so that the trap is no darker than the darker color. This makes the trapping less conspicuous.

The trap color may also be reduced in overprint strokes. A reduced tonal value of the original color has to be assigned to the stroke. If successful, the trap color created by mixing should have the same brightness or neutral density as the darker of the two colors to be trapped.

Trapping strokes

One cannot trap strokes with the Pathfinder panel. If one has to trap strokes manually, a second overprint stroke is set over or under whichever stroke is thicker than the original. The best way to produce an exact copy is with the command Paste in Front in the edit menu. The thicker stroke is set to overprint in the Graphic Attributes palette.

When the stroke is brighter than its background, the duplicated stroke is thicker than its original and prints over the background. When the stroke is darker than its background, the duplicated stroke is thinner than its original, and the thicker original prints over the background.

When dotted lines need trapping, it is easier to expand the strokes into fills. These can be assigned to an outline as traps. Strokes are expanded into fills with the command Object > Expand or Object > Path > Outline Stroke.

They can subsequently be trapped using the Pathfinder panel. One has to bear in mind that the line width will be difficult to control or change later. If it needs to be done, strokes should be expanded into fills at the end.

Trap settings

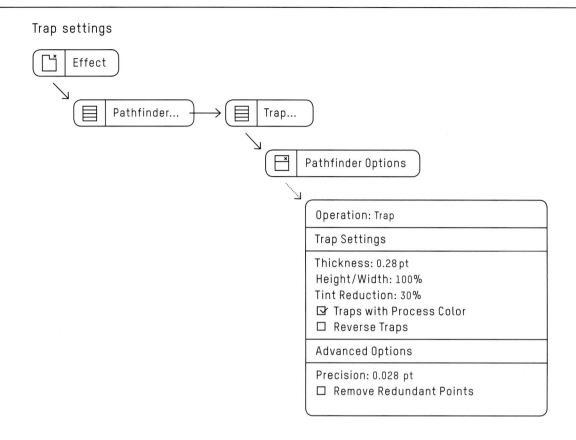

Operation: Trap

Trap Settings

Thickness: 0.28 pt
Height/Width: 100%
Tint Reduction: 30%
☑ Traps with Process Color
☐ Reverse Traps

Advanced Options

Precision: 0.028 pt
☐ Remove Redundant Points

<u>Trap height/width</u> One can increase or reduce the strength of the horizontal traps in relation to the default value under Height/Width in the Pathfinder options. For example, at 200 percent they are double the strength—and at 50 percent half the strength—of the default trap value. This way one can counter one-sided stretching of the paper during printing. At 100 percent, horizontal and vertical traps are the same.

<u>Trapping as an effect</u> The strength of a trap created with the Pathfinder panel cannot be changed later on unless the trap is an effect (Effect > Pathfinder > Trap). An effect is listed in the Appearance palette. One opens the trap settings by double clicking on the effect. These can be changed at any time.

Notes

5. Color

Colors are subject to trends in society and are an indicator of changes in taste. They give an object character and decisively influence its appearance. Does something look serious or implausible, modern or crazy? Different people perceive colors differently. Many great thinkers have investigated the science and laws of color, and its physical, biological, and psychological effects.

The perception of color changes from person to person because every eye reacts differently to light stimulus and the brain processes it and perceives it differently. The human eye has various color receptors for the three colors red, green, and blue. All colors in our spectrum can be mixed from these three base colors, with the color information completed by brightness information. The recognition threshold is not the same for each color tone. It is 20 times lower for green recognition than for blue, meaning that green tones are easier to distinguish than blue ones.

An experienced and sensitive approach to color is necessary in order to produce the same color perception in print design and reproduction. The following sections look at the most important basic aspects of color, including everything about the various color modes, a basic knowledge of color management, and everything important about color proofs. The chapter ends with a few practical examples of color conversion in Photoshop, InDesign, and Illustrator.

<u>5.1 Color basics</u> One can explain a color given the necessary background knowledge, and also measure and mathematically describe it. The following mostly physical basics form the basis for the practical use of color in everyday graphic design.

<u>Light colors and body colors</u> There is a fundamental difference between light and body colors. The former are produced from a light source in the three base colors red, green, and blue. The various brighter color mixtures are created from the meeting of these base colors. This is called additive color because the spectral colors are added together. White is created when all three base colors are added together in equal measure. When none of the base colors are present, the color stays black. Monitors and televisions work according to this system. Their pixels are composed of the three different luminescent substances red, green, and blue.

Body colors, on the other hand, are the colors with which we see our environment through trichromatic color perception. One can differentiate body colors because the incident light is absorbed in different parts and only partially reflected back. The color impression is created by this reflected light, which is again composed of different parts of the base colors red, green, and blue. One can differentiate light and dark colors because different colors and materials absorb light to varying degrees. When body colors are mixed, as they are in painting, they become darker. This is called subtractive color because the color brightness diminishes due to the absorption of the light rays.

The base body colors are cyan, magenta, and yellow. In theory, when cyan, magenta, and yellow are

Additive color mix

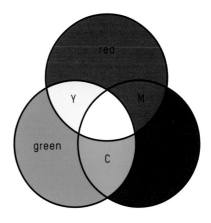

Subtractive color mix

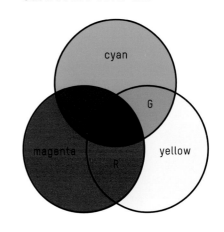

Color space

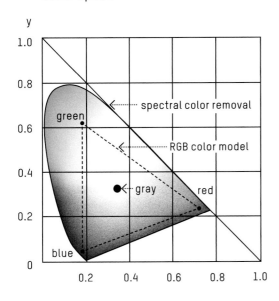

Color triangle

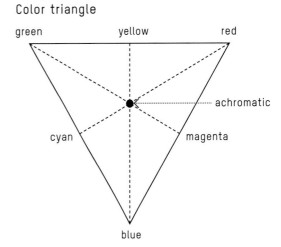

RGB color model

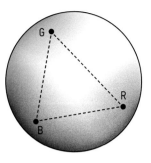

CMY color model

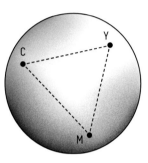

mixed, they create black. However, for technical reasons, in practice pure black does not ensue, but a sort of brown tone in its place. Adding pure black as a printing ink makes reproducing neutral tones, such as black or gray, easier.

The complementary colors of additive colors are subtractive colors. When two of the additive base colors red, green, or blue are mixed, cyan, magenta, or yellow ensue. The ensuing color is the complementary color to whichever third base color has not been mixed. The same thing applies to subtractive color mixing. Complementary colors are capable of mutually canceling out or strengthening one another. The color triangle that shows complementary colors opposite one another is very useful for work such as correcting the color balance of a picture.

<u>Color space</u> A color space contains all the colors that are possible within a particular coordinate system. It may also be described as a color model. The coordinate system or color space area is determined by the color space system used. A color

model is a model of all the colors in the particular color space used.

There are device-dependent and non-device-dependent color models. The former are limited to the possible colors of an input or output device, such as the RGB color space of a monitor or the CMYK color space of a printer. Non-device-dependent color models have no limitations and contain all conceivable colors within a coordinate system, like for example, the CIE Lab color system.

<u>Color model</u> The respective color range of a color space is fundamentally determined by its base colors. There are different color models for this. In prepress the relevant color spaces are mostly limited to the RGB, CMY, CIE Lab and HSB color models. When one depicts a cross section of a color space, one gets a two-dimensional area with the respective base colors on its corners.

The RGB color model consists of the three base colors red, green, and blue, from which all possible colors can be mixed in theory. The device-dependent RGB color spaces are limited to the colors they can produce.

The CMY color model consists of the three base colors cyan, magenta, and yellow. When these three colors are printed over one another at 100 percent, it will theoretically produce black. However, black ink is introduced because the absorption properties of pigments for printing ink produce a brownish black in practice. The K in CMYK stands for key black. Black may also be distributed across the entire tonal value range and be

Lab color model

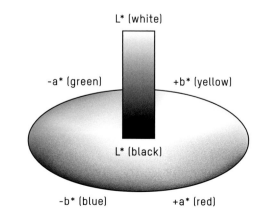

CIE Lab color model

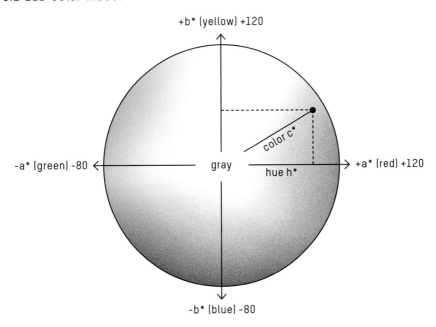

Color and hue are defined on the chrominance level with the coordinates a* (red-green axis) and b* (yellow-blue axis).

present in the midtones and highlights, depending on the separation technique.

The Lab color model (luminance, a, b) belongs to the non-device-dependent color models, which include all perceivable colors. It consists of the two horizontal color axes a and b with two base colors each, so four colors altogether. Red and green are opposite each other on the a axis, with blue and yellow on the b axis. The vertical brightness axis L (luminance) indicates the brightness of colors: 0 for black and 100 for white.

Luminance and chrominance, i.e., brightness and colorfulness, may be adjusted independently from each other in the Lab mode. All colors with the same brightness are on one horizontal level due to the horizontal arrangement of both color axes. The vertical arrangement of the L axis means that one measures the saturation of a color by its distance from the L axis.

The Lab color model is also often called CIE Lab. It was developed by the International Commission on Illumination and touches on the previously described complementary color model. This purely imaginary, mathematically created color space knows

no limitations. The CIE Lab color space is also used as a bridge between source colors and destination colors. It is the reference color space that considers human color recognition and contains all the colors that we can perceive. All device-dependent color spaces contain only some of these colors.

The CIE XYZ color model is based on the imaginary color space that is created with the coordinates X, Y, and Z. Within the coordinates X and Y there are all conceivable colors. The Z axis defines color brightness, similar to the L axis in the Lab color space. However, the colors within this coordinate system do not correspond to human color distance perception and do not take into consideration human visual perception like the CIE Lab color space does.

The LCH color model defines luminance (brightness), color, and hue. Color increases and decreases with changes in brightness. Colors on the outermost edge are the most saturated, while those on the inside are less saturated. In black or white and all neutral tones in between it is zero. Inside both axes is the hue, which indicates the color tone; for example, whether it is a red or green tone. Thus hue, brightness, and saturation are all defined.

Color settings in the HSB color model

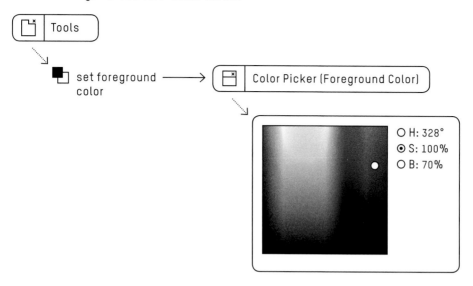

In Photoshop one can set the hue, saturation, and brightness of a color in the HSB model independently of each other.

The HSB color model defines hue, saturation, and brightness. HSB means the same thing as LCH, with the S for saturation corresponding to C for color, and the B for brightness to L for luminance.

When one compares various color spaces or models, it becomes clear why some colors cannot be perfectly reproduced. The various color spaces are not identical. Colors that are outside of a working color space can only be reproduced approximately. When the different colors are superimposed on top of each other, only the colors that overlap can be reproduced exactly. All the other colors that do not overlap can only be reproduced with the closest color tone in the destination space.

Color space comparison (diagram)

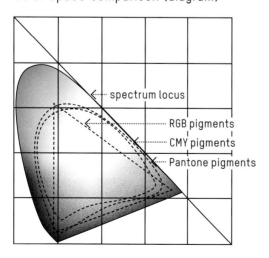

Color matching system

Color matching systems or catalogs, also called swatch color libraries, are a limited collection of certain colors by different manufacturers. The most commonly used ones in the printing industry are HKS, Pantone, and RAL. The HKS collection comprises 86 spot colors for different grades of paper. The suffix K (in German *Kunstdruckpapier*) is for coated art paper, N (*Naturpapier*) is for uncoated paper, Z (*Zeitungspapier*) is for newsprint, and E (*Endlospapier*) is for continuous paper. The suffix follows the number of the color and designates the grade of paper. There are official process color conversions for different grades of paper—although some colors can be reproduced better than others in the Euroscale.

The Pantone collection comprises 1114 colors, which are mostly presented on coated and uncoated swatches. The spot colors look more or less the same on different types of paper. However, the official Pantone CMYK conversions are identical in the C (coated) and UC (uncoated) swatches, so that colors simulated using process colors look totally different on different types of paper. This is mostly due to the fact that process colors have to be screened to reproduce a Pantone color. This leads to fluctuations in tonal value on different types of paper, which in turn leads to differences in color.

The Pantone Solid Coated table in the InDesign Swatch Options dialog box is especially relevant to the use of Pantone spot colors. The Pantone Color Bridge CMYK EC table is extremely useful for CMYK conversions because these are specially made for Europe, and the process colors generally look most like the real colors. One should adapt the conversions for other types of paper using color management and current color profiles. Pantone reworks the swatches every couple of years. It can occur that a certain Pantone color changes its color tone over time. This is impractical for a company color, so HKS colors are somewhat more recommendable as far as color reliability goes.

There is always the possibility of creating a custom company color, exclusively available as a print color for the company. As a rule, only large businesses can afford this.

RAL colors are also called the RAL color system. They are composed of various standard colors for the construction and machine manufacture industries. The RAL Classic System contains 210 colors. The RAL Design System contains 1,688 colors in the CIE Lab color space. This color standardization is important for the graphic designer when adhesive film or varnish refer to this color system.

Apart from these much-used color matching systems there are also other swatch color libraries. These include DIC Color, with 1,200 CMYK spot colors by Dainippon Ink & Chemical of Tokyo; Toyo Color Finder with over 1,000 colors from Japanese inks; Focoltone, with 763 colors in 5 percent gradations; and Truematch, with over 2,000 digital colors that cover over the visible CMYK spectrum in even steps.

Pantone guides

Pantone Color Bridge CMYK EC Coated paper, for Europe
Pantone Color Bridge CMYK PC Coated paper, for US
Pantone Color Bridge CMYK UP Uncoated paper
Pantone Metallic Coated
Pantone Pastel Coated
Pantone Pastel Uncoated
Pantone Process Coated
Pantone Process Uncoated
Pantone Solid Coated
Pantone Solid Matte
Pantone Solid to Process Euro No longer available
Pantone Solid to Process No longer available
Pantone Solid Uncoated

<u>5.2 Color mode</u> An image has to be set in a certain color mode that determines which color system the colors are defined in. In Photoshop one can choose from the color modes RGB, CMYK, Lab, Grayscale, and Duotone. Images and colors may be separated in the individual color channels according to the set color mode.

Bitmap

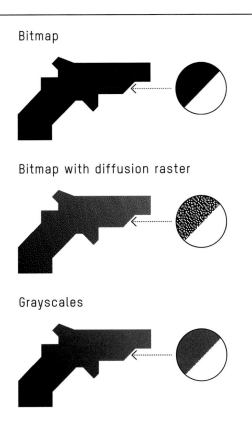

Bitmap with diffusion raster

Grayscales

Duotone mode image

In the Duotone mode, a single grayscale channel with its 256 possible gradations from black to white can be reproduced with more than one print color. This mode is good for high-quality grayscale image reproduction. By using two print colors, it is possible to reproduce the midtones and highlights with an additional gray, which allows for a more dynamic reproduction.

The Duotone mode is also used a lot to reproduce grayscale images with a varying degree of color shading. This entails printing the highlights with a color, such as a Pantone or HKS color. The options Monotone, Duotone, Tritone, and Quadtone are available. These determine the amount of print colors.

A duotone image is a single channel image. The individual colors may only be worked using the curves in the Duotone options by repeating the command Image > Mode > Duotone. The image has to be converted in the Multichannel mode (Image > Mode > Multichannel) in order to have access to the individual color channels. The print colors are converted to spot colors so that each color is represented in the Channel palette.

Bitmap mode image

This mode is only available in Photoshop. In the Bitmap mode each pixel can only be either black or white. This mode is very useful for line drawings, i.e., for logos or illustrations. A bitmap can also have a screen added to simulate the various grayscales.

Grayscale mode image

The Grayscale mode image consists of only one channel. Black can be distributed across the entire tonal value range in 256 gradations from white to black. However, most printing machines are not capable of reproducing that many grayscales. Therefore, a grayscale should be reproduced with more than one print color, in the CMYK or Duotone mode, for instance. This introduces the risk of a color cast when absolute color accuracy cannot be guaranteed and the color balance cannot be maintained. This risk is higher in newspaper printing, as there can be major fluctuations in color within a print run.

Indexed Color mode

This color mode is particularly good for internet or multimedia use. The individual pixels do not contain any color information themselves but a link to a color in a separate color table. This table contains a maximum of 256 colors. The fewer colors it contains, the smaller the file size is. One can edit the individual colors by opening the color table (Image > Mode > Color Table).

One comfortable option to achieve an image with indexed colors is with the command Save for Web. In this dialog window, the color table can be optimized with different options. The file size and estimated loading time in the internet are also shown.

RGB color mode image

The RGB mode mixes all colors from the base colors red, green, and blue. RGB are not print colors; RGB is mainly used for creating graphics and colors for the internet or for Office software on a computer screen.

Duotone image black and
Pantone Warm Gray

Black color separation

Pantone Warm Gray color
separation

Duotone options

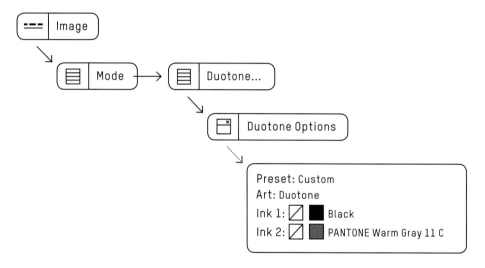

Duotone curves for black

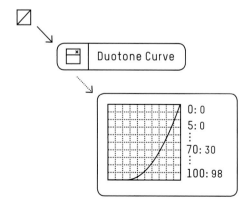

Duotone curves for Pantone Warm Gray 11C

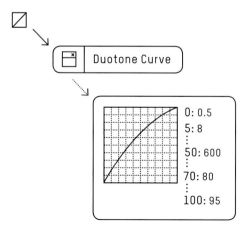

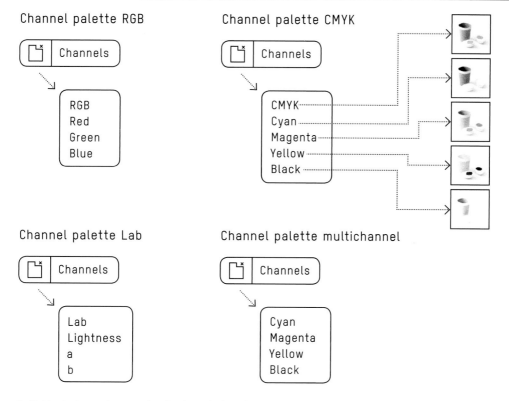

Channel palette RGB

Channels

RGB
Red
Green
Blue

Channel palette CMYK

Channels

CMYK
Cyan
Magenta
Yellow
Black

Channel palette Lab

Channels

Lab
Lightness
a
b

Channel palette multichannel

Channels

Cyan
Magenta
Yellow
Black

Individual channels can also be targeted and corrected where necessary.

CMYK color mode image
CMYK are the print colors cyan, magenta, yellow, and black. Nearly all colors can be mixed from these base colors. The K in CMYK stands for key black, and is the description for black printing ink. In theory, black can be mixed from cyan, magenta, and yellow, but in practice these produce a brownish black. Depending on the method of separation, black is usually added to the shadows, midtones, and neutral tones, although the other colors can also be reduced accordingly. The total color application is reduced, as it cannot be too high for technical reasons. Black is also needed for type so that it can be printed in one color alone. A screened type color would mean a loss in quality, particularly for small type sizes or fine typefaces.

Lab color mode image
The Lab mode separates the image into three image channels. The first channel defines the luminance (L), which corresponds to brightness; the second channel (a) consists of the red-green axis; and the third channel (b) is the blue-yellow axis. The brightness can be set independently of image color in this mode.

Multichannel mode image
The multichannel mode separates the image into individual spot colors. When, for example, a CMYK image is converted in the multichannel mode, the image consists of four spot colors with the descriptions cyan, magenta, yellow, and black. The individual channels can be renamed or erased. Like the other modes, further color channels can also be added. One gets to the spot color channel by double clicking on a channel in the Channel palette. Here one can change the name and solidity or intensity of a print color.

A print color is simulated at an intensity of 100 percent that completely covers all the print colors underneath it, such as would occur with a metallic color. An intensity of 0 percent simulates print colors that are totally transparent, such as

Spot color channel options

```
┌─────────────────┐
│ 🗋× │ Channels   │
└─────────────────┘
         ↘
    ┌──────────────────────────┐
    │ ☰ │ Channel Options...   │
    └──────────────────────────┘
             ↘
       ┌──────────────────────────────┐
       │ 🗋× │ Spot Channel Options    │
       └──────────────────────────────┘
                 ↘
          ┌────────────────────────┐
          │ Name: Silver           │
          ├────────────────────────┤
          │ Ink Characteristics    │
          ├────────────────────────┤
          │ Solidity: 70%          │
          └────────────────────────┘
```

One can simulate the opacity of a print color by changing its intensity in the spot color channel options.

clear varnish. Adjusting the strength of a color has no effect on the printed separation; it only changes its appearance onscreen.

Colors in InDesign

An important part of the final artwork is determining the right kind and mode of color. Although it is possible to convert spot colors into process colors using the Ink Manager in Printing or during PDF export, all colors are separated in the same way, which can lead to poor results. A tidy color palette is part of good artwork.

It can be a good idea to delete all the colors that are not used in the color palette, in order to better control the colors that are used. To do this, there is the command Select All Unused Colors in the Color palette menu. After this, one should check that all the remaining colors conform to the output requirements. These include color mode, kind of color, and the composition of the process colors.

It is fundamental that one makes sure that spot colors in Illustrator or Photoshop are labeled the same as they are in InDesign. Otherwise, there will be doubly defined spot colors in the Color palette, for instance a HKS 27 K and a HKS 27 N. When that happens the wrong color should be substituted for the correct one.

The quickest way to do this is by deleting the wrong one and replacing it with the correct one. If the color is still in use, a dialog will appear in which one color may be replaced by another. If an undesired spot color cannot be deleted, it is presumably because an imported graphic contains it.

In InDesign one can always define a color in the Lab, CMYK, and RGB color modes or as a mixed print color. One also has access to the various swatch color libraries, such as the HKS or Pantone tables, in the color mode.

Regardless of the colour mode used, the type of color is defined as a process color, spot color, or mixed ink. This determines whether a color ought to be separated. The type of color is indicated in the Color palette by an icon. A process color is composed exclusively of cyan, magenta, yellow, and black for printing. A spot color is printed as a separate print color. A mixed print color can be composed of all available colors; for example, a spot color and a process color. In this way, one can create darkened spot colors by mixing a spot color with a little black. A mixed print color is often used to mix a color with a varnish to create a spot varnish to cover a particular print color.

The choice of color type is important for ensuring that the colors used are in the right color separations. For instance, it is possible to define a spot color but mix it in the CMYK color mode. One can give a spot color the descriptions "varnish" or "Pantone 123" and mix these individually in the CMYK mode. In this case the color mode influences the screen display above all. On the other hand, choosing the right color mode is important when clear specifications or expectations determine the color.

Ink Manager

When one is working with many imported graphics that do not correspond to the correct output requirements, the ink manager is a quick and convenient aid. It can either be accessed through the Color palette menu or later in the print or export dialog.

All output colors are shown in the upper window. All colors may be assigned an Ink Alias. Spot colors that have been defined twice or incorrectly can thus be assigned the correct spot color so that all elements have the right ink variety for output.

All spot colors may also be printed as process colors using the option Convert All Spots to Process Colors. One must be careful that all ink aliases are

Deleting and replacing colors

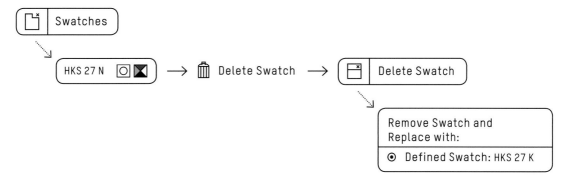

Color types in InDesign

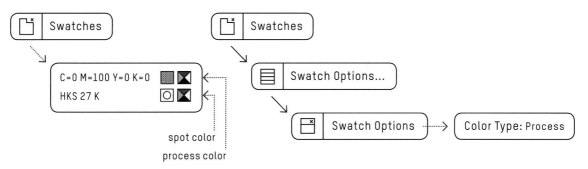

spot color
process color

Ink Manager in InDesign

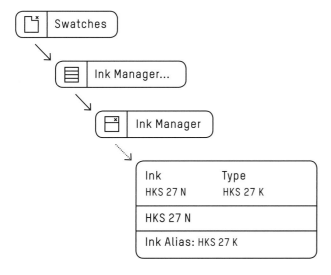

The spot color HKS 27 N is defined as the ink alias HKS 27 K.

Color palette in Illustrator

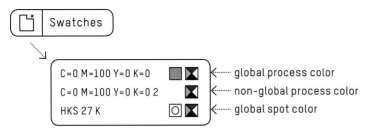

When a color defined as global is changed all objects containing this color are automatically updated.

removed. Individual spot colors can be converted to process colors by clicking on the ink type icon on the left. The separation ensues with the CMYK values of the spot colors.

Alternatively, a spot color can be separated using the option Use Standard Values for Spots. One can separate spot colors in the color preferences in relation to the output profile with this setting. However, the results are not previewable and do not necessarily correspond to expectations. Hence, this way is not really suitable for final artwork in which precise color specifications play a role.

Colors in Illustrator

Colors in Illustrator documents are defined by the output conditions, as they are in InDesign. So if one is printing in the Euroscale alone, one must define the colors as CMYK colors, taking care to label them correctly. The spot color description has to be identical to the description in InDesign, so that no unnecessary colors are output during color separation. When a spot color is printed, there must be only one definition of it in the Color palette and not, for example, one HKS 27 K and one HKS 27 N.

In this context one should use Global in the Swatches options. A color defined as global is linked to the color in the Color palette. Thus all objects that contain a color defined as Global will keep that color. All objects with a non-Global color retain the original definition of it if it is subsequently changed, because their color is not linked to one in the Color palette.

In many cases, it is worth defining a color as Global. This is because if the color is redefined from, say, HKS 27 to HKS 28 during the course of a layout, all objects will automatically receive the newly defined color. One can see whether a color is defined as Global by the icon in the Color palette.

Notes

<u>5.3 Color management</u> Color management enables the faithful reproduction of colors throughout the work process. The mode of operation is based mainly on the interaction between three components: the color management module, color profiles, and application support. The color management module is the engine that drives the color management system. The color profiles describe the various color spaces that need compensating.

Color view in various RGB color spaces

R=181 G=53 B=23   R=178 G=0 B=106

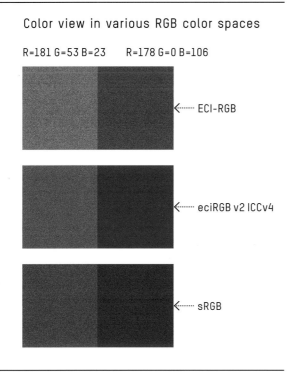

←······ ECI-RGB

←······ eciRGB v2 ICCv4

←······ sRGB

and output devices in order to do this. Different print conditions and types of paper also have to be taken into consideration. This information is contained in ICC-compatible color profiles, also called ICC profiles. They contain a precise description of the color spaces. The device-independent reference color space CIE Lab, which contains all possible colors, is needed to convert a color into different device-dependent color spaces. This way each device-specific color can be transferred to the CIE Lab color space, from where it is transferred to another device-specific color space.

ICC stands for International Color Consortium, a group of well-known industrial businesses that have agreed to a standard method for producing consistent, predictable, and reliable colors within a digital workflow. The ICC was formed in 1993 on the initiative of Fogra. Various prepress providers, such as Adobe, Apple, Microsoft, Agfa, and Kodak, have come together to unify color management systems. They developed a color management system (CMS) and the ICC profile format specification, which is the basis of all ICC profiles.

Due to the fact that the color spaces of the various input and output devices are not identical, the color management system's main task is to convert the colors from one color space to the next, either to display them on-screen or to print them. If they were not converted, certain color values would be represented differently in each color space. For example, a red with the RGB values R=181, G=53, B=23 would look slightly different in each RGB color space, just as a CMYK color composition would look different in each CMYK color space.

An ICC-supported color management system is capable of interpreting this color information and converting it to the various color spaces so that a red will look as similar as possible in each input and output device. This red displayed is very close to the print result on the monitor. The print result in turn must correspond to the proof. Color management compensates the technical differences between the various devices. The degree to which a color is represented the same on different devices depends on whether that color is in both color spaces, and if not, to what degree it can be simulated using the base colors of the respective color spaces.

A color management system requires precise information about the properties of the various input

Color management module
The basis of color management is the color management module, or CMM. It is also described as a color engine. There is a choice of various color management modules in the color settings. Two engines are automatically installed in the Adobe Creative Suite for Mac OS: The CMM by Heidelberg, a leading printing machine manufacturer, which is also used by Microsoft's ICM (Image Color Management) and which is the system standard for ColorSync; and the Adobe Engine, or ACE (Adobe Color Engine).

The color management module is responsible for converting colors into the various specific color spaces. Here a CIE Lab color space is required, which produces the connection between the color spaces and is also called the Profile Connection Space (PCS). This imaginary, device-independent color space is large enough to represent all device-dependent color spaces. It enables the colors to be converted into the various input and output device color spaces, to be as true to the original as possible on-screen, and to be reproduced on different types of paper. The colors can be converted from one color space to another, taking different intents into consideration. We shall look at the different intents in more detail later on in this chapter under "Rendering intent." (See p. 214ff.)

Color profile The color management module can only perform its work with the help of color profiles. They are the mathematical descriptions of particular color spaces and contain all relevant data about the specific properties of the input and output devices—which color space a scanner or digital camera has, for instance, or which color space particular inks on different types of paper have. The CMYK profiles are available for the various printing processes on different types of paper. They take into account the properties of the inks, the tonal dot gain of the paper, and the right preferences for color separation, including black generation and the maximum total ink application.

When the relevant color profiles have been embedded in all the files, a color management system can display and output consistent colors by compensating the differences of the various devices. Colors and images are converted from one color space to another to adapt them to the various output conditions. This means that the image on-screen or a printout will pretty much match the subsequent print result.

There is always a color space transformation when working with a color management system. So, for example, a print image has to be converted from a scanner color space or a general RGB color space to a CMYK color space. The colors also always have to be converted to the specific color space of the monitor in order to guarantee color accuracy on-screen. In this context one uses the terms source and destination space. Source color space is the input color space, and destination is the output.

Device-dependent and device-independent color profiles
A color management system differentiates between device-dependent and device-independent profiles. The former describe color models that may have different color spaces. These include the RGB and CMYK models. Although every monitor works in the RGB model, the destination color space is always slightly different, which is why each monitor receives a device-dependent color profile. This applies in general to all input devices, such as scanners or digital cameras, and for various output devices, such as printers. Device-independent profiles describe color models with fixed color spaces such as the CIE Lab model. These profiles are device-independent and describe a theoretical, imaginary color space.

Color temperature and gamma in prepress

White point	5000–6000 K or color balance with paper
Gamma	1.8 or L*
Absolute brightness	160 cd/m² or brightness balance with unprinted paper (a typical ambient lighting intensity of 5000 lux corresponds to an absolute brightness of around 160 cd/m²)

Color space	Color temperature	Gamma/gradation
Adobe-RGB	6500 K	2.2
sRGB	6500	2.2
Apple-RGB	6500	1.8
ECI RGB	5000	1.8
ECI RGB v2	5000	L*
ISO Coated v2	~5000	~1.8

The color temperature of the monitor in prepress should be adapted to match the white point of the unprinted paper.

Device-dependent profiles are divided into monitor, input device, output device, and document profiles. Monitor profiles describe the specific color space of a monitor. The monitor profile is needed for the color management system to correctly display the colors within the workflow. Therefore the first thing to do is calibrate the monitor—which should be done at regular intervals—and produce a monitor profile.

Input device profiles describe the color space of the various input devices, such as a scanner or a digital camera. Output device profiles usually concern printers and printing machines. An output device profile takes into consideration the different print conditions, such as the various printing processes and types of paper, but also country-specific features. There are special ISO profiles for this that define national and international print standards.

Document profiles define in which RGB or CMYK color space one is to work in. This guarantees that the colors in a file are represented properly and reproduced correctly. When a document is not given a color profile, it only contains the raw color numbers that are represented differently on each device. A document meant for printing will generally receive the pertinent output profile—ISO Coated for coated paper or ISO Newspaper for newsprint, for example.

Calibration

User-defined ICC profiles of the various input and output devices have to be created so that the color management has all the information it requires. This entails calibrating the devices. Calibration consists of adjusting a device so that its output values correspond to the desired destination values and that its colors are consistent when the input data is the same. Subsequently, the device is characterized, in which the attained measured data is written in a device-specific color profile. This profiling makes it possible to calculate the device-independent CIE Lab color values from the device-dependent values in order to get correct output values on a printer or monitor.

Calibrating input devices

Special software is used to calibrate a scanner or a digital camera and to create profiles. Generally a standardized color table is scanned or photographed. Here a special printout, slide, or film with a series of swatches of various standard colors and grayscales is used as as original. The software then compares the collected data with the actual color values of the original.

A scanner or a digital camera only has to be calibrated once as a rule. The color profiles that have been created can be embedded in the color management system to deliver the necessary information in order to interpret the input data correctly, display it, and convert it into another color profile if required. The specific scanner profile is attached to the raw scan and not a device-independent RGB profile. Only one profile has to be created for a scanner. However, several profiles should be created for the different lighting conditions for a digital camera.

Calibrating monitors

A major requirement for on-screen color accuracy is monitor calibration. Taking the technical possibilities of the device into account the white point (i.e., the color temperature of the monitor), the gradation, and the absolute brightness are all adapted to desired destination values.

A monitor should only be calibrated once it has been in use for a while. This is because it takes a little time to warm up and reach a stable condition which normally takes about an hour. However, to be on the safe side, one should wait two hours before calibrating. It should also be repeated at regular intervals. It is recommendable to check or repeat calibration once a month, or even weekly at the beginning. That way one can even out color mismatches that arise over time.

High-quality calibration is carried out using color measuring devices. The radiated colors of the monitor are measured using a colorimeter or spectrometer. The monitor colors can be compared with the destination body colors much more precisely like this than they can with the human eye. Special software then writes the attained data in a user-defined color profile.

The brightness, white point, and gradation of a reference original are compared with the screen view so that the screen view and the print result correspond exactly. One gets the best results when the original is in a special viewing cabinet, which is right next to the screen, has a standard light source, and protects the original from interfering light sources or other influences. The reference original should be very precise when it comes to visual fine adjustment, or else a good monitor calibration gray balance might be lost again.

The white point, which is the color temperature of the monitor, should be set so that the screen proof with the chosen paper simulation matches the white point of the original paper. The white point of the monitor and the brightness of the viewing cabinet are adapted using the dimmer to get the monitor white and the paper white to match.

A color temperature of 5000 to 6000 kelvin (K) is regarded as optimal for comparing the standard light. Some users prefer values between 5300 and 5800 K. The white point and the brightness of the monitor are compared with white point of the paper. The color effect changes depending on the color temperature. A high white point of up to 8000 K has a cold bluish effect, whereas a white point of 5000 to 6000 K produces a warmer yellowish effect. Hence colors often look warmer after calibration.

The curves of the base colors red, green, and blue are set for gradation so that the created colors have optimum neutrality and brightness. This guarantees that the monitor does not have a color cast and that the brightness of the colors is reproduced correctly. This process is often referred to as gamma correction, or gamma adjustment. In practice a gamma between 1.8 and 2.2 has proved successful. The gradation of the screen and the working color space should correspond to the gradation of the print result. A gamma of 1.8 roughly corresponds to the characteristic print curve in offset printing. The L* gamma (pronounced "el star") corresponds to the brightness of a CIE Lab color space.

The absolute brightness of the monitor is finally set so that the brightness of unprinted paper corresponds to the brightness of a white area on-screen. This can be achieved either visually or by measuring. The absolute brightness must be neither too gray nor blindingly high. It should be around 50 percent of the maximum brightness. If the ambient brightness changes drastically, the monitor brightness should be adjusted accordingly.

In general, a distinction is drawn between hardware and software calibration. In the former, adjustments are made on-screen with the help of the monitor color conversion tables. If this cannot be used, the adjustments have to be carried out within the graphics card or with an ICC monitor profile. This is called a software calibration. Software calibration is of lower quality because the colors only have an 8-bit precision to the destination values. In hardware calibration, however, gradient smoothness can be lost in adjustments

using the three characteristic curves for red, green, and blue. Instead of making manual adjustments, one can achieve the desired results through calibration with readapted destination values.

The operating system utility programs can also be used to create profiles. These include the Apple Calibration Assistant, which can be accessed via the monitor configuration. No color measuring device is used for this sort of calibration.

The same colors are displayed on every monitor within a work group when the calibration is correct. One must be aware that the ambient colors influence the colors on the monitor. These include the lighting conditions, the colors of the walls and floors, and the pictures and objects in the workplace, including the clothes one is wearing.

Ideally therefore high quality image processing is carried out under diffused light in a color-neutral room. The room should not be too light or too dark—2000 lux is ideal, which is roughly that of a pleasantly lit room. A professional image-processing room is equipped with a standard light source: D50, 5000 K or 2000 lux, for example. Neutral lighting is vital because judging the gray balance depends on the colorfulness of the white point and is judged in reference to the white point. Therefore the white point of the room should match the white point of the monitor as much as possible.

The monitor should also not be right next to a light source that can reflect in the monitor. It must also not be backlit by a window. The monitor should have a neutral background so that the colors in an image can be judged correctly and not be influenced by anything. Colored or black screen backgrounds or pictures on the walls can affect judgment of the gray balance of an image. This is because the eye looks for a reference point to judge the gray balance with. The Photoshop neutral gray background is perfect for this.

Apple Calibration Assistant Calibrating a monitor using the Apple Calibration Assistant is comparatively simple. The program leads the user step by step through the application. On the preceding pages and above, a monitor calibration using the Apple Calibration Assistant is displayed. Steps 1 through 9 are explained in conjunction with the preceding section "Monitor calibration."

Calibrating output devices Output device calibration mainly affects printers, which include all desktop printers, proof printers, and, of course, printing presses. Calibration is partly carried out automatically in high-quality devices. The Lab values of the color originals are measured and compared with the corresponding output colors using a color measuring device called a spectrophotometer. If the measured color difference is not within a permitted tolerance, the output device has to be calibrated. The respective tolerances are defined by ISO standards. The gamma curves of the individual colors are adjusted so that the contrast and brightness of the output colors match the desired value.

Profiling is similar to the process for input devices. First, a series of swatches is printed out on the

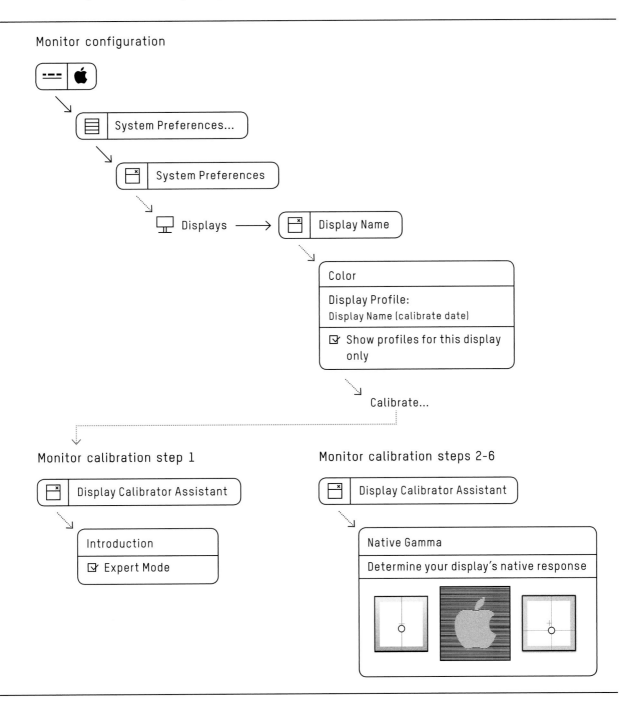

Monitor calibration step 7

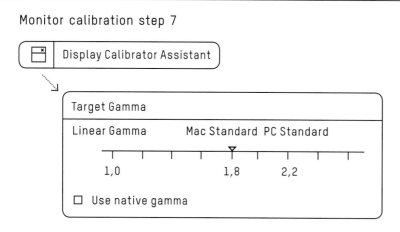

Monitor calibration step 8

Monitor calibration step 9

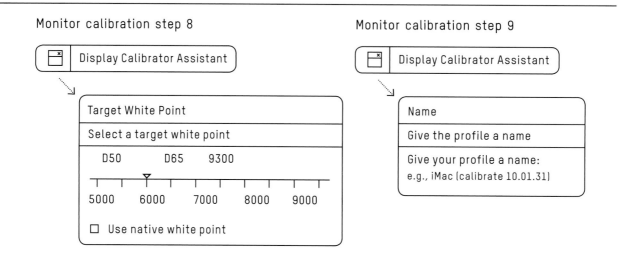

device. These swatches are measured using a color measuring device. The values are passed onto the software for profiling. The software compares the actual values with the desired values and produces the custom color profile. The more swatches measured, the more precise and protracted the profiling is. There are also mechanical swatch readers on the market.

A few color printers can also be adjusted without separate color measuring devices. Some color copiers provide the possibility of placing the printed-out swatches on the glass plate of the device. These are 10 gradations each per ink as a rule. The actual values are then measured by a densitometer so that the gamma curves of the output colors may be corrected accordingly. Calibration using a color-measuring device is usually more precise, especially when more swatches have

to be imported. There are programs that can process over 1000 swatches for creating a profile.

Output device calibration also has to be repeated at regular intervals. These intervals depend on the amount that the printer is used. It is virtually impossible to attain all the desired values, even with a calibrated device. Hence print standards define certain tolerances within which color mismatch has to be accepted. Printer profiling has to be corrected or completed by further profiles when outside factors such as paper or ink change or vary.

A standard profile, such as ISO Coated v2, can be used as an alternative to the custom profile. These generic profiles are based on normal conditions and can therefore also be used for proof prints. Nevertheless, regular adjustment of the device is still necessary.

Color settings in Adobe Bridge

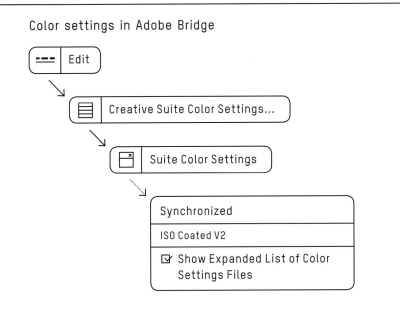

found in this list. These can be preinstalled settings such, as Europe Prepress 2. The default color setting North America Prepress 2 should be changed to Europe Prepress 2 if one is working in Europe.

In the color settings there are also custom saved options, i.e., all settings made in Photoshop, InDesign, or Illustrator and stored in the usual folders for color settings. The right storage location is automatically chosen when the setting file is saved. In Mac OS this is under Macintosh HD > Library > Application Support > Adobe > Color > Settings, or under Macintosh HD > User > User Name > Library > Application Support > Adobe > Color > Settings. After the desired setting has been chosen, all one has to do is click the Apply button and all color settings within the Creative Suite will be synchronized. A custom color setting can be created in Photoshop, for example.

Application support The third component of the color management system is application support. All relevant programs enable work using a color management module and color profiles. This means that a file—no matter with which program it was created—can be assigned a color profile and the colors may be converted from one color space to another with regard to the various intents.

Color settings Color settings regulate the general performance having to do with color management. They are fundamental program settings that affect not only the file that happens to be open. They also regulate how color profiles are opened and how files are inserted. Among other things, the color settings determine which color space or color profile is activated as the base setting, how this deals with profile variation, and how a file may be converted into another profile.

Color settings in Adobe Bridge In Adobe Bridge, the color settings of all Creative Suite programs can be synchronized. The option Show Expanded List of Color Setting Files should be activated. All color settings saved up to date are

Color settings in Photoshop Compared to the base settings, the color settings may be optimized and adapted to further print conditions where necessary. The following options are recommended as default settings, although some variation might be needed depending on the work environment. To begin, one selects saved default settings under Settings. These are any that are included with delivery, but also custom settings. It is recommendable to save at least one default setting with an up-to-date color profile that one uses a lot, to be able to switch quickly after any readjustments. It may make sense to save further settings for different print conditions with various color spaces. These custom color settings are then available in all programs and also in Adobe Bridge. One can choose RGB, CMYK, Gray, and Spot under Working Spaces.

It makes sense to choose the color spaces that one works with most often for the default settings. In the printing industry these are usually the color spaces eciRGB v2 ICCv4 for RGB, ISO Coated v2 for CMYK,

Color setting in Adobe Photoshop

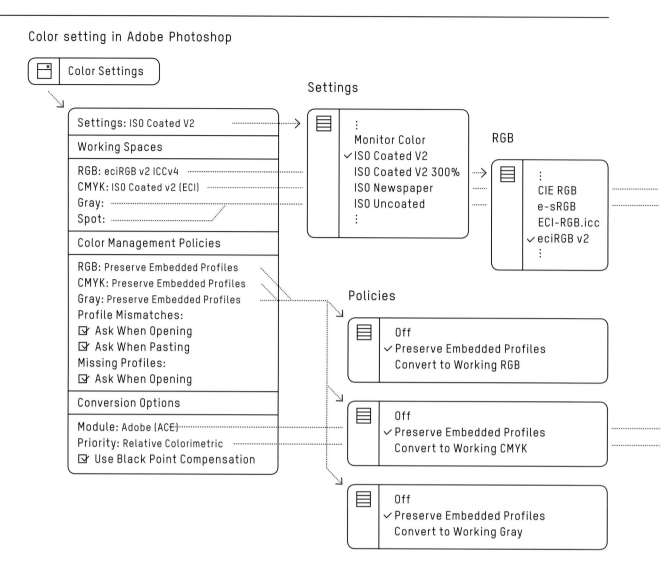

and Black Ink – ISO Coated v2 for Gray and also for Spot; eciRGB v2 ICCv4 is relatively large and contains nearly all the colors that are possible in sheet-fed and web offset as well as gravure or newspaper printing. It guarantees that the colors of an RGB image can be reproduced in CMYK. ISO Coated v2 is a color profile for coated paper, such as art paper. One should select the color space for grayscales or spot colors. Users who normally produce for uncoated paper can select a color space for CMYK, grayscales, and spots that meet their special requirements. There is more information about the individual color profiles in "The most important color profiles." (See p. 205.)

Under Color Management Policies one chooses the settings for the default behavior of color profiles. They mostly affect reading and embedding color profiles. One must choose Preserve Embedded Profiles under RGB, CMYK, and Grayscale. This setting guarantees that when a file is opened, the embedded profile is preserved even when it does not match the current program settings. A file is displayed in the color space in which it has been stored. If the profile is not embedded in the file, it will look different on every monitor because the color information only contains the pure color numbers that are displayed differently in each color space. The Off setting ignores all embedded profiles when images

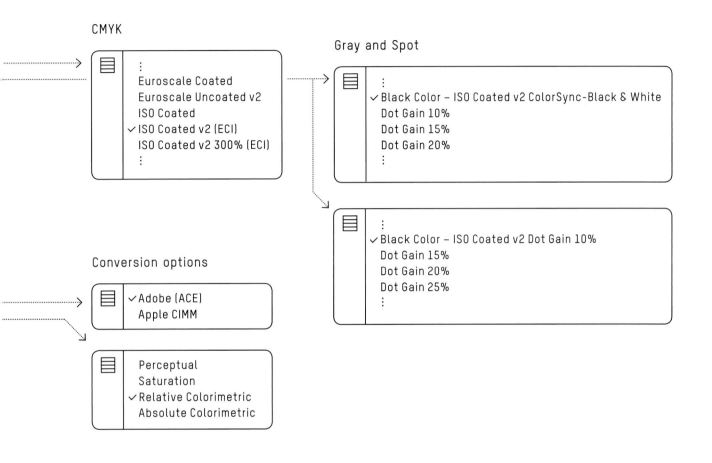

CMYK

Euroscale Coated
Euroscale Uncoated v2
ISO Coated
✓ ISO Coated v2 (ECI)
ISO Coated v2 300% (ECI)

Gray and Spot

✓ Black Color – ISO Coated v2 ColorSync-Black & White
Dot Gain 10%
Dot Gain 15%
Dot Gain 20%

✓ Black Color – ISO Coated v2 Dot Gain 10%
Dot Gain 15%
Dot Gain 20%
Dot Gain 25%

Conversion options

✓ Adobe (ACE)
Apple CIMM

Perceptual
Saturation
✓ Relative Colorimetric
Absolute Colorimetric

are opened and imported, so the profiles are not embedded in new documents.

Convert to Working RGB, CMYK or Gray converts each file automatically into the current color space when it is opened if the embedded profile does not match the color space. Often this is not a good option, because the color profile selected in the color settings is not always the best preference for every original in combination with the chosen conversion intent.

The subsequent options Ask When Opening and Ask When Pasting should be activated because that way one retains the option of choosing a color management policy when opening or pasting a file if one opens an image that has another profile embedded or none at all. One can convert or assign a profile if one already knows which profile has not been embedded, or which profile the image should be converted to, and which conversion intent selected in the presets matches the original. Otherwise, it is best to convert or assign a profile after opening with the command Convert to Profile or Assign Profile, using the preview.

One can choose the color management module and the intents for color conversion under the conversion options. There is more information about the modules under "Color management module." (See p. 195.) It is best to choose Relative Colorimetric in

Profile error

| ▣ | Embedded Profile Mismatch |

> Embedded: sRGB IEC61966-2.1
> Working: eciRGB v2 ICCv4
>
> What would you like to do?
>
> ⦿ Use the embedded profile (instead of the working space)
> ○ Convert document's colors to the working space
> ○ Discard the embedded profile (don't color manage)

| ▣ | Missing Profile |

> What would you like to do?
>
> ⦿ Leave as is (don't color manage)
> ○ Assign working RGB: eciRGB v2 ICCv4
> ○ Assign Profile: sRGB IEC61966-2.1

One can react to profile errors when opening or inserting.

combination with Black Point Compensation as an intent in the conversion options. The option Use Dither should not be activated in this context. However, it is generally better to convert images or colors via the menu with the command Convert to Profile where one can choose the intent.

Each intent has to be adapted to the original when files are converted. Before deciding on an intent, one should compare different conversion intents with the preview. Absolute Colorimetric is only useful for very few originals. More precise information will be found later in the section "Rendering intent" and in the practical examples of color conversion. (See p. 214ff.)

When converting between color spaces with 8 bit per channel, missing colors that are among the source colors but not the destination colors may be simulated under the option Use Dither (8-bit/channel images). A dither can simulate colors by mixing pixels with available colors. Thus block-like stripes that may occur in images when colors are missing can be reduced. When images are compressed for the web, the dither creates larger files.

The following settings under More Options are not defined in any ICC workflow and thus should not be activated. Using the option Desaturate Monitor Colors, missing colors of the monitor color space can be simulated when the monitor color space is smaller than that of the image. This should prevent different colors from being displayed the same. It is, however, also possible that a color is displayed differently from how it is output.

The option Blend RGB Colors Using Gamma allows RGB colors to be mixed in the color space of the gamma defined here during filling or painting in layers. A gamma value of 1.0 is correctly described as colorimetric and so has the least sharp edges. When the option is deactivated, RGB colors are filled with the document color space.

Color settings in InDesign and Illustrator

Once the color settings created in Photoshop have been applied in Adobe Bridge to all the Creative Suite programs, no more settings have to be made in InDesign or Illustrator. The color setting then mostly correspond to those in Photoshop, although the working color spaces for gray and spot colors are missing.

The color management policy should be set to Preserve Embedded Profiles in the RGB originals. This means that RGB values are converted into the document CMYK for output.

However, in the CMYK preferences the Preserve Numbers (Ignore Linked Profiles) option is active. Thus the CMYK profile is preserved when a document is opened. On the other hand, when CMYK objects are placed they are ignored by default. This policy prevents unwanted color conversions during printing or making a PDF since all CMYK contents use the document profile. Thus the composition of all CMYK colors remains intact even when some placed objects have a different profile. The custom colors of the document and the placed contents may still be converted.

The option Ask When Opening should always be activated so that one has the possibility to react differently when opening or pasting a file with a missing or different profile.

The most important color profiles

One must know the properties of the color profiles in order to work with a color management system. The differences in the RGB profiles are largely a matter of the size of the color space, the color temperature, and the gamma.

The CMYK profiles are first split into three groups for the various printing processes. Hence there are profiles for commercial offset printing (sheet-fed and heatset web offset), profiles for newspaper printing (coldset web offset), and profiles for gravure printing. A few printing houses or publishers also provide their own profiles.

Within the printing process a distinction is drawn between different types of paper and separation methods. For screen-printed products, the ISO Coated v2 or ISO Uncoated profile is used. (There is more information about the different printing methods in the chapter "Print technology," p. 60ff.)

By now there are quite a lot of ISO profiles. Therefore on the following pages there is a list of the most important working color spaces, explaining when to use which profile. Anybody unfamiliar with this topic or unsure about a special type of paper can also inquire about what profile to use at the printing or publishing house, or even the paper manufacturer. The recommended color or grayscale profile is usually to be found in the terms and conditions or advertising information.

People who work with color profiles have to check the relevant websites from time to time for updates or completions. All color profiles are ready to download from www.eci.org, fogra.org, and ifra.de.

RGB profiles [1]

Adobe RGB This color space has a relatively large color range that includes nearly all print colors. This makes it a good color space for the production of artwork. With a gamma of 2.2 and a color temperature of D65 it does not, however, quite conform to printing industry requirements. Since cyan is clearly outside of the Adobe RGB color space, not all print colors can be reproduced.

Apple RGB This color space corresponds to that of an average Mac OS monitor. It was formerly used by many DTP programs, such as Photoshop 4.0.

ECI RGB 1.0 and 2.0 The RGB color space recommended by the European Color Initiative (ECI) for printing contains nearly all the colors used today in sheet-fed offset, web offset, gravure, and newspaper printing. The 1.0 and 2.0 versions have different gamma characteristics. The 1.8 gamma of the first version is replaced by the L* characterization in the second version. This reduces errors during color conversion.

sRGB This color space corresponds to that of an average monitor. Many scanners, printers, and various programs now use it as a default color space. It is comparatively small and is therefore particularly useful for web graphics, as most monitors can reproduce the colors in an sRGB color space. Due to its limited color space it is not suitable for prepress. Nevertheless, many digital photos use this color space.

CMYK profiles for commercial offset printing[2]

The following color profiles reproduce the ICC profiles for standard print conditions in commercial offset printing, or more precisely for sheet-fed offset and heatset web offset printing. Commercial offset printing includes things with comparatively small print runs, such as business cards, postcards, leaflets, pamphlets, or catalogs. Two profiles are also provided for continuous printing. There is a whole series of color profiles for commercial offset printing. In offset printing the entire range of print products can be produced, from business cards to catalogs. The different profiles within this group chiefly differentiate between different types of paper, seeing as each one has a special surface texture. In conventional screen processes this means there are different dot gain curves, so that the applied color leads to a different result on each kind of paper. Slightly yellow paper is also taken into consideration. There is more information about the various paper grades in the chapter on paper under "Finish," "Grades of paper and paperboard," and "Paper grades." (See p. 11ff.)

Furthermore, there are special profiles for frequency-modulated screening. The default periodic screen is called amplitude-modulated screening or AM screening; the less commonly used non-periodic screen is also called frequency-modulated screening or FM screening. The profiles for the non-periodic screen can be recognized by the suffix NPScreen in their description. The NP profiles are available because CMYK spot colors with the same tonal value and identical CIE Lab values show clear differences of color even with the same tonal gain when FM and AM screening are compared. In general, both screen processes have completely different dot gain curves. Different types of paper have no noteworthy bearing on the dot gain curves in FM screening. All four print colors have the same dot gain curves in FM screening anyway, whereas in conventional AM screening the dot gain is 2 to 3 percent higher for black than it is for the chromatic colors cyan, magenta, and yellow.

There are five different dot gain curves in the various color profiles, in which all profiles have curve F for NP screening, that is to say, the highest dot gain. The dot gain curves measured on a 40 percent control field are characterized thus: curve A, 13 percent; curve B, 16 percent; curve C, 19 percent; curve D, 22 percent, and curve F, 28 percent.

The maximum surface coverage indicates the maximum permissible total ink application. In the ISO Coated v2 profile, for example, the total ink application when all four colors are printed must never be higher than 330 percent, and must never contain more than 95 percent black. In ISO Coated v2, a rich black with a brightness of 0 is separated with, say, 95 percent cyan, 95 percent magenta, 45 percent yellow, and 95 percent black.

The ISO Coated v2 300 profile has a total ink application of maximum 300 percent and is recommended for web offset. A rich black is separated with 85 percent cyan, 85 percent magenta, 35 percent yellow, and 95 percent black—although the exact proportion of each individual color depends on the conversion options used.

An ICC profile can be created with the help of a profiling program based on the characteristic properties of a type of paper. One attains the data by printing a standard color table and measuring it colorimetrically. The ICC profile can be generated with the help of additional information, such as the desired color composition. Several profiles can be generated from a single characterization file. The initials PSO used in some profile descriptions stands for Process Standard Offset, while SNP stands for Standard Newsprint.

ISO Coated v2 (ECI)
– File name: ISOcoated_v2_eci.icc
– Standard: ISO 12647-2
– Print condition: Paper type 1 and 2, gloss or matte coated art paper
– Dot gain curves: A (CMY) and B (K)
– Total area coverage: 330%
– Total black: 95%
– Characterization data: FOGRA39L

ISO Coated v2 300% (ECI)
– File name: ISOcoated_v2_300_eci.icc
– Standard: ISO 12647-2
– Print condition: Paper type 1 and 2, gloss or matte coated art paper
– Dot gain curves: A (CMY) and B (K)
– Total area coverage: 300%
– Total black: 95%
– Characterization data: FOGRA39L

PSO LWC Standard (ECI)
– File name: PSO_LWC_Standard_eci.icc
– Standard: ISO12647-2
– Print condition: Paper type 3, improved LWC paper, gloss coated
– Dot gain curves: B (CMY) and C (K)
– Total area coverage: 300%
– Total black: 98%
– Characterization data: FOGRA46L

PSO Uncoated ISO12647 (ECI)

- File name: PSO_Uncoated_ISO12647_eci.icc
- Standard: ISO12647-2
- Print condition: Paper type 4, uncoated white, offset
- Dot gain curves: C (CMY) and D (K)
- Total area coverage: 300%
- Total black: 98%
- Characterization data: FOGRA47L

ISO Uncoated Yellowish

- File name: ISOuncoatedyellowish.icc
- Standard: ISO 12647-2
- Print condition: Paper type 5, uncoated yellowish, offset
- Dot gain curves: C (CMY) and D (K)
- Total area coverage: 320%
- Total black: 100%
- Characterization data: FOGRA30L

SC Paper (ECI)

- File name: SC_paper_eci.icc
- Standard: ISO 12647-2
- Print condition: Paper type SC, supercalendered, commercial offset
- Dot gain curves: B (CMY) and C (K)
- Total area coverage: 270%
- Total black: 100%
- Characterization data: FOGRA40L

PSO MFC Paper (ECI)

- File name: PSO_MFC_paper_eci.icc
- Standard: ISO 12647-2
- Print condition: Paper type MFC, machine finished coated, commercial offset
- Dot gain curves: B (CMY) and C (K)
- Total area coverage: 280%
- Total black: 98%
- Characterization data: FOGRA41L

PSO SNP Paper (ECI)

- File name: PSO_SNP_paper_eci.icc
- Standard: ISO 12647-2
- Print condition: Paper type SNP, standard newsprint, heatset web offset
- Dot gain curves: C (CMY) and D (K)
- Total area coverage: 260%
- Total black: 98%
- Characterization data: FOGRA42L

PSO Coated NPScreen ISO12647 (ECI)

- File name: PSO_Coated_NPScreen_ISO12647_eci.icc
- Standard: ISO 12647-2
- Print condition: Paper type 1 and 2, gloss and matte coated art paper, non-periodic screen, commercial offset
- Dot gain curves: F (CMYK)
- Total area coverage: 330%
- Total black: 98%
- Characterization data: FOGRA43L

PSO Coated 300% NPScreen ISO12647 (ECI)

- File name: PSO_Coated_300_NPScreen_ISO12647_eci.icc
- Standard: ISO 12647-2
- Print condition: Paper type 1 and 2, gloss and matte coated art paper, non-periodic screen, commercial offset
- Dot gain curves: F (CMYK)
- Total area coverage: 300%
- Total black: 98%
- Characterization data: FOGRA43L

PSO Uncoated NPScreen ISO12647 (ECI)

- File name: PSO_Uncoated_NPScreen_ISO12647_eci.icc
- Standard: ISO 12647-2
- Print condition: Paper type 4, uncoated white, non-periodic screen, offset
- Dot gain curves: F (CMYK)
- Total area coverage: 300%
- Total black: 98%
- Characterization data: FOGRA44L

ISO Continuous Forms Coated

- File name: ISOcofcoated.icc
- Standard: ISO 12647-2
- Print condition: Paper type 2, matte coated art paper, offset endless
- Dot gain curves: n/a
- Total area coverage: 350%
- Total black: 100%
- Characterization data: FOGRA31L

ISO Continuous Forms Uncoated

- File name: ISOcofuncoated.icc
- Standard: ISO 12647-2
- Print condition: Paper type 4, uncoated white, offset endless
- Dot gain curves: n/a
- Total area coverage: 320%
- Total black: 100%
- Characterization data: FOGRA32L

CMYK profiles for coldset newspaper printing

The ISO Newspaper profile and the SNAP 2007- is normally used in newspaper offset printing with coldset web offset machines. Normal daily newspapers are printed using coldset web offset. One can usually see what profile should be used in the newspaper printing house or publishers' advertising information—sometimes only by defining the ISO standard. Some publishers have a conversion table for HKS colors in the Euroscale that have been produced according to this standard on their website. The ECI works together with Ifra in newspaper printing. The following newspaper profiles may be downloaded from the Ifra website and the International Color Consortium. The ISO Newspaper profile applies to both color and black and white originals.

ISOnewspaper26v4 (for color artwork)
ISOnewspaper26v4_gr (for black & white artwork)
- File name: ISOnewspaper26v4.icc or ISOnewspaper26v4_gr.icc
- Standard: ISO 12647-3
- Print condition: Paper type standard newsprint, coldset web offset, newspaper offset
- Dot gain: 26%
- Total area coverage: 240%
- Total black: 95%
- Characterization data: IFRA26

SNAP 2007
- File name: SNAP 2007.icc
- Standard: ISO 12647-3
- Print condition: Newsprint paper, coldset web offset, CTP plates
- Dot gain: 26%
- Total area coverage: 240%
- Total black: 80%
- Characterization data: CGATS TR002

CMYK profiles for gravure printing

In gravure printing, high-quality print products are produced in large print runs. Typical examples are magazines and mail-order catalogs, but also bank bonds, stamps, and banknotes. Gravure printing is distinguished by its high image quality, which makes it good for illustration printing. Gravure printing presses are almost exclusively built as web-fed machines. **(For more information about gravure printing see the chapter "Print technology," p. 60ff.)**

The following profiles may be downloaded from the ECI website. The initial PSR in the profile names stand for Process Standard Rotogravure. The LWC profiles are suitable for coated paper, and the SC profiles and the MF profile are for uncoated paper.

PSR_LWC_Standard_V2_PT
- File name: PSR_LWC_STD_V2_PT.icc
- ISO standard: ISO 12647-4
- Print condition: Paper type LWC, lightweight coated, rotogravure
- Dot gain curves: n/a
- Total area coverage: 360%
- Total black: 85%
- Characterization data: PSR_LWC_STD_V2

PSR_LWC_PLUS_V2_PT
- File name: PSR_LWC_PLUS_V2_PT.icc
- ISO standard: ISO 12647-4
- Print condition: Paper type LWC plus, gloss coated, lightweight coated, optically improved, rotogravure
- Dot gain curves: n/a
- Total area coverage: 360%
- Total black: 85%
- Characterization data: PSR_LWC_PLUS_V2

PSR_SC_Standard_V2
- File name: PSR_SC_STD_V2_PT.icc
- ISO standard: ISO 12647-4
- Print condition: Paper type SC, supercalendered, rotogravure
- Dot gain curves: n/a
- Total area coverage: 360%
- Total black: 85%
- Characterization data: PSR_SC_STD_V2

PSR_SC_PLUS_V2
- File name: PSR_SC_PLUS_V2_PT.icc
- ISO standard: ISO 12647-4
- Print condition: Paper type SC plus, whiter supercalendered, optically improved, rotogravure
- Dot gain curves: n/a
- Total area coverage: 360%
- Total black: 85%
- Characterization data: PSR_SC_Plus_V2

PSRgravureMF
- File name: PSRgravureMF.icc
- ISO standard: ISO 12647-4
- Print condition: Paper type MF, machine finished, improved newsprint, 55 g/m^2, rotogravure
- Dot gain curves: n/a
- Total area coverage: 375%
- Total black: 80%
- Characterization data: PSRgravureMF_ECI2002

Endnotes for USreaders

1 – ROMM RGB (Reference Output Medium Metric RGB) is the ANSI (American National Standards Institute) standard RGB color space for printing with a gamma of 1.8.

2 – <u>GRACoL2006_Coated1v2</u>
- File name: GRACoL2006_Coated1v2.icc
- Standard: ISO 12647-2
- Print condition: US Grade #1 paper, glossy coated, wood-free art paper
- Dot gain curves: 17%
- Total area coverage: 310%
- Total black: 100%
- Characterization data: CGATS TR006

<u>SWOP2006_Coated3v2</u>
- File name: SWOP2006_Coated3v2.icc
- Standard: ISO 12647-2
- Print condition: US Grade #3 paper, coated freesheet, web offset, CTP plates, variable screen frequency
- Dot gain curves: 17%
- Total area coverage: 300%
- Total black: 100%
- Characterization data: CGATS TR003

<u>SWOP2006_Coated5v2</u>
- File name: SWOP2006_Coated5v2.icc
- Standard: ISO 12647-2
- Print condition: US Grade #5 paper, coated groundwood, web offset, CTP plates, variable screen frequency
- Dot gain curves: 17%
- Total area coverage: 300%
- Total black: 100%
- Characterization data: CGATS TR005

<u>5.4 Color conversion</u> When documents for different output conditions are prepared, the colors have to be converted into the corresponding color spaces. This affects all objects in a document, i. e., all the colors used and all imported graphics and images. The color management system's automatic conversion makes adapting a file to different print conditions easy. Some presets are important, however.

Assigning a missing profile

| Edit |

| Assign Profile... |

| Assign Profile |

○ Don't Color Manage This Document
○ Working RGB: eciRGB v2 ICCv4
◉ Profile: sRGB IEC61966-2.1

eciRGB v2 ICCv4   ECI-RGB   sRGB

When there is a profile error, one should assign the image to the matching profile before editing. This may be the profile in which the image was originally produced, but also the profile that delivers the desired result.

In theory, all colors can be converted into another color space when a print PDF is created. However, only one conversion intent is used for all objects, and this can lead to undesired or flawed results in individual cases. In order to achieve the best results, it is advisable to check and control the conversion results individually.

The main argument against color conversion when creating a PDF is the fact that pure black is also converted and is then composed of four colors, which is unfortunate from a technical point of view, particularly for type and small objects. The option Convert to Destination (Preserve Color Numbers) does not necessarily lead to optimum results either. Although the images alone are converted to the destination so that the black remains pure black, all the other colors of the InDesign document are not converted.

Assigning color profiles

In addition to a destination color space, a source color space is also required for color conversion. This applies whether it is an InDesign document, an Illustrator file, or a Photoshop image. Assigning the right working color space is extremely important when a file does not have a profile embedded in it. A source color space is always needed if a file is displayed on-screen, in order to convert the colors to the monitor color space. When one opens a file that has not had a profile embedded, it is displayed in the color space that happens to be chosen in the color settings—even when the command to eject the embedded profile appears on opening the file. After all, some kind of color space has to be used to be able to display the image on the monitor. This working color space

Converting profiles in Photoshop and InDesign

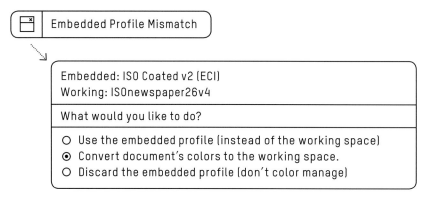

| --- | Edit |

| ▤ | Convert to Profile... |

| ▣ | Convert to Profile |

| **Destination Space** |
| Profile: ISOnewspaper26v4 |
| **Conversion Options** |
| Engine: Adobe (ACE)
 Intent: Perceptual |

Photoshop

| **Destination Space** |
| RGB-Profile: Working RGB – eciRGB v2 ICCv4
 CMYK-Profile: ISOnewspaper26v4 |
| **Conversion Options** |
| RGB-Profile: Working RGB – eciRGB v2 ICCv4
 CMYK-Profile: ISOnewspaper26v4 |

InDesign

Converting to profile in Illustrator

| ▣ | Embedded Profile Mismatch |

| Embedded: ISO Coated v2 (ECI)
 Working: ISOnewspaper26v4 |
| What would you like to do? |
| ○ Use the embedded profile (instead of the working space)
 ◉ Convert document's colors to the working space.
 ○ Discard the embedded profile (don't color manage) |

In Illustrator one can only convert to another color profile when opening a file by using a created profile mismatch.

would also be used as the source color space when a file without an embedded profile is converted to another color space. However, when the working color space chosen in the color settings does not accord with the working color space in which the file was actually created, the image is interpreted incorrectly. Without an embedded profile the file merely contains the pure color numbers that look somewhat different in each color space.

Therefore it is important to assign a color profile to a document or image before conversion to another color space. One can assign a profile in Photoshop, InDesign, and Illustrator with the command Assign Profile.

The following practical example in Photoshop shows why assigning a profile is so important and what effect it can have. First, the Photoshop color settings should be selected according to the instructions previously described in "Color settings in Photoshop."

Info palette in Photoshop

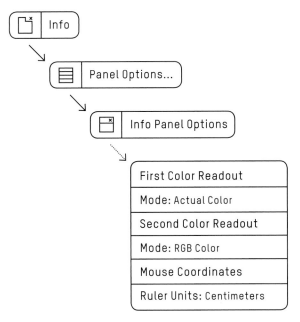

When converting colors in Photoshop one should compare the various rendering intents using preview and the info palette.

(See p. 201ff.) Here it is important to activate Ask When Opening under Missing Profiles in the color management policies.

Upon opening an image that does not have a profile there are various possibilities for how to deal with the profile error. In our example the option Preserve (No Color Management) is active in order to subsequently assign the right profile. Alternatively, a profile may be assigned to the image while it is being opened in this dialog box, although one has to do this without a preview. Therefore it is better to assign a profile in this case if one knows which color space the file was created in.

Our practical example is an RGB image without a profile. After opening it and choosing Preserve (No Color Management) it is first displayed in the RGB color space that was chosen in the Photoshop color settings. In this example it is in the eci-RGB v2 ICC v4 color space. This means that our image has quite a lot of saturation. Subsequently one can check which profile fits the image best with the preview. One should try as many color spaces as possible before deciding on a profile. In our example the most suitable color space is sRGB, but it could be any other one.

There are many cases where it is worthwhile to assign a missing profile. It can make the subsequent image editing much quicker when there are color casts that are particularly disruptive on skin tones. At most, it may have to be converted into a CMYK profile.

Convert to profile A file must always be converted to another color space with the command Convert to Profile. Although this can happen in Photoshop by changing the mode, profile conversion has the advantage that the conversion options can at the same time be adapted to the original. This is because the conversion options selected in the color settings, which include the color management module and conversion intent, do not necessarily deliver the best result for all originals. The command Convert to Profile is present in Photoshop and InDesign but not in Illustrator (Edit > Convert to Profile).

First, one can choose the color management module in the conversion options. There is more information about this in this chapter under "Color management module." (See p. 195.)

In Illustrator colors can only converted to another profile when there is a profile error upon opening a file. One must produce this error on purpose by tagging a source profile to the file, saving it as an Illustrator file (not an EPS), thereby adding the profile. Subsequently one has to close the file and choose its destination profile in the program color settings. When the file is reopened the warning Embedded Profile Mismatch appears. One can convert the colors of the document into the working space in this dialog box. See the practical example under "Converting in Illustrator." (See p. 242–243.)

Rendering intent
In the color settings there are four different intents available for converting colors to other color spaces: Perceptual, Saturation, Relative Colorimetric, and Absolute Colorimetric. As the names suggest, all the options set different intents for the converted color. The color composition changes according to intent, which leads to different color effects. The results of the different methods can be compared using the preview in the conversion dialog in Photoshop and InDesign. In Photoshop there is also the Info palette, where the converted color values can be seen in the destination space. One has to set the matching color space, say, CMYK, in the Info palette. One can then read the different CMYK results using the preview in the Info palette before deciding on a conversion intent.

The main intent of a conversion ought to be color fidelity in most cases. The results should look as similar as possible in all color spaces. Furthermore, certain printing requirements could play a role. With some originals it may be important that neutral tones be composed purely of black, for instance for logos or screenshots. In some circumstances the highest possible saturation might be most important, for instance for info graphics. In this respect it is perfectly possible that each color and each object should have a different conversion intent.

The Perceptual setting is very good when the destination space is smaller than the source space, like it is for images that contain a large amount of colors outside of the destination space. With Perceptual the relation between the colors mostly remains intact, i.e., the distance between each color. The result should be as true to perception as possible. Individual colors can be changed though. Take, for instance, two colors that were different from each other in the source color

space, but have the same coordinates in the destination space. Since at least one of them cannot be reproduced precisely in the destination space, the coordinates of at least one of the two colors are shifted so that they keep the same distance to one another in the destination space and can still be differentiated. Perceptual is a perception-oriented conversion method.

The intent Saturation renders the colors to produce maximum saturation, albeit at the expense of color accuracy. This method is particularly good for strong colors in diagrams, for example, in which the perceptually accurate reproduction of a color is unimportant.

With Relative Colorimetric more original colors are preserved than with Perceptual. In principle Relative Colorimetric is an exact colorimetric conversion method carried out in relation to paper white, where the white point of the source space is compared with the white point of the destination space. Colors outside of the source color space are reproduced using the most similar color from the destination space. During conversion all the colors are moved so that, in combination with the option Use Black Point Compensation, the visual result is very close to the original. Relative Colorimetric is the default setting for color conversion n Europe. In many cases it delivers good, perceptually accurate results that can hardly be discerned from their originals. This method is so useful because it is good for adapting colors to different print conditions—ISO Coated to ISO Newspaper, for example. To achieve optimal results with Relative Colorimetric, the option Use Black Point Compensation should nearly always be active or else the colors will be too dark.

Absolute Colorimetric renders the individual colors as accurate as possible without comparing them with each other. Colors inside the destination space are reproduced colorimetrically perfect and are therefore always preserved. Colors outside the destination space are cut and replaced by the closest color. This method is good for proofing: to simulate colors on a particular output device and judge to what degree the color of the paper influences the printed color. That way one makes sure that the colors of the proof cannot be more radiant than the subsequent print result.

In order to find out which intent delivers the best result, different versions may be produced and compared on-screen with the original in soft proofing. (There is more information about soft proofing in "Color proofs" in this chapter under "Soft

Perceptual, ISO Coated v2

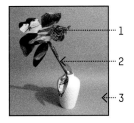

1) CMYK 53/45/36/27
2) CMYK 22/53/22/20
3) CMYK 65/24/8/5

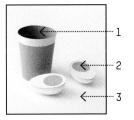

1) CMYK 78/43/18/27
2) CMYK 2/55/98/5
3) CMYK 13/9/10/1

1) CMYK 2/25/86/1
2) CMYK 2/93/85/3
3) CMYK 63/62/23/22

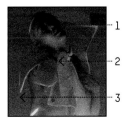

1) CMYK 76/67/73/84
2) CMYK 58/51/52/46
3) CMYK 53/58/57/50

1) CMYK 0/0/0/0
2) CMYK 53/51/36/29
3) CMYK 12/35/30/3

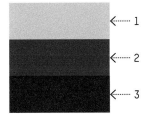

1) CMYK 26/19/19/4
2) CMYK 1/100/12/2
3) CMYK 24/95/10/42

Relative Colorimetric with black point compensation, ISO Coated v2

1) CMYK 55/47/37/29
2) CMYK 23/52/22/20
3) CMYK 62/22/10/7

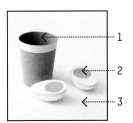

1) CMYK 77/44/20/28
2) CMYK 1/54/96/3
3) CMYK 13/9/10/1

1) CMYK 1/25/84/0
2) CMYK 2/87/82/3
3) CMYK 64/62/24/24

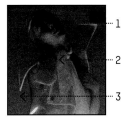

1) CMYK 80/70/68/85
2) CMYK 61/53/51/51
3) CMYK 55/60/59/54

1) CMYK 0/0/0/0
2) CMYK 55/52/37/31
3) CMYK 11/35/30/2

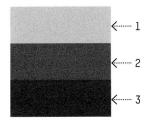

1) CMYK 27/20/20/4
2) CMYK 0/98/3/0
3) CMYK 32/93/0/33

Relative Colorimetric without black point compensation, ISO Coated v2

1) CMYK 56/48/38/31
2) CMYK 22/55/22/22
3) CMYK 64/22/10/7

1) CMYK 81/44/18/31
2) CMYK 1/54/100/3
3) CMYK 13/9/10/1

1) CMYK 1/25/87/0
2) CMYK 2/91/91/3
3) CMYK 66/65/23/25

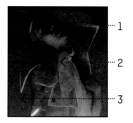

1) CMYK 93/84/58/95
2) CMYK 63/56/56/55
3) CMYK 55/64/63/60

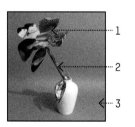

1) CMYK 0/0/0/0
2) CMYK 56/54/38/33
3) CMYK 11/35/30/3

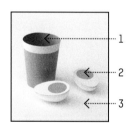

1) CMYK 27/20/20/5
2) CMYK 0/100/2/0
3) CMYK 33/100/7/32

Saturation, ISO Coated v2

1) CMYK 17/25/1/55
2) CMYK 0/56/15/23
3) CMYK 78/35/0/11

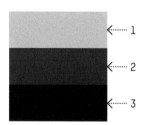

1) CMYK 87/49/0/32
2) CMYK 0/62/99/6
3) CMYK 0/1/1/14

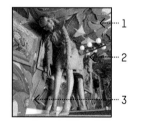

1) CMYK 0/36/90/7
2) CMYK 0/97/81/3
3) CMYK 44/62/2/29

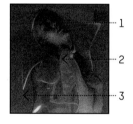

1) CMYK 5/3/11/92
2) CMYK 0/9/12/75
3) CMYK 0/41/35/68

1) CMYK 0/0/0/0
2) CMYK 11/38/1/54
3) CMYK 0/41/32/7

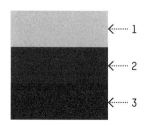

1) CMYK 2/2/0/29
2) CMYK 0/99/29/5
3) CMYK 9/92/10/33

Absolute Colorimetric, ISO Coated v2

1) CMYK 53/46/38/28
2) CMYK 18/53/21/20
3) CMYK 60/18/9/5

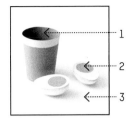

1) CMYK 78/42/18/27
2) CMYK 0/53/100/0
3) CMYK 6/5/8/0

1) CMYK 0/23/89/0
2) CMYK 0/89/92/0
3) CMYK 63/63/22/22

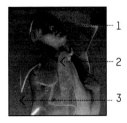

1) CMYK 92/82/62/95
2) CMYK 61/54/56/52
3) CMYK 53/62/63/56

1) CMYK 0/0/3/0
2) CMYK 53/51/37/30
3) CMYK 5/33/29/1

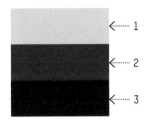

1) CMYK 22/16/18/3
2) CMYK 0/100/4/0
3) CMYK 31/100/6/28

Perceptual, Eurostandard Coated, GCR, maximum black

1) CMYK 13/11/0/73
2) CMYK 4/51/4/40
3) CMYK 72/4/6/22

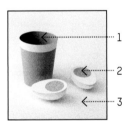

1) CMYK 73/11/2/62
2) CMYK 0/73/98/1
3) CMYK 0/1/1/18

1) CMYK 0/36/91/0
2) CMYK 0/97/92/1
3) CMYK 51/49/1/56

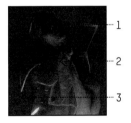

1) CMYK 1/1/2/98
2) CMYK 0/3/3/87
3) CMYK 0/14/9/88

1) CMYK 0/0/0/0
2) CMYK 15/20/1/74
3) CMYK 0/41/25/16

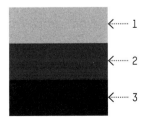

1) CMYK 1/1/0/38
2) CMYK 1/100/10/1
3) CMYK 28/98/0/44

Gray curve separation

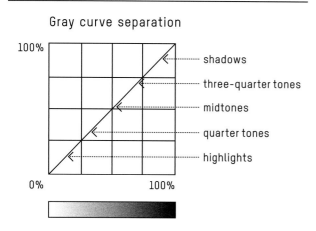

shadows
three-quarter tones
midtones
quarter tones
highlights

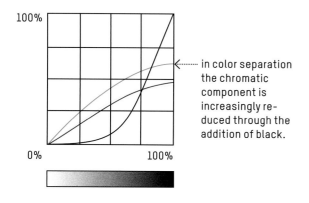

in color separation the chromatic component is increasingly reduced through the addition of black.

proofing," p. 225ff.) Ideally the different results are checked with proofs.

The choice of intent generally depends on the original and the destination profile. For normal color photos it is normally enough to compare the perceptual and the relative colorimetric intents. Perceptual often results in more saturation than relative colorimetric does. This means that the quality of newsprint can sometimes be compensated for. The relative colorimetric method tends to deliver the result most true to the original though. Therefore in general Relative Colorimetric can be used together with black point compensation as the default setting for color photos. One should also consider Relative Colorimetric without black point compensation for individual colors such as those of a logo or background color. In order to understand the different intents better, the illustrations on pp. 215–217 show the separation results with different intents in conversion form RGB to CMYK.

Separation options

Although the composition of a mixed color can change when a particular rendering intent is chosen, it always matches the conditions of the respective destination profiles. The choice of ISO profile cannot affect the individual separation options such as separation type, type of black generation, or the limit for black ink and total ink. This would not do justice to the idea of the ISO profiles, since these profiles provide a print standard that should not be changed individually.

Should the separation result fall short of expectations, it can be corrected using the gradation curves. We will now explain how to affect the separation result with the Photoshop ink and separation options.

One gets to the separation options in Photoshop via the conversion dialog, where one selects Custom CMYK... as the choice of destination space, or alternatively via the color settings in the working space pop-up menu under CMYK. There are various inks to choose from under the ink color options. Under Custom... one can change the inks individually by entering different Lab values. Then the dot gain can be changed. The different dot gain curves are in this chapter under the properties of the color profiles. (See pp. 206–208.)

Next one can choose between GCR and UCR in the separation options. The gray curves in the dialog window show how the chromatic component is reduced in the neutral tones when black is added. One can add black or generate the neutral tones in two different ways, which are called GCR and UCR.

In UCR (under color removal) a part of the chromatic colors cyan, magenta, and yellow is replaced by black in the achromatic—gray—component of a color. As this saves on ink, UCR is mainly used for newsprint and uncoated paper because the dot gain is particularly high there. Compared to GCR one can achieve more depth to the shadows in UCR.

In GCR (gray component replacement) black replaces the chromatic colors cyan, magenta, and yellow in the entire achromatic component of a color. Since the black generation is higher in GCR than in UCR, it is easier to preserve the gray balance on the printing machine. There is, however, the risk of the colors graying slightly and losing saturation, and of the shadows looking comparatively flat. The subsequent use of chromatic addition can counter this by replacing part of the black once again by the chromatic colors. Having less chromatic color saves on production costs and cuts the time that the printing machine requires, and also reduces the amount of wasted sheets of paper.

Black generation

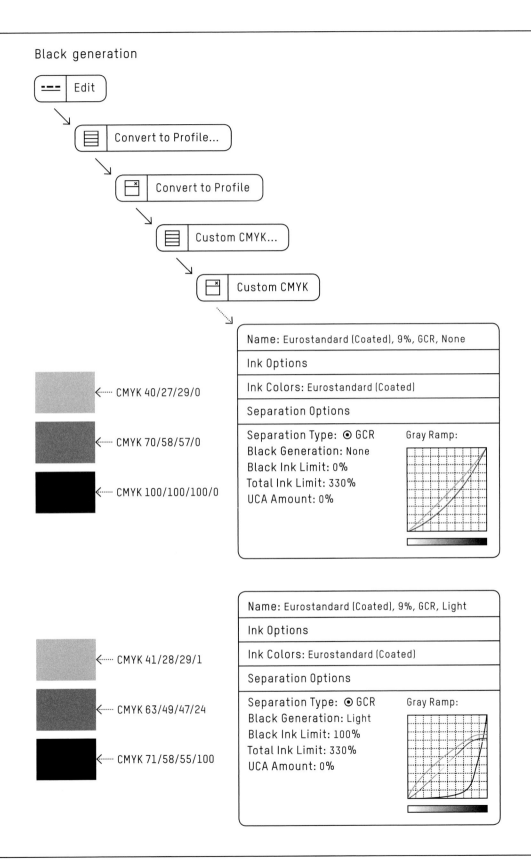

--- | Edit

▤ | Convert to Profile...

▣ | Convert to Profile

▤ | Custom CMYK...

▣ | Custom CMYK

CMYK 40/27/29/0

CMYK 70/58/57/0

CMYK 100/100/100/0

Name: Eurostandard (Coated), 9%, GCR, None

Ink Options

Ink Colors: Eurostandard (Coated)

Separation Options

Separation Type: ⊙ GCR
Black Generation: None
Black Ink Limit: 0%
Total Ink Limit: 330%
UCA Amount: 0%

Gray Ramp:

CMYK 41/28/29/1

CMYK 63/49/47/24

CMYK 71/58/55/100

Name: Eurostandard (Coated), 9%, GCR, Light

Ink Options

Ink Colors: Eurostandard (Coated)

Separation Options

Separation Type: ⊙ GCR
Black Generation: Light
Black Ink Limit: 100%
Total Ink Limit: 330%
UCA Amount: 0%

Gray Ramp:

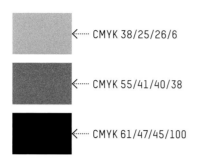

<----- CMYK 38/25/26/6

<----- CMYK 55/41/40/38

<----- CMYK 61/47/45/100

Name: Eurostandard (Coated), 9%, GCR, Medium
Ink Options
Ink Colors: Eurostandard (Coated)
Separation Options

Separation Type: ⊙ GCR
Black Generation: Medium
Black Ink Limit: 100%
Total Ink Limit: 330%
UCA Amount: 0%

Gray Ramp:

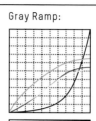

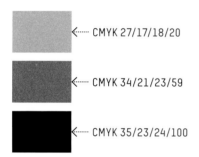

<----- CMYK 27/17/18/20

<----- CMYK 34/21/23/59

<----- CMYK 35/23/24/100

Name: Eurostandard (Coated), 9%, GCR, Heavy
Ink Options
Ink Colors: Eurostandard (Coated)
Separation Options

Separation Type: ⊙ GCR
Black Generation: Heavy
Black Ink Limit: 100%
Total Ink Limit: 330%
UCA Amount: 0%

Gray Ramp:

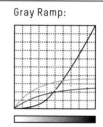

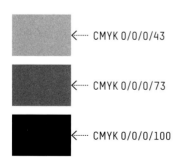

<----- CMYK 0/0/0/43

<----- CMYK 0/0/0/73

<----- CMYK 0/0/0/100

Name: Eurostandard (Coated), 9%, GCR, Maximum
Ink Options
Ink Colors: Eurostandard (Coated)
Separation Options

Separation Type: ⊙ GCR
Black Generation: Maximum
Black Ink Limit: 100%
Total Ink Limit: 330%
UCA Amount: 0%

Gray Ramp:

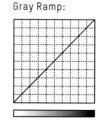

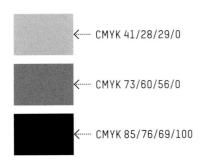

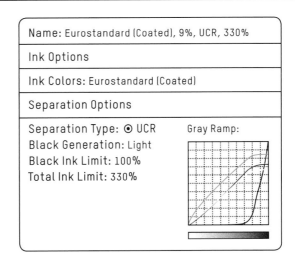

Name: Eurostandard (Coated), 9%, UCR, 330%

Ink Options

Ink Colors: Eurostandard (Coated)

Separation Options

Separation Type: ⊙ UCR   Gray Ramp:
Black Generation: Light
Black Ink Limit: 100%
Total Ink Limit: 330%

CMYK 41/28/29/0

CMYK 73/60/56/0

CMYK 85/76/69/100

(See the section "Black composition" in the chapter "Print technology," p. 77ff.)

After choosing GCR one can change the black generation from None to Maximum. With None all colors without black are separated. With Maximum, on the other hand, neutral tones only contain black, and the CMY component is reduced to zero. This option is good for separating logos or screenshots so that the neutral tones contain nothing but black.

Subsequently one can change the total ink limit, which should be set according to the type of paper. The settings for normal total ink coverage are in this chapter in the section on color profiles. (See p. 206ff.) Undercoat addition makes the dark colors richer in reproduction by raising the chromatic component.

Rich black In this context rich black plays a special role. Rich black is not composed purely of black. It contains other Euroscale colors in order to give the ink more depth. Pure black sometimes looks flat on larger objects or large type, particularly in contrast to other colors. Added to this is the fact that when black prints over a color background it can lead to an undesired irregular color cast. This is why objects and type in excess of a certain size are preferably composed of rich black. However, if the black is against an even background that does not give the black an undesired tone, or if the tone fits in well, then one can do without a specially mixed rich black.

Black and rich black

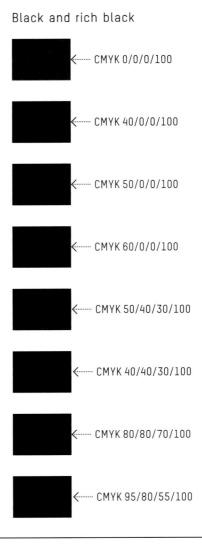

CMYK 0/0/0/100

CMYK 40/0/0/100

CMYK 50/0/0/100

CMYK 60/0/0/100

CMYK 50/40/30/100

CMYK 40/40/30/100

CMYK 80/80/70/100

CMYK 95/80/55/100

Custom CMYK

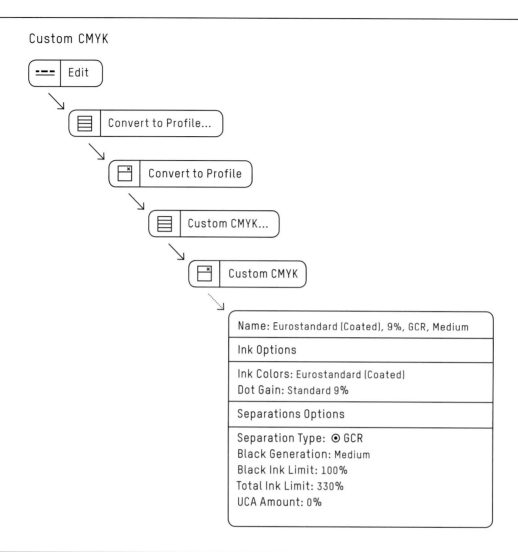

Adding cyan is the main way to achieve more depth in black. The optimum mix ratio is 100 percent black and 40 to 60 percent cyan. Here 40 percent cyan has the advantage that the halftone dots do not touch, so the effect is smoother; 60 percent cyan has a higher opacity, which can be an advantage when rich black is set against a very dark background.

A rich black composed purely of black and cyan has a slight blue tinge that can be jarring or might not fit in, so a rich black may also be mixed from all four process colors. One must take care not to exceed the maximum ink limit or area coverage of each type of paper. One should recheck the mix ratio of the rich black and perhaps optimize it manually when one converts a document to another space.

Notes

<u>5.5 Color proofs</u> Although it is possible to create pre-viewable colors using color management, one should nevertheless create a proof before going to press. A proof simulates the later print result in relation to the type of paper chosen. A proof serves to control the data before printing and subsequently a color proof is made to check the result of the printer.

Before going to press the colors and images are checked with a proof. Once it is passed to the printing house it is used as a color proof with which the print result is compared. A non-color proof is called a layout proof, as it is used solely to check the layout and imposition rather than color accuracy. There is a general distinction between analog and digital proofing. Proofs ought to be printed on the same paper as the end result, or at least as close as possible in feel and color. One can also produce what is known as a soft proof on a calibrated monitor. In the most color-accurate view on-screen the paper that will be used for printing is also taken into account.

Analog proofing

One has to produce films for analog proofing. As with manual exposure of printing plates, these films are for making the proof. Each color film is exposed individually onto a paper-like carrier material, in which the print films show the later halftone screen. This method is relatively laborious compared to digital proofing.

Digital proofing

Nowadays digital proofing is normally used. High-quality dye-sublimation and inkjet printers are used to simulate the print result, taking into account the various color profiles. If the product is produced in a digital printing method, there is also the possibility that the proof is produced on the same system as the entire print run.

Today digital proofing can deliver a similar quality to analog proofing. Since inkjet colors have a comparatively large color space, inkjet systems are often used for proof printers. The carrier material should be a paper as close as possible to the paper that will be used for printing, although in practice standardized papers are used. Some proof printers are capable of producing a proof on the paper that will be used for printing, even when it is produced with a conventional printing method. Standard papers are not really suitable because they are often too white for normal digital printers in comparison with the paper for printing. Furthermore, with some printers the halftone dots used correspond to or simulate those in print, thereby creating a noticeable moiré effect.

Printed result

Normal view

One can see in the example of black with dark colors why the shadows are often too dark in the normal view. On the top is the visual result of the printed ink; below, it is simulated in the normal view in Photoshop.

Soft proofing

A soft proof is a representation on-screen of the print result that is as color accurate as possible. The monitor has to simulate the interplay between the ink colors and the paper. Using a soft proof one can already judge the result on the screen in the layout stage or during data preparation with some degree of color accuracy. Soft proofing is becoming increasingly common in the print room.

Monitor calibration is a major requirement for a soft proof with maximum possible color accuracy. This can be carried out with as much detail as needed. (See p. 197ff.) The input and output devices also have to be calibrated regularly. This mainly affects the monitor, proof printer and printing machine.

The difference between a soft proof and the normal view in Photoshop is that in the normal view the image contrast is scaled to the complete monitor contrast, possibly making the shadows too dark and the highlights too bright. This is due to the relative

Proof setup

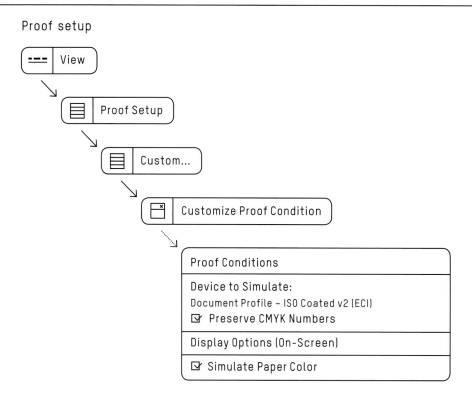

When the device to be simulated fits the document profile, Preserve CMYK Numbers should be active.

colorimetric conversion of the image data in the monitor profile. This method of conversion in combination with black point compensation is usually very good for converting RGB data to CMYK, but the screen view does not yield accurate results because of the higher contrast. There is more information about conversion methods under "Rendering intent." (See p. 214ff.)

Soft proof settings

In order to get the most exact view of the later print result, one must choose the settings in Photoshop, InDesign, or Illustrator for the proof that correspond to the print conditions (View > Proof Setup > Custom... or > Customize...in Illustrator).
Next one chooses the destination space under Device to Simulate. For instance, the ISO Newspaper profile must be chosen to represent an original for a daily newspaper in the soft proof view.

Preserve CMYK Numbers must be active when there is an image or document that is already in the destination space. This ensures that the exact previously set values that are printed are also represented. When the CMYK values are not yet in the destination space and the image or colors still need to be converted, this option must not be active.

The rendering intent indicates how the document or image file colors are converted to the destination space for soft proofing on the monitor. The colors are not actually converted. The setting merely defines the way in which the colors are temporarily represented on-screen for soft proofing. If the colors are already in the destination space, one must choose the intent Absolute Colorimetric. This guarantees that the actual color values are represented in the soft proof view. If, on the other hand, the colors are not yet in the destination space, the best option is usually either Relative Colorimetric with black point compensation active, or Perceptual. There is more detailed information about rendering intents under "Rendering intent." (See p. 214ff.)

Output preview in Acrobat

```
[ --- | Advanced ]
        ↘
      [ ☰ | Print Production ] ——→ [ ☰ | Output Preview... ]
                                              ↘
                                          [ ▣ | Output Preview ]
                                                  ⇲
```

Simulation Profile: ISO Coated v2 (ECI)
☑ Simulate Paper Color
☑ Simulate Overprinting
Show: All
Warning Opacity: 100%
Preview: Separations

Under Display Options (On-Screen) one should select Simulate Paper Color in order to achieve a representation of the print result as color-accurate as possible. When the paper color is simulated, Simulate Black Ink becomes active automatically. Then the soft proof view (View > Proof Colors) is the best way to check the document colors and images on-screen before going to press or before the digital proof.

One should look at a soft proof of the print PDF in Acrobat as a final check of the print data. The soft proof in Acrobat is called Output Preview. One gets to this via the advanced menu (Advanced > Print Production > Output Preview...). Normally the destination profile with which the PDF was written is selected automatically. One should select Simulate Paper White for soft proofing, which automatically activates Simulate Black Ink.

<u>5.6 Color conversion step by step</u> On the following pages we will look at how images or individual colors are converted from RGB to CMYK, and from one CMYK color space to another. We will also see how color images are converted to grayscale, how duotone images are created, and what to watch out for when using spot colors.

RGB > CMYK, photograph – Step 1: Open a file without a color profile

View in the working space "eciRGB v2 ICC v4"

Missing Profile

What would you like to do?
- ◉ Leave as is (don't color manage)
- ○ Assign working RGB: eciRGB v2 ICCv4
- ○ Assign Profile: sRGB IEC61966-2.1

RGB > CMYK, photograph – Step 2: Assign missing profile

View in ECI-RGB

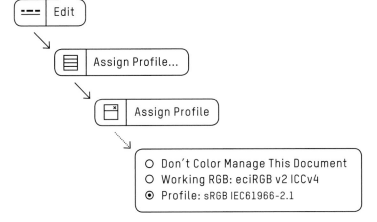

Edit → Assign Profile... → Assign Profile

- ○ Don't Color Manage This Document
- ○ Working RGB: eciRGB v2 ICCv4
- ◉ Profile: sRGB IEC61966-2.1

View in sRGB

Converting from RGB to CMYK, photograph

The first example shows how an RGB image is converted to the CMYK mode.

Step 1 The following example does not have an embedded color profile. That is why the corresponding profile warning is displayed when the file is opened. Here one chooses the option Preserve (No Color Management) when one does not know the RGB profile of the image. The image is displayed in the RGB profile chosen in the color settings; in our example it is eciRGB v2 ICC v4. However, in case an RGB image is opened that already has an embedded profile, one should preserve that profile. A warning is displayed when there is a mismatch with the profile chosen in the color settings. When this occurs one

RGB > CMYK, photograph – Step 3: Convert to profile

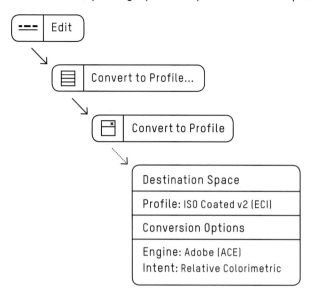

Perceptual

Relative colorimetric

must choose Use the Embedded Profile (instead of the Working Space).

Step 2 Next there is the command Assign Profile (Edit > Assign Profile), and with the help of the preview one can find out which RGB working space the image was created in. One can try out all the available RGB profiles in the preview before opting for one. In our example the sRGB profile is selected. This step is superfluous if an image already has a profile, unless the image looks better in another color space. In that case it might make sense to assign another color space to the image if it saves on unnecessary tweaks.

Step 3 Subsequently the command Convert to Profile (Edit > Convert to Profile) is carried out to convert the image to the CMYK mode. One should choose the profile as the destination space that corresponds to the output conditions in which the image is printed. In this case it is ISO Coated v2. One must choose the module Adobe (ACE) in the conversion options. Before deciding on an intent one should compare the differ-

ent intents with the preview to see which is best suited. As a rule, the best result for a color image is a CMYK conversion that it most similar to the RGB view. Here the intent Relative Colorimetric is selected, in combination with Black Point Compensation. That way the image looks almost exactly the same in the CMYK mode as it does in the RGB mode.

Converting RGB to CMYK, drawing
The second example is a line drawing in the form of a pixel image in the RGB mode.

In this example there are only two colors: a saturated red and black.

Step 1 When the file is opened, a profile mismatch is displayed because the image is not in the RGB color space chosen in the Photoshop color settings. Since the image ought to be displayed the way it was created, one should activate the option Use the Embedded Profile (instead of the Working Space).

RGB > CMYK, drawing – Step 1: Open a file with profile mismatch

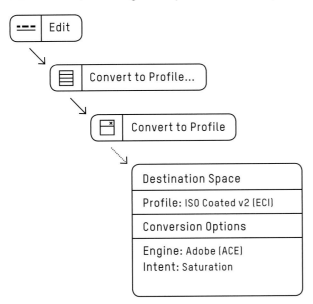

Embedded Profile Mismatch

Embedded: Adobe RGB (1998)
Working: eciRGB v2 ICCv4

What would you like to do?

⊙ Use the embedded profile (instead of the working space)
○ Convert document's colors to the working space
○ Discard the embedded profile (don't color manage)

View in color profile of Adobe RGB file

RGB 0/0/0

RGB 203/75/27

RGB > CMYK, drawing – Step 2: Convert to profile

Edit

Convert to Profile...

Convert to Profile

Destination Space

Profile: ISO Coated v2 (ECI)

Conversion Options

Engine: Adobe (ACE)
Intent: Saturation

Relative Colorimetric

CMYK 78/68/58/95

CMYK 0/81/98/0

Saturation

CMYK 0/0/0/95

CMYK 0/91/95/3

Step 2 One should choose Saturation so that the black is composed mainly of black ink. In the other rendering intents, black would be composed of all four process colors. This could lead to color gaps in the case of misregister, particularly in delicate patterns.

Step 3 Next the composition of the colors can be corrected in different ways. In the example shown, black can be raised to 100 percent using the gradation curve, seeing as the ISO Coated v2 profile limits black ink coverage to 95 percent. One can also correct red using the gradation curve when it contains too much magenta after conversion with Saturation. (There is more information about gradation curves in the chapter "Image Editing," p. 246ff.)

Converting from CMYK to CMYK, photograph

In order to adapt an image to different print conditions, one often has to convert it from one CMYK space to another.

<u>Step 1</u> First, one opens the image in the ISO Coated v2 profile. No profile error is displayed since the document profile corresponds to the Photoshop working space. The ISO Coated v2 profile is a good starting point for adapting images to different print conditions that are supposed to look the same on all types of paper.

CMYK > CMYK, photograph – Step 1: Open the file in the ISO Coated v2 profile

If one chooses an RGB space instead of the ISO Coated v2 profile as a starting point, one must choose an RGB space that contains all inks. This is nearly always the case with an ECI RGB space.

<u>Step 2</u> One should choose Convert to Profile to prepare the image for printing onto newsprint, for instance. In our example only Relative Colorimetric together with Black Point Compensation, or Perceptual can be considered. Different versions of the image are produced in order to find out which is the best conversion method; in this case two versions.

<u>Step 3</u> The best way to check the intents is by comparing the conversion results with the original in the soft proof view. This view is closer to the print result than the normal view is. One opens all created images in the ISO Newspaper profile, and the original in the ISO Coated profile, and then one places the windows next to each other so that they can be directly compared. That way it is easier to choose the version that looks most like the ISO Coated version.

The soft proof view must be set to correspond to the output profile (View > Proof Setup). One must choose the document profile under Device to Simulate. In this case it is the ISO Newspaper profile. The options Preserve CMYK Numbers and Simulate Paper Color must also be active. The soft proof view must also be active for the original; only that one must choose the color space of the original instead of the ISO Newspaper profile. In our example, it is the ISO Coated v2 profile. (See "Soft proof settings" in the chapter "Color proof," p. 226–227.)

In the normal view of our example the version with the intent Relative Colorimetric is the one that looks most like the original. However, in the soft proof view, one can see that the slightly brighter version with the intent Perceptual better compensates the low quality of the newsprint.

CMYK > CMYK, photograph – Step 2:
Producing different conversion results

ISO Newspaper, normal view

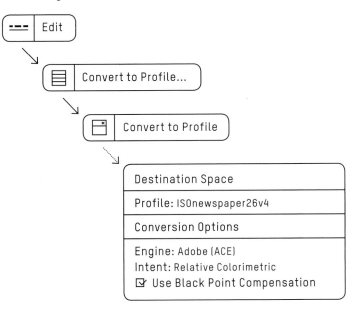

| --- | Edit |

↘

| ▤ | Convert to Profile... |

↘

| ⊟ | Convert to Profile |

⤑

| Destination Space |
| Profile: ISOnewspaper26v4 |
| Conversion Options |
| Engine: Adobe (ACE) |
| Intent: Relative Colorimetric |
| ☑ Use Black Point Compensation |

ISO Newspaper, soft proof view

| ⊟ | Convert to Profile |

⤑

| Destination Space |
| Profile: ISOnewspaper26v4 |
| Conversion Options |
| Engine: Adobe (ACE) |
| Intent: Perceptual |
| ☐ Use Black Point Compensation |

ISO Newspaper, normal view

ISO Newspaper, soft proof view

CMYK > CMYK, colors – Step 1:
Place files in ISO Coated v2 profile

CMYK > CMYK, colors – Step 2:
Convert colors to destination profile

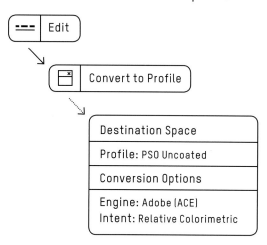

CMYK > CMYK, colors – Step 3:
Compare results in the soft proof view

Perceptual

Relative Colorimetric with black point compensation

Relative Colorimetric without black point
compensation

Converting from CMYK to CMYK, colors

When one converts individual colors, such as a logo color or a background color, all the available conversion intents should be compared with one another. Photoshop works best for converting colors because the results are easier to judge. Moreover, it is harder to convert colors to another space in Illustrator because it lacks the command Convert to Profile.

Step 1 First, one must create a new file in the ISO Coated v2 profile whose area is filled with the color that is to be converted. One should then save these files, which now include the embedded profile, and name them accordingly. In our example three colors need to be converted. A light red, a pink composed solely of magenta, and a warm gray-brown. The size and resolution are irrelevant.

Step 2 The colors are subsequently converted in the destination space using various conversion options, and then named accordingly. The destination space in our example is PSO Uncoated for uncoated paper. One should choose Relative Colorimetric once without Black Point Compensation with the other conversion options.

Step 3 Now one must open all results and compare them with the original colors. The soft proof view should be active for all files. It is virtually impossible to find color compositions that look the same on coated and uncoated paper. This particularly applies to saturated colors such as red and pink. With brown, on the other hand, it is relatively easy to choose relative colorimetric conversion without black point compensation because the other results are too lifeless.

In our example the red looks too bright in the Perceptual result. It is difficult to opt for or against black point compensation in relative colorimetric conversion since both results are almost identical. With black point compensation the color composition is almost identical to the original bright red, which means that the red is more vivid without black point compensation. When one reduces the magenta component instead, it produces a red that never appears darker than the original. A proof on the paper to be used for printing, which in this case is uncoated paper, makes the decision easier. Therefore it is better to print pure magenta unchanged at 100 percent. Thus one produces a pure color on the uncoated paper that looks most like the original.

Grayscale, variant 1 - Step 1: Open the file in the ISO Coated v2 profile

Grayscale, variant 1 - Step 2: Convert colors to destination profile

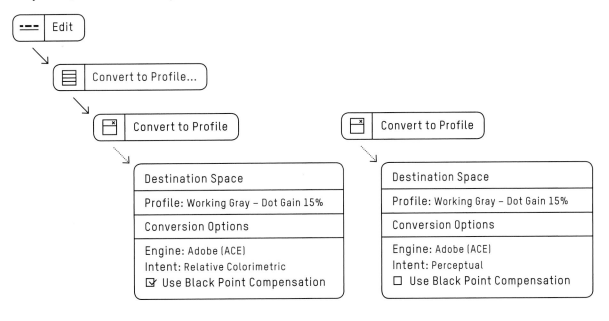

Relative Colorimetric

Perceptual

Step 4 It is recommendable to make a proof of the conversion results on the paper for printing, which in our example is uncoated paper. One should then compare them under a daylight lamp before deciding.

Step 5 The chosen colors are transferred to the respective Illustrator graphics or InDesign documents. The color definitions have to be manually adjusted in the Color palette. It is useful in Illustrator for the colors to be defined as global. (See "Colors in Illustrator," p. 192.) Subsequently one assigns the new color profile to the document.

Converting to grayscale, photograph variant 1

One converts an image to grayscale with the command Convert to Profile, like conversion to any other color space. One must choose a gray space for a profile that corresponds to the destination space.

Step 1 First, one has to open the color image. It generally makes no difference whether the original is in the RGB or CMYK mode. Our example is a CMYK image that has been saved in the ISO Coated v2 profile.

Step 2 One converts the image to a gray space with the command Convert to Profile. The right choice depends on the type of paper and printing method used. One should choose Working Gray – Black Ink – ISO Coated v2 as the destination space for printing on coated art paper, at the top inside the conversion dialog pop-up, provided one has selected the corresponding gray space in the color settings. (See "Color settings in Photoshop," p. 201ff.) ISO Newspaper26v4_gr is the correct gray space for coldset newspaper printing.

When converting to a gray space one should also compare the different intents using the preview.

Step 3 Should none of the conversion results in the preview match expectations due to some areas being too dark or too bright, or if there is too little contrast, one should edit the colors before converting to gray. As long as the image is still in color, one can brighten or darken areas to give the image more contrast using selective color adjustment. A blue—especially a dark blue—sky often looks too dark after converting to gray.

In our example, we will brighten the blue areas before conversion using selective color adjustment or by adjusting tone, saturation, and balance. That way the background will not be too dark in gray.

It is useful to display the image during color adjustment in the gray soft proof view. One must first adjust the soft proof view accordingly (View > Proof Setup > Custom...). In the proof conditions under "Device to Simulate" one must choose the gray space that the image is to be converted to. The image is then displayed in gray, even though it is still in the color mode.

Step 4 The background becomes brighter when the image is subsequently converted to the gray space. The result may still be optimized by increasing the contrast or by targeting areas for brightening.

Converting to grayscale, photograph variant 2

There is an even easier way to create a gray image. The colors are taken out of the image, while at the same time specific areas can be made brighter or darker. In Photoshop the command is the Image menu (Image > Adjustments > Black & White...).

Step 1 This command does not work for a CMYK image, so first it is converted to an RGB profile. In our example the image was converted to the eciRGB v2 ICC v4 space with the command Convert to Profile.

Step 2 Next one goes to Black & White... in the image menu. There one can make individual color areas brighter or darker. In our example we have made the blue and cyan tones brighter and the magenta tones darker.

Step 3 Where necessary, one can subsequently increase the contrast by adjusting the gradation curve.

Step 4 Finally, the image must be converted to a gray, duotone, or CMYK space with the command Convert to Profile. (One should follow the directions under "Grayscale mode image" and "Duotone mode image" in the section "Color mode," p. 187.)

Grayscale, variant 1 - Step 3 A: Adjust proof conditions to gray

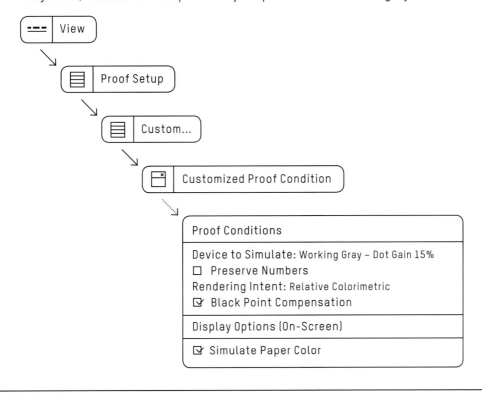

```
[---] View
      ↘
      [≣] Proof Setup
           ↘
           [≣] Custom...
                ↘
                [▣] Customized Proof Condition
```

Proof Conditions
Device to Simulate: Working Gray – Dot Gain 15% ☐ Preserve Numbers Rendering Intent: Relative Colorimetric ☑ Black Point Compensation
Display Options (On-Screen)
☑ Simulate Paper Color

Grayscale, variant 1 – Step 3 B: Color adjustments

Corrected color image

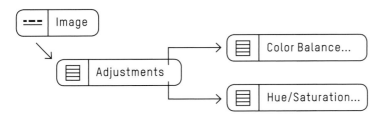

```
[---] Image
      ↘
      [≣] Adjustments ──→ [≣] Color Balance...
                      └──→ [≣] Hue/Saturation...
```

Result in grayscale

After color adjustment one can still optimize the gray image in different ways, for instance by altering the gradation curve or by partially brightening or darkening it using the dodge or burn tools.

Grayscale, variant 2 – Step 2: Black & White command

Result in grayscale

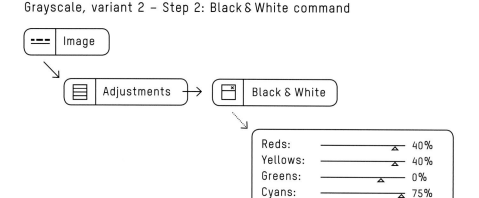

Converting to Duotone mode

The Duotone mode is good for reproducing monochrome plus one or more added colors. One can create high-quality reproductions of grayscale images by using more than one ink. One usually uses black plus a Pantone or HKS color. A process color, such as magenta, can also be used instead to give the image a certain tone. (See "Duotone mode image" in the section "Color mode," p. 187.)

Step 1 The motif must be in the Grayscale mode in order to convert it to Duotone. One must first convert a color image to a gray space with the command Convert to Profile.

Step 2 One cannot convert to Duotone mode with the command Convert to Profile, since the Duotone mode cannot be linked to a special color profile. Instead one converts grayscale images to Duotone via the image mode (Image > Mode > Duotone).

Step 3 In the Duotone mode the dialog box appears with the Duotone options. Under Type one can choose how many inks to use for the Duotone image. There are up to four inks available. Photoshop offers a whole series of ready-made Duotone, Tritone and Quadtone settings.

In Presets there are various CMYK Duotone settings with black and cyan, magenta and/or yellow. There are several settings for all color combinations

that produce color casts to varying degrees. Furthermore, there are Duotone settings with black plus one or more Pantone gray tones for high-quality reproduction of grayscale images. There are further black plus Pantone combinations with varying degrees of color cast.

The sequence of inks from 1 to 4 should correspond to the actual sequence for printing, so that the screen image accords with the print result. The actual printing sequence is crucial for the color result. Under Overprint Colors one can set how the color result looks when the individual colors are printed over one another. Customarily one prints the darkest color first and the lightest last. The usual sequence of the process colors in offset printing is: black, cyan, magenta, yellow, but sometimes also black, magenta, cyan, and yellow.

Step 4 When one clicks on one of the curves, a dialog opens in which the Duotone curves can be altered manually or numerically. In the numbers on the right one can enter the percentage of ink that each black component of the original grayscale image should use for reproduction.

If under 0 one enters 10, all the areas that had no tone in the original grayscale image are printed with 10 percent of this Duotone ink. Or if under 50 one enters 70, all the areas that had 50 percent shading in the grayscale image are printed with 70 percent of the Duotone ink.

Duotone mode – Step 1:
Grayscale image

Duotone mode –Step 3:
Choose Duotone options

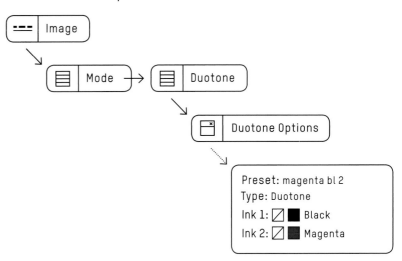

Duotone mode – Step 4: adjust Duotone curves

Duotone image

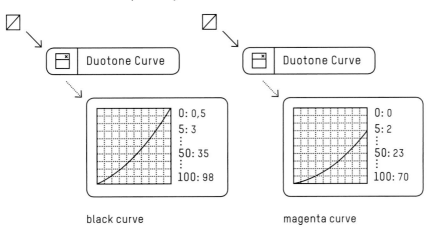

black curve

magenta curve

In our example all 5 percent grayscales are reproduced with 3 percent black and 2 percent magenta, while 50 percent grayscales are 35 percent black and 23 percent magenta, and 100 percent black grayscales are 98 percent black and 70 percent magenta.

Step 5 Where required, one can keep these curves but change the inks. When one clicks on one of the color swatches in the Duotone options, the dialog opens with the usual color selector or the chosen color library for choosing or mixing another ink. The ink is automatically given a name, but it can be changed. One

may have to be careful that the description is not different from the color used in InDesign. (See "Colors in InDesign," p. 190.)

Duotone images cannot be saved as TIFF files. They may be Photoshop or Photoshop EPS format files. Color profiles cannot be embedded in Duotone images.

Multichannel mode – Step 1: Multichannel mode

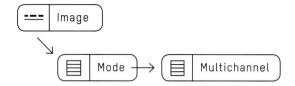

Converting to multichannel mode

The multichannel mode is good for images partially or entirely reproduced using a spot color.

An example is an image in which a certain area is emphasized with a spot color. This is easier to do in the multichannel mode than in the Duotone mode, as one can access the individual color separations in the Channel palette.

Step 1 One converts an image to the multichannel mode via the command Image > Mode > Multichannel. Since the example is in the grayscale mode, there is only one channel in the Channel palette, called Black. In a CMYK image the four process colors would be named in the Channel palette.

Step 2 Further channels may now be added to the Channel palette. Double-clicking on the channel one gets to Options, where one can define the color and its solidity. One should enter 0 percent for low opacity process colors like in our example. This ensures that the screen view corresponds to the later print result, as the colors from the individual channels mix with each other. One should enter 100 percent for a high-opacity color, such as a metallic color. (See "Multichannel mode image," p. 189–190.)

Step 3 Now one can choose the new channel and filled or painted as desired. In our example a circle was drawn first before being filled with 100 percent of the color.

Step 4 Multichannel images cannot be saved as Tiff files. One can use the Photoshop DCS 2.0 format to embed them in an InDesign document. In the "Save As" dialog the "Spot Colors" option must be active. A color profile cannot be embedded in a multichannel image.

Multichannel mode – Step 2: Add channel

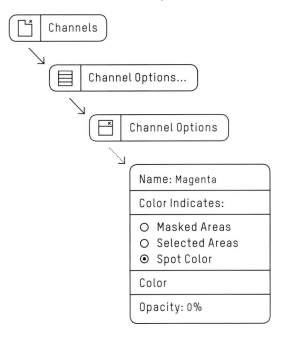

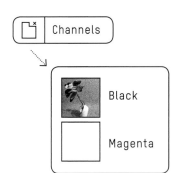

Multichannel mode – Step 3: Fill channel

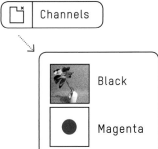

Multichannel mode – Step 4: Save as EPS

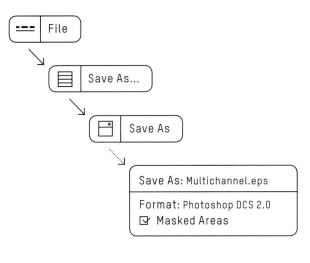

CMYK > CMYK, Illustrator – Step 1:
Save Illustrator file with profile

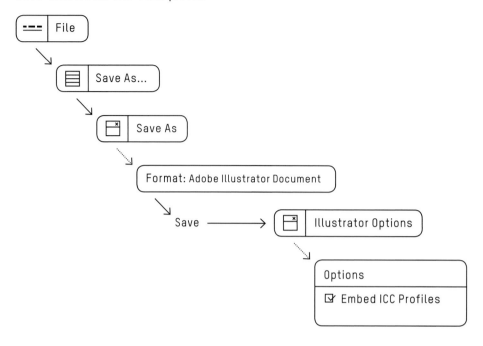

Converting from CMYK to CMYK in Illustrator

Illustrator does not have the command Convert to Profile.... Nevertheless, colors in Illustrator can be adapted to different spaces by previously converting the colors in Photoshop and transferring the results to the colors in Illustrator. If this method is too time-consuming, one should do as follows.

Step 1 First, the file must be saved as an Illustrator file. The current ICC profile is embedded in this file, since color profiles cannot be embedded in an EPS. In our example the ISO Coated v2 profile is embedded. Next, one must close the file.

Step 2 Next, the new color space is chosen in the color settings (Edit > Color Settings...); our example shows PSO Uncoated.

Step 3 One then reopens the file. A profile error appears on opening. Here one has the option of converting the colors in the previously chosen working space. One only has the conversion options chosen in the color settings available. When one wishes to com-pare different intents, one must change the color settings in order to convert the file on opening again.

Step 4 When one is satisfied with the colors one should rename the converted file (Logo-uc.ai, for example).

CMYK > CMYK, Illustrator – Step 2: Change color settings

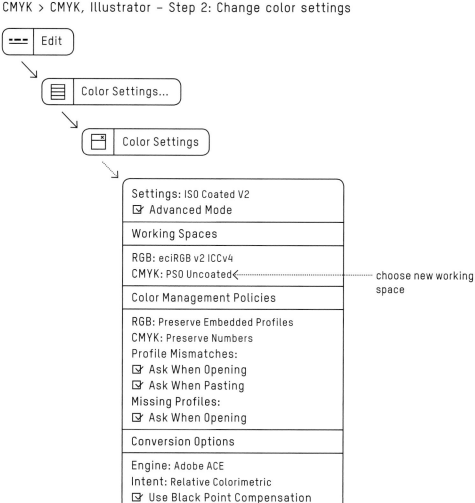

choose new working space

CMYK > CMYK, Illustrator – Step 3: Convert colors when opening

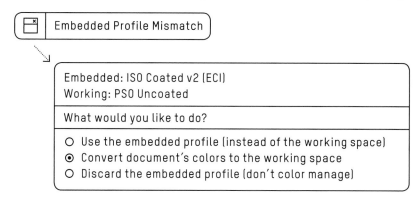

CMYK > CMYK, InDesign – Step 1: Assign profile

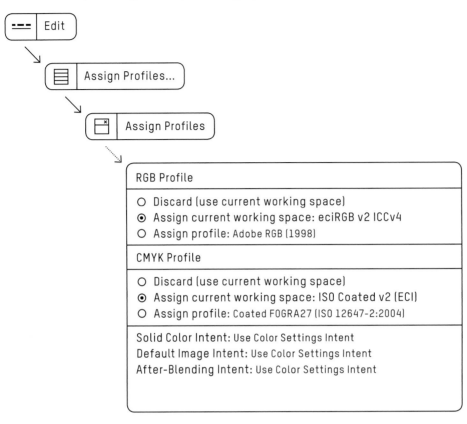

Converting from CMYK to CMYK in InDesign

Like Photoshop, InDesign offers the possibility of converting the document colors in another working space (Edit > Convert to Profile...). This converts all colors created in InDesign, but not those of placed Illustrator or Photoshop files.

<u>Step 1</u> In case it does not already have one, the document should be assigned a profile before conversion. Our example is for coated offset paper, so the ISO Coated v2 (ECI) profile is assigned.

<u>Step 2</u> The destination space and conversion options can be defined via the command Convert to Profile. In case the color composition does not change in the preview when one changes the conversion intent from, say, Relative Colorimetric to Perceptual, one must break off the process and start the command again.

<u>Step 3</u> Finally, the conversion results have to be checked and optimized where necessary. The colors Black, Paper, and Registration are not converted as a rule. All other colors are mixed again according to the chosen conversion options. In the color palettes on the right it is best to avoid converting the base colors cyan, magenta, and yellow, in case these are used in the document.

CMYK > CMYK, InDesign – Step 2: Convert colors to destination space

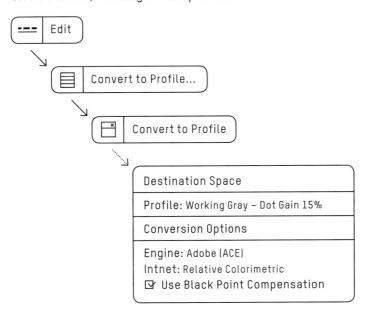

CMYK > CMYK, InDesign – Step 3: Check color palette

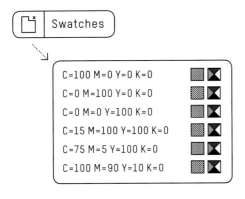

before conversion

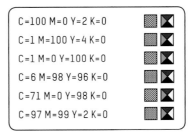

before relative colorimetric conversion

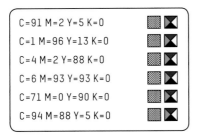

after perceptual conversion

6. Image Editing

Perfection is everywhere. It is suggested in almost every image we see—particularly in advertising. No blemishes, bold colors, pure skin. From models to pictures of products to background landscapes: images tempt the viewer with a perfect world. To produce such images, one needs both image editing and a good photographer with high-quality equipment and a trained eye, but also good lithography.

The following chapter looks at the necessary basics for judging and editing images. This knowledge is also vital for scanning and retouching. After that, we will look at image optimization, which will help understand the working steps and how best to apply them.

<u>6.1 Basics</u> This chapter explains the basics about how to judge, edit, and reproduce an original or digital image. There are various types of images that have to be treated differently. The main distinguishing features of a digital image are its bit depth, the corresponding color model, gamut, and image resolution.

1 bit (two possible states per pixel)

2 bits (four possible states per pixel)

8 bits (256 possible states per pixel)

1 bit	2 bits

Bi-level image black and white	Grayscale image four grayscales

8 bits

Grayscale image
256 grayscales

3 x 8 bits	3 x 16 bits

RGB color image 256^3 colors	RGB color image $65,536^3$ colors

Bit depth A major feature of an image is its bit depth, also called color depth. A digital image consists of a series of pixels. Each of these image dots contains a certain amount of information. The bit depth indicates how many bits there are to describe each pixel. The higher the bit depth, the more information a pixel can contain, and the more colors a pixel and an image can display. The usual bit depths are 1, 2, 8, and 16.

An image with only 1 bit per pixel is also known as a bi-level image. Due to its limited bit depth such an image can only display two states—black or white. That makes this bit depth optimal for line drawings. A depth of 2 bits already makes four grayscales possible. Normal grayscale images have a depth of 8 bits, which makes 256 different grayscales, including black and white, possible per pixel; 256 grayscales are sufficient for a continuous gradation from black to white.

RGB color images have three color channels with 8 bits each, meaning they can represent 16.7 million colors ($256 \times 256 \times 256$). This number is generally enough for reproducing color photos. A CMYK color image with four 8-bit channels also makes possible 16.7 million colors, seeing as the additional channel with black ink is only needed for technical reasons for reproduction. Image editing software, such as Photoshop, also offers the opportunity to edit images with a depth of 16 bits per channel. This large increase in gradations per pixel makes it easier to edit originals with a high density, i.e., with many different colors. An image with

16-bit color depth is more flexible for color adjustment, plus it makes numerous shadow details possible.

High bit depth is also a great starting point for converting RGB images to the CMYK mode. Although the downsampling to 8 bits that occurs reduces the bit depth, one does not altogether lose the fine details in the shadows. It is important that the scanner software or digital camera record these differences and that they are not lost during image editing, while adjusting the tonal value, for instance.

A relatively high bit depth is not exclusively useful for color originals. It can make sense to have a high bit depth per pixel for editing and reproducing black-and-white photographs. Although a grayscale image

Number of colors per bit depth

Pixel depth	Mode	Number of colors
1-bit	Bitmap	Black and white
2 bits	Grayscale	4 grayscales
8 bits	Grayscale	256 grayscales
16 bits	Grayscale	65,536 grayscales
24 bits	RGB (3 x 8 bits)	16.7 million (256 x 256 x 256 colors)
32 bits	CMYK (4 x 8-bits)	16.7 million (256 x 256 x 256 colors)
48 bits	RGB (3 x 16 bits)	281 trillion colors

The number of colors increases with the bit depth and number of channels.

Narrow gamut

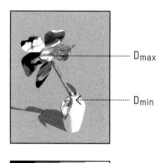

D_{max}

D_{min}

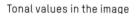

Tonal values in the image

Broad gamut

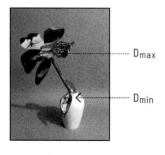

D_{max}

D_{min}

Tonal values in the image

with a mere 8-bit depth allows 256 grayscales, including black and white, conventional printing and screening processes are not capable of perfectly reproducing that many grayscales. Therefore a grayscale image should use more than one color where possible so that it can reproduce more differences in tonal value. The CMYK mode is also a good image mode for grayscale images. The Duotone mode is another method for high-quality reproduction of grayscales. In it one can use the different tonal values of several colors for printing; often black and Pantone gray.

Gamut One of the most important aspects of image editing is knowing how to judge and manage the tonal range, or gamut. A high-end scanner or digital camera should be capable of managing the entire tonal range of an image. One gets this value from the difference between the image point with the highest density (D_{max}) and the point with the lowest density (D_{min}), in other words, the darkest and lightest image points. The entire gamut of an image is between D_{max} and D_{min}.

The density is proportional to the opacity logarithm. This indicates how much light is reflected for non-transparent originals, and how much light is let through—transmitted—for transparent originals. One reaches the figure by dividing the entire amount of incident light by the amount of reflected or transmitted light.

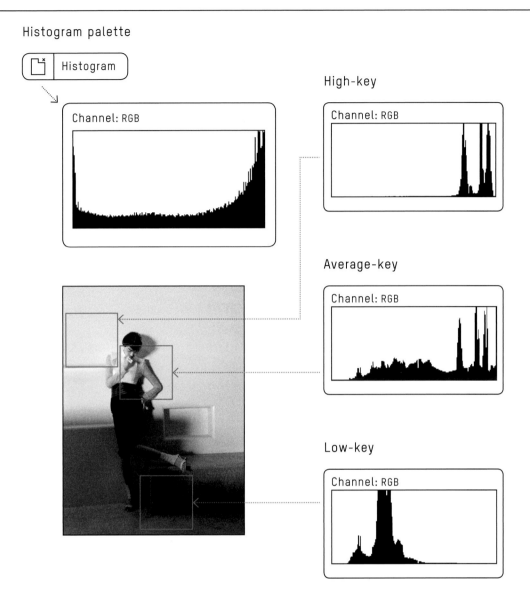

Histogram palette

Channel: RGB

High-key

Channel: RGB

Average-key

Channel: RGB

Low-key

Channel: RGB

In the advanced view of the palette, there is detailed information about the tonal distribution of the image, and one can activate different channel views.

Thus if 100 percent of the incident light is reflected off the original, it has an opacity of 1 (100/100 = 1); if only 50 percent is reflected, it has an opacity of 2 (100/50 = 2).

A slide, for example, with a D_{max} of 3.3 and a D_{min} of 0.3 produces a gamut of 3.0. Compared with paper, slides can have more than double the gamut. Non-transparent originals generally have a maximum gamut of 2.0. The density in print is, depending on the type of paper, roughly between 1.9 for coated paper and 0.9 for newsprint.

Histogram A histogram is the graphic representation of the gamut, or of the pixel distribution in an image. It shows the pixel distribution along a horizontal intensity scale from 0 (left) to 255 (right), or from black to white. The bar height indicates how many pixels with what intensity there are in the image. Thus one can see whether an image has sufficient detail in the shadows, midtones, and highlights, or whether the tonal values need to be adjusted.

Histogram

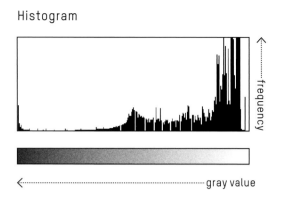

The histogram makes the tonal distribution of an image clearer. The higher a bar is, the more pixels there are with this tonal value in the image.

In the advanced view of the Histogram palette in Photoshop there is additional information about the tonal distribution of an image. The mean value shows the average brightness from 0 to 256. The standard deviation shows just how much the intensity values vary. The median value is the middle value in the whole intensity range. Pixels is the total number of pixels in the image; Level indicates at what intensity level the cursor is on the histogram; Count shows the total number of pixels at the level where the cursor is; and Percentile shows the percentage of pixels in the palette that are at, or to the left of, the cursor. The cache level shows the image cache with which the histogram was created. In cache level 1 the histogram is created from the current image pixels. The higher the cache level, the faster the histogram is updated, since in a cache level above 1, four neighboring pixels are grouped into one pixel value.

One can generally read on the histogram what kind of image one is dealing with, i.e., whether the main image points and details are likely to be in the shadows, midtones, or highlights. Different image types are called key types. In an image with a broad gamut the pixels are distributed more or less evenly. Images with this even tonal distribution are described as average-key. Images with mainly dark colors and few light areas are termed low-key, and images with mainly light colors and few dark areas are high-key.

This uneven tonal distribution can also mean that the image is either under- or overexposed. However, an image does not have to have the entire gamut

from black to white. A motif can have a limited gamut or an unusual color balance. It is important when scanning or editing to pay precise attention to this limited tonal range or color cast, and not to distort it with automatic gamma adjustment.

A gray wedge can be scanned in at the same time as the original in order not to distort the limited tonal distribution when scanning with automatic lighting control. This is generally included in delivery with a high-quality scanner.

Image resolution

Image resolution A digital image consists of a series or collection of pixels. The more pixels per inch an image has, the higher its resolution is. An image needs a sufficiently high resolution in order to be reproduced well. Image resolution is measured in dpi (dots per inch).

The image pixels are not reproduced one to one on a printing machine. Instead, they are transformed to the pixel distribution of the printer. In conventional reproduction methods, the different grayscales of an image pixel are reproduced with halftone dots of varying sizes. Each dot is composed of several printer pixels, or spots. This transformation of image pixels into dots takes place in the printer's PostScript RIP.

The higher the printer resolution and the wider the screen ruling, the more printer pixels there are available for a halftone dot. Likewise, there are fewer printer pixels for a halftone dot the finer the screen ruling becomes. In conventional AM screening, a dot matrix should consist of at least 8 x 8 printer pixels in order to create continuous gradations. This ensures that a single halftone dot can assume 64 different states or sizes. This is the required amount for reproducing continuous gradations. (See "Continuous gradation" in the chapter "Printing Technology," p. 86–87.) The output resolution of the printer and the screen ruling determine the maximum number of grayscales that can be represented, plus the sharpness of the image details.

Since the image pixels are transformed from halftone images to halftone dots, the image resolution does not have to correspond to the output resolution of the printer. Instead, the required image resolution is in relation to the screen ruling connected to the printer resolution. There are special formulas for calculating the optimal resolution of halftone images and line graphics.

Image pixel

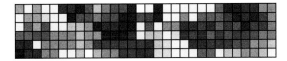

Printer pixel AM screen

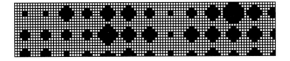

The halftones of the image pixels are simulated by dots with varying amounts of printer pixels.

Resolution rules for AM screening

Line graphics
output device resolution
x scale factor

Grayscales and color images
screen ruling x quality factor
x scale factor

Quality factor

Screen ruling	Quality factor
Up to 133 lpi	2
Over 133 lpi	1.5

A line graphic should generally have a higher image resolution than a halftone original.

A certain quality factor is included for AM screening in these formulas. Factor 2 is used for screen widths up to 133 lpi in frequency-modulated screening and images with geometric shapes. Quality factor 1.5 is used for screen widths in excess of 133 lpi in conventional screening. On the other hand, halftone dots are not needed for line graphics. In this case, the resolution of the graphics should correspond to the output device resolution.

Image resolution in AM screening with a quality factor of 1.5

	25%	50%	75%	100%
53 lpi	20 dpi	40 dpi	60 dpi	80 dpi
60 lpi	23 dpi	45 dpi	68 dpi	90 dpi
85 lpi	32 dpi	64 dpi	96 dpi	128 dpi
100 lpi	38 dpi	75 dpi	113 dpi	150 dpi
133 lpi	50 dpi	100 dpi	150 dpi	200 dpi
150 lpi	56 dpi	113 dpi	169 dpi	225 dpi
175 lpi	66 dpi	132 dpi	197 dpi	263 dpi

Calculating the scale factor

desired size / original size

Image resolution in AM screening with a quality factor of 2

	25%	50%	75%	100%
53 lpi	27 dpi	53 dpi	80 dpi	106 dpi
60 lpi	30 dpi	60 dpi	90 dpi	120 dpi
85 lpi	43 dpi	85 dpi	128 dpi	170 dpi
100 lpi	50 dpi	100 dpi	150 dpi	200 dpi
133 lpi	67 dpi	133 dpi	200 dpi	266 dpi
150 lpi	75 dpi	150 dpi	225 dpi	300 dpi
175 lpi	88 dpi	175 dpi	263 dpi	350 dpi

The resolution tables can be understood by example.
It is recommendable to adapt the image resolution of an image placed in InDesign to its exact scale factor and then use the Unsharp Mask tool if needed.

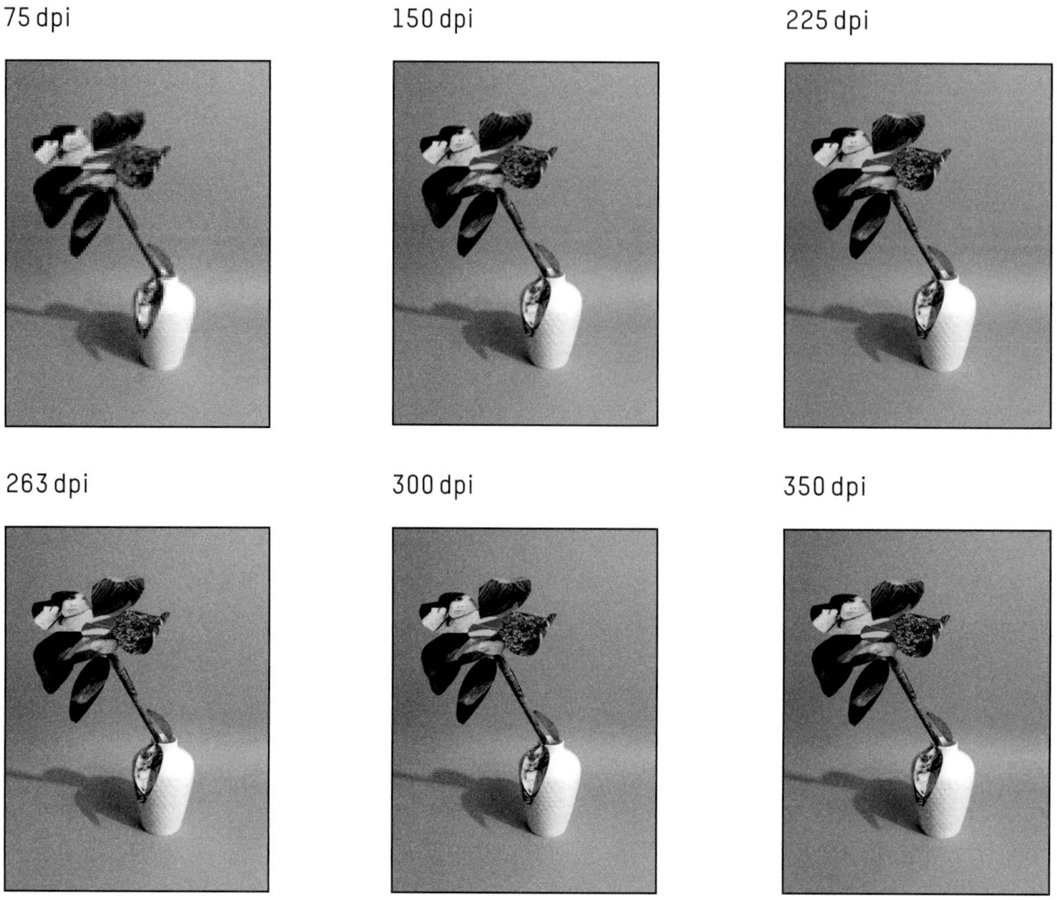

75 dpi 150 dpi 225 dpi

263 dpi 300 dpi 350 dpi

The resolution of halftone images depends on the screen ruling and the screening process used.

Line graphics must have a higher resolution than halftone images. The resolution of a line graphic should correspond to that of the output device. One calculates the image resolution by multiplying the printer output value by the scale factor of the graphic. The output resolution of a line graphic should be at least 1200 dpi, although it does not have to be higher, seeing as the human eye cannot recognize higher values.

The line drawing shown here was scanned in using different resolutions. In the 300 dpi scan, one can see pixels without a magnifying glass. One can barely see the difference between the 600 dpi and the 1200 dpi scans. The difference between 1200 dpi and 2400 dpi is not noticeable at all. In line graphics and halftone images, one must always take into account the scale factor, i.e., with how much percent an image is placed in InDesign. It is best to scan an image in the required output resolution, taking the scale factor into regard.

When an image with 200 percent is placed, the output resolution is only half the size of the input resolution. If, however, the image were reduced to 50 percent, the output resolution would be twice the size.

When images are in digital form, one should lower the resolution in respect to the scale factor in Photoshop when using AM screening. Thus one can avoid stepped breaks in gradients, for example. Each form of recalculating the resolution is connected to a loss of quality, since pixels are taken away during downsampling. This leads to a usually undesired blurring of the image, which can be corrected as far as possible using the Unsharp Mask tool.

In case the resolution of an image is not enough, interpolating pixels will not necessarily improve the result. Depending on the method of interpolation, the image will lose sharpness. It does make sense to use interpolation for line graphics to prevent visible step-

Image resolution
300 dpi

Image resolution
600 dpi

Image resolution
1200 dpi

Image resolution
2400 dpi

Line drawings should generally have higher resolutions than halftone originals.

Original

Pixel repetition

1 pixel

2 pixels

Bilinear

Bicubic

2 pixels

2 pixels

Bicubic smoother

Bicubic sharper

2 pixels

2 pixels

like effects. The resulting lack of sharpness is the reason why the image resolution should not be calculated at, say, 300 dpi when the PDF is written. Instead, the resolution for each image should be interpolated individually in Photoshop where the lost sharpness can be compensated using an unsharp mask. In FM screening the image resolution generally depends on the imagesetter resolution and the selected cluster. The size of the cluster defines how many imagesetter points comprise a halftone dot. This may be 2 x 2 or 3 x 3 pixels, for example. At an imagesetter resolution of 2400 dpi and a cluster of 2 x 2 pixels, this produces an image resolution of 1200 dpi. Thus much smaller halftone dots are created, meaning that more details are reproduced than by using conventional screen processes.

A very fine screen of 2 x 2 or even 3 x 3 imagesetter pixels is particularly good for high-quality art and commercial printing. At an imagesetter resolution of 2540 dpi, which corresponds to a resolution of 1000 l/cm, this produces 20 or 24 µm halftone dots. In other printing methods, such as silkscreen, flexo or newspaper printing, or when using uncoated paper, one should use bigger halftone dots. In that case it is best to use clusters of 2 x 3 or 3 x 3 pixels which at an imagesetter resolution of 2540 dpi produce 24 or 30 µm halftone dots. The optimum image resolution depends on the platesetter resolution together with the cluster resolution, which in turn depends on the printing method and type of paper used. For metal printing plates, the customary resolution is around 2400 dpi; for coated art paper with

Original with
200 dpi

Interpolated to
600 dpi

Original with
75 dpi

Interpolated to
300 dpi

The illustrations above were printed in FM
screening. The resolution of the illustrations
on the right has been heightened. In the line
graphic, the pixel repetition method was used,
while the halftone image uses the
smoother bicubic method.

The different interpolation methods determine how new pixels are introduced. Pixel repetition is the simplest method, where each new pixel receives the color of the nearest pixel. In the bilinear method, the color of a new pixel is a mix of the colors of the two nearest pixels to the right and left. In bicubic interpolation, the colors of all neighboring pixels are ascertained in order to determine the color of the new pixel.

Screenshots are an exception. Their resolution should not be adapted to the printer output resolution and the screen ruling. Screenshots lose quality when their resolution is changed. They have exclusively straight edges and do not look bad with a very low output resolution.

a cluster resolution of 2 x 2 pixels, this produces an optimum image resolution of 1200 dpi. This dot size is too small for polyester plates. Instead, one could choose an imagesetter resolution of 2800 dpi and a cluster of 3 x 3 pixels, which would produce an image resolution of 933 dpi. In newspaper printing, the normal resolution is 1270 dpi. With a cluster size of 2 x 2 pixels, an image resolution of 635 dpi would be optimal. Clusters of 16 x 16 pixels can be optimal for silkscreen printing, depending on the resolution of the screens.

In general, the image resolution in FM screening should be as high as possible, in particular when there are fine details. A low output resolution of, say, 300, 400, or 600 dpi can, however, still yield good results for a motif.

Screenshot in original resolution

| --- | Image |

↓

| ▤ | Image Size... |

↓

| ▣ | Image Size |

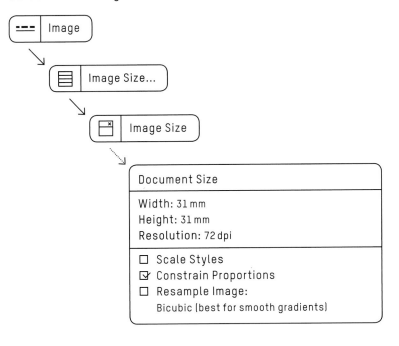

Document Size

Width: 31 mm
Height: 31 mm
Resolution: 72 dpi

☐ Scale Styles
☑ Constrain Proportions
☐ Resample Image:
    Bicubic (best for smooth gradients)

Bicubic smoother interpolation to
300 dpi

Document Size

Width: 31 mm
Height: 31 mm
Resolution: 300 dpi

☐ Scale Styles
☑ Constrain Proportions
☑ Resample Image:
    Bicubic (best for smooth gradients)

Interpolation to 300 dpi with pixel
repetition

Document Size

Width: 31 mm
Height: 31 mm
Resolution: 300 dpi

☐ Scale Styles
☑ Constrain Proportions
☑ Resample Image:
    Nearest Neighbor (preserve hard edges)

The reproduction quality of a screenshot does not improve by recalculating the image resolution.

<u>6.2 Image optimization</u> When the tonal distribution of an image is wrong or does not meet expectations, one can change it by adjusting the tonal value curve. Even an undesired color cast can be corrected by adjusting the tonal value curves of the individual color channels. Heightening the image sharpness also belongs to image optimization.

Image optimization should be carried out in the following sequence where possible: After judging the image using the histogram, errors or weaknesses in the tonal distribution can be solved by adjusting the tonal value curve. Next, possible color casts or an undesired color balance can be corrected. Selective color adjustment offers added possibilities for making targeted adjustments in specific color areas. After calculating the output resolution, the image sharpness is optimized using the Unsharp Mask tool.

Tonal correction

One method of tonal correction is to use the gradation curve. The unchanged input values are on its horizontal axis, and the new output values of the image are on its vertical axis. At a straight 45-degree line the tonal values stay the same. The direction of the gradation curve can be changed in the curve display options under Show Amount Of..., so that the highlights are at the top or bottom of the curve.

In general, there is linear and nonlinear tonal correction. The latter is also called gamma correction. In linear tonal correction, only the position of a straight tonal curve changes. The brightness and contrast of all image points change. Nonlinear tonal correction allows individual points on the gradation curve to be changed more precisely.

By changing the gradation curve, the new distribution of the tonal values discards certain gray values in an image and replaces them with others. Thus simply raising the mid- and quarter tones of the image brightens the image in general. Shadow details come to the fore, while highlight details are lost to a varying degree. By raising the highlights and quarter tones and lowering the shadows and three-quarter tones, one can increase the contrast of a dull image. The S-shaped curve

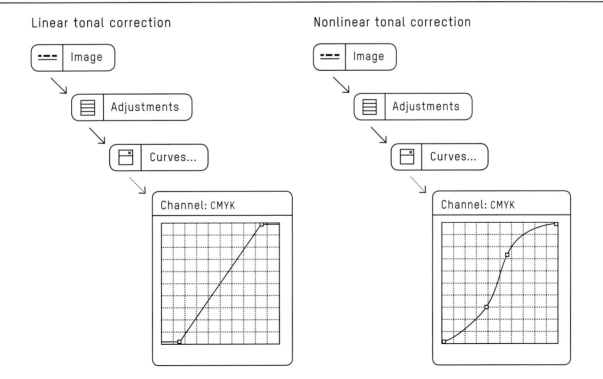

Unchanged gradation curve

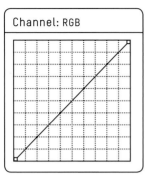

Before

Change brightness

After

One can alter the brightness and contrast of an image by raising or lowering the gradation curve.

One can change the image brightness by shifting the curve up or down without changing its shape.

Change contrast

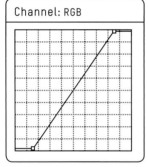

After

Change brightness and contrast

After

When the increase angle of the curve changes while the shape remains the same, the contrast of the image increases or decreases.

Nonlinear correction changes brightness and contrast. The corrections have different effects depending on the tonal range.

that ensues increases the contrast in the midtones. The highlights and shadow details are compressed but not lost, as they would be in linear correction. The rotated S-shaped curve, in which the highlights and quarter tones are lowered and the shadows and three-quarter tones raised, corrects an image with too much contrast. Although the midtones are compressed, this does not necessarily affect motifs with few midtones.

Color cast correction
A color cast in an image can be both intentional or unintentional. Recognizing and determining a color cast is a trained skill. An undesired color cast is easiest to spot in neutral gray tones. However, not every motif has gray tones. An image can also have a color cast on purpose.

A color cast can be corrected by moving the color balance to the complementary color of the color cast. (For more about complementary colors, see p. 182.) In the Photoshop color balance dialog, colors

Raising the mid- and quarter tones

Before/after

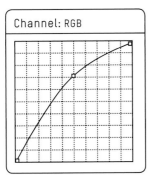

The missing shadow details become noticeable by raising the curve. The image is better illuminated as a whole.

Lowering the shadows, raising the highlights

Before/after

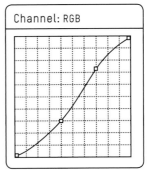

The contrasts are increased in the image by lowering the shadows and three-quarter tones and raising the highlights and quarter tones.

Raising the shadows, lowering the highlights

Before/after

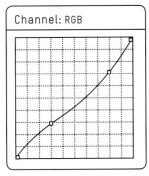

The highlights and shadow details are brought to the fore by raising the shadows and three-quarter tones and lowering the highlights and quarter tones.

are opposite one another like they are in the color circle. In a cyan cast, for example, the color balance is shifted towards red. Should an image have a red cast, one reduces the red component by adding mainly cyan. The intensity of the color cast determines how far one needs to move the slider.

The color balance can also be changed with the gradation curve. A single gradation curve changes the tonal distribution in all color channels. By specifically targeting the base color curves, one can remove or add a color cast. This is easiest to do when the

images has neutral color areas. One must correct the respective curves so that the red, green, and blue components are more or less the same. The RGB mode is best for this method of correcting color casts by setting white, gray, and black points in the image using the pipettes underneath the curve. These image points should already be defined in the automatic color correction options. One can define the destination colors by clicking on the shadows, midtones, and highlight swatches. In principle, every color can be defined, including colors that are not neutral but

Color cast correction with color balance

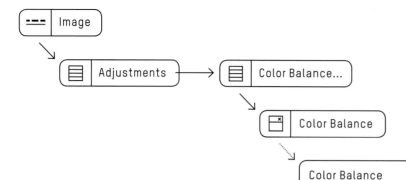

Before

After

Color Balance

Color Levels: +5 -5 +20
Cyan ———————————△————— Red
Magenta ————————△———————— Green
Yellow ——————————————△—— Blue

Tone Balance

○ Shadows ○ Midtones ⊙ Highlights

☑ Preserve Luminosity

Color Balance

Color Levels: -30 +6 -25
Cyan ———————△——————————— Red
Magenta ————————————△——— Green
Yellow —————————△————————— Blue

Tone Balance

○ Shadows ⊙ Midtones ○ Highlights

☑ Preserve Luminosity

Color Balance

Color Levels: -15 -7 -25
Cyan ——————————△———————— Red
Magenta ——————————△———————— Green
Yellow —————————△————————— Blue

Tone Balance

⊙ Shadows ○ Midtones ○ Highlights

☑ Preserve Luminosity

Color cast correction with gradation curve

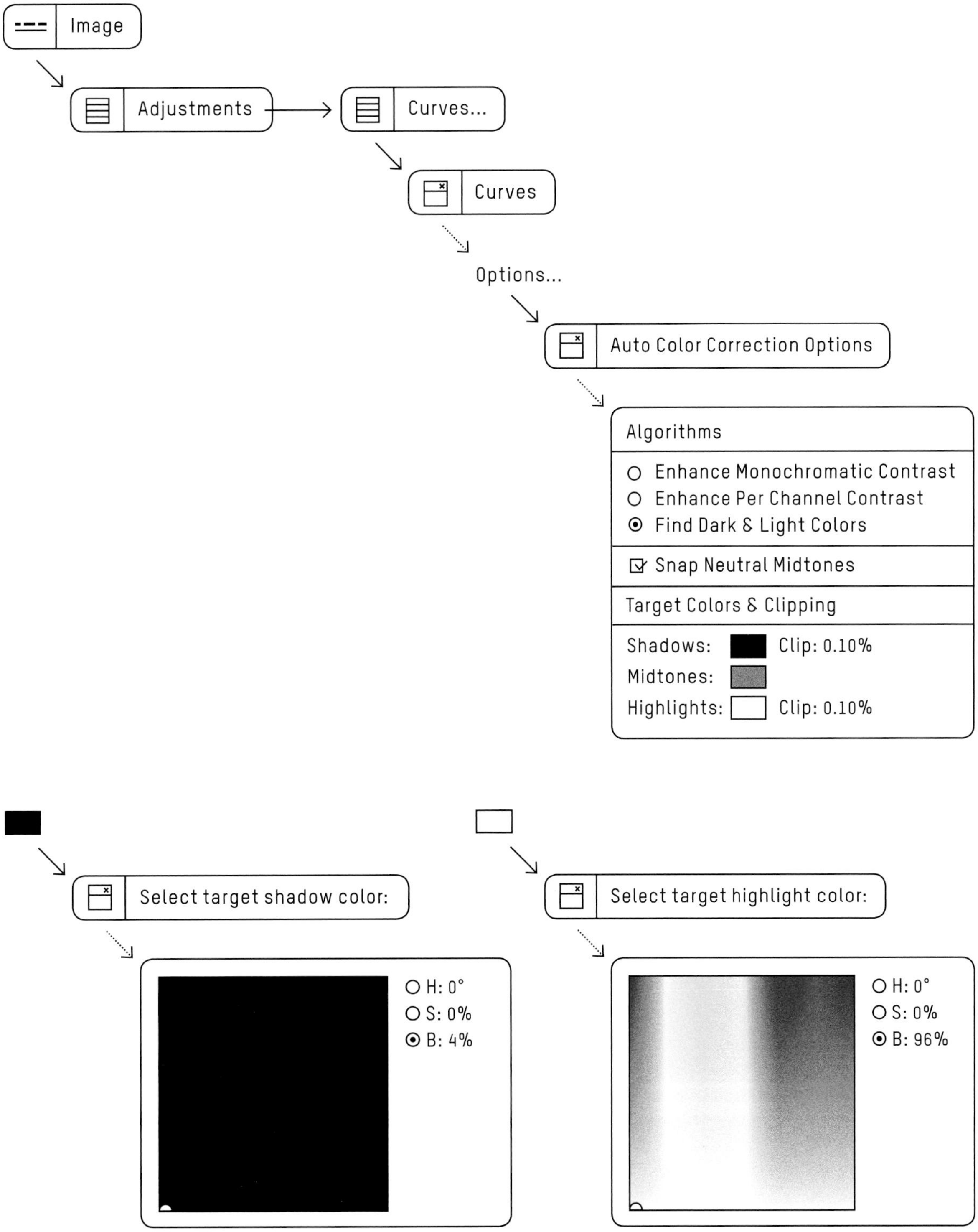

--- Image

目 Adjustments ⟶ 目 Curves...

□ Curves

Options...

□ Auto Color Correction Options

Algorithms

○ Enhance Monochromatic Contrast
○ Enhance Per Channel Contrast
⊙ Find Dark & Light Colors

☑ Snap Neutral Midtones

Target Colors & Clipping

Shadows: ■ Clip: 0.10%
Midtones: ▦
Highlights: □ Clip: 0.10%

□ Select target shadow color:

○ H: 0°
○ S: 0%
⊙ B: 4%

□ Select target highlight color:

○ H: 0°
○ S: 0%
⊙ B: 96%

have a specific color cast. The brightness swatch in the HSB area is the best place to define the brightness of the colors.

When one places the individual pipettes on, say, a red-cast white, gray, or black point, Photoshop automatically changes the color composition of these image points and moves the colors accordingly. One can also carry out color cast correction by setting only the white and black points. If one only sets the white point on a red-cast white point, all color will be removed from this point, leaving it neutral white. One then applies this to black in diminishing intensities. If one only sets the black point on a red-cast black point, the red cast is corrected toward white in diminishing amounts.

One can also automatically determine the lightest and darkest points in an image. Clicking on Auto in the gradation curve dialog, Photoshop searches for these image points and moves the colors according to the preset options.

Selective color correction
Using selective color correction one can carry out corrections in very specific color areas. For instance, one can change the color of a sky by correcting the cyan and blue tones. By correcting the red tones, one can target specific skin tones to match certain expectations. One can also improve the general effect of the image with specific color correction by increasing certain color contrasts.

Selective color corrections are easiest to judge in the CMYK mode because the inks reproduce the effect better. It is also easier to target and remove black from red skin tones that need to look brighter and fresher, or yellow from a sky that is meant to look clearer and more summery.

Image sharpness correction
One can improve the sharpness of image with an unsharp mask. The contrast on the object edges increases so that the details come to the fore. The object edges stand out, giving the impression of sharpness. An unsharp mask is particularly good for correcting blur after recalculating the image resolution. The term "unsharp mask" comes from its earlier use in the manual reproduction of images. An unsharp negative was mounted over the original. During the subsequent exposure only the edges were emphasized, which gave the impression of sharpness.

In Photoshop's digital Unsharp Mask, the threshold determines which pixels are seen as object edges and made sharper. The lower this value is, the smaller the difference needs to be between neighboring pixels in order to be reinforced as object edges.

The radius indicates the width of the unsharp mask. The value depends on the image resolution. The lower the image resolution, the lower one must set this value. If the radius is set too high, it produces unwanted halos. One can reduce these somewhat by only applying the filter to the brightness channel in the Lab mode. In general, the strength of an unsharp mask has to be set individually so that there are no undesired effects.

In Photoshop, the effect of the filter can only be judged correctly in the 100-percent view. The sharpness effect is less pronounced in print than on the monitor. The screening reduces the emphasis on the edges. Where possible, one should try various settings and check them with proofs.

Increasing the image effect with selective color correction

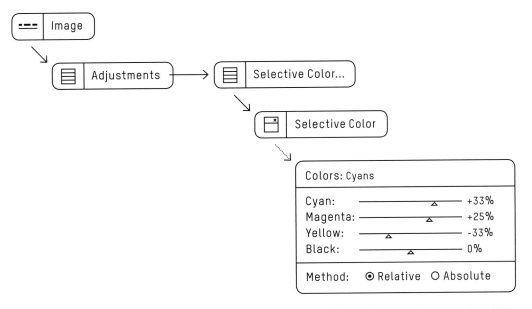

Before

Colors: Cyans

Cyan:	+33%
Magenta:	+25%
Yellow:	-33%
Black:	0%

Method: ⊙ Relative ○ Absolute

Colors: Blues

Cyan:	+25%
Magenta:	+25%
Yellow:	0%
Black:	0%

Method: ⊙ Relative ○ Absolute

Colors: Magentas

Cyan:	0%
Magenta:	+75%
Yellow:	0%
Black:	0%

Method: ⊙ Relative ○ Absolute

After

Changing specific color areas

```
┌─────────────────────────────────┐
│ Colors: Cyan tones              │
│                                 │
│ Cyan:     ──────△──────  0%     │
│ Magenta: △──────────────  -50%  │
│ Yellow:   ──────────△────  +15% │
│ Black:    ─────△──────────  -20%│
│                                 │
│ Method:  ⊙ Relative  ○ Absolute │
└─────────────────────────────────┘
```

```
┌─────────────────────────────────┐
│ Colors: Blue tones              │
│                                 │
│ Cyan:     ─────────△──────  +15%│
│ Magenta: ──────△───────────  -30%│
│ Yellow:   ────────────△────  +40%│
│ Black:    ──────△──────────  -30%│
│                                 │
│ Method:  ⊙ Relative  ○ Absolute │
└─────────────────────────────────┘
```

```
┌─────────────────────────────────┐
│ Colors: Neutral tones           │
│                                 │
│ Cyan:     ───────△────────  -5% │
│ Magenta: ────────△─────────  0% │
│ Yellow:   ──────△──────────  -20%│
│ Black:    ────────△────────  0% │
│                                 │
│ Method:  ⊙ Relative  ○ Absolute │
└─────────────────────────────────┘
```

Changing the image effect with selective color correction

```
┌─────────────────────────────────┐
│ Colors: Cyan tones              │
│                                 │
│ Cyan:     ─────────△──────  -5% │
│ Magenta: ──────────────△───  +10%│
│ Yellow:   ─────────────△───  +25%│
│ Black:    ─────────────△───  +20%│
│                                 │
│ Method:  ⊙ Relative  ○ Absolute │
└─────────────────────────────────┘
```

```
┌─────────────────────────────────┐
│ Colors: Blue tones              │
│                                 │
│ Cyan:     ──────────△──────  0% │
│ Magenta: ──────────△───────  0% │
│ Yellow:   ────────────△────  +33%│
│ Black:    ─────────────△───  +20%│
│                                 │
│ Method:  ⊙ Relative  ○ Absolute │
└─────────────────────────────────┘
```

```
┌─────────────────────────────────┐
│ Colors: Magenta tones           │
│                                 │
│ Cyan:     ─────────────△───  +10%│
│ Magenta: ──────────△───────  -15%│
│ Yellow:   ─────────────△───  +5% │
│ Black:    ──────────────△──  +40%│
│                                 │
│ Method:  ⊙ Relative  ○ Absolute │
└─────────────────────────────────┘
```

Before

After

Before

After

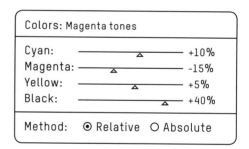

Unsharp mask

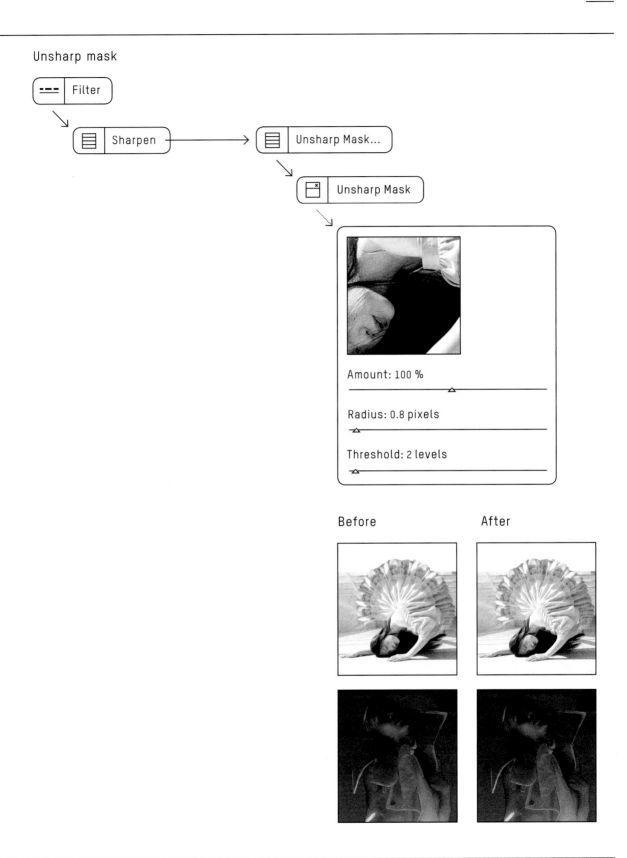

Before   After

7. PDF

Final artwork is normally sent to the printers or publishers in the form of a PDF. The advantage is that the file is relatively small and the recipient does not need to have the program or system with which the text or images were created.

In the chapter on trapping, we explained how to create a PDF with traps. On the following pages, we will explain what a PDF/X format is and how to create a normal print PDF without traps.

<u>7.1 Basics</u> A print PDF should be created as a PDF/X. This ensures that the basic prepress requirements are met. This mainly affects the color, transparency, and integration of type in the PDF.

PDF/X formats

Format	Standard	Compatibility
PDF/X-1a	PDF/X-1a:2001 PDF/X-1a:2003	Acrobat 4.0/PDF 1.3 Acrobat 5.0/PDF 1.4
PDF/X-3	PDF/X-3:2002 PDF/X-3:2003	Acrobat 4.0/PDF 1.3 Acrobat 5.0/PDF 1.4
PDF/X-4	PDF/X-4:2008	Acrobat 7.0/PDF 1.6

Format	Colors
PDF/X-1a	CMYK, spot
PDF/X-3	CMYK, spot, RGB,Lab, ICC-based
PDF/X-4	CMYK, spot, RGB, Lab, ICC-based colors

PDF/X

PDF/X—particularly the formats PDF/X-la, PDF/X-3 and PDF/X-4—are official ISO standards for the international standardization of PDF settings for prepress. PDF/X files must conform to certain rules. For X-la and X-3, this means that fonts and images have to be embedded, OPI comments are not allowed and neither is LZW compression due to licensing reasons, transparencies may not be included, the file must include information on whether the PDF contains traps, and the output conditions must be defined.

The main difference between the various formats is that a PDF/X-la may only include device-dependent process colors or spot colors, whereas PDF/X-3 may also have a device-independent RGB or Lab color space. Thus one does not have to choose a concrete output method for a PDF until output. PDF/X-4 is the only format that may contain transparencies, which are only reduced with the appropriate resolution during output. Otherwise, it is based on PDF/X-3 and can theoretically also include RGB and Lab colors.

In digital printing PDF/X-3 is generally recommended, or else PDF/X-la. The presets for the artwork are in the publishers' advertising information or at the printing houses. The PDF/X-2 standard was developed so that PDF files could be created in which the images and fonts are not embedded.

Creating a printable PDF file is comparable to a printing process. The printability depends on the correct color output, the perfect image resolution, high-resolution transparency flattening, sufficient stroke widths, and the integration of all fonts used. Where required, the PDF may have to include traps. When these preferences are set it really makes no difference whether it is a PDF/X-1 or X-3.

7.2 PDF export from InDesign for printing

In general, one has already reworked the layout and finished the artwork before creating a print PDF. On the following pages, we will explain how to create a PDF for the printer or the publisher step by step using the example of a PDF export from InDesign.

PDF presets

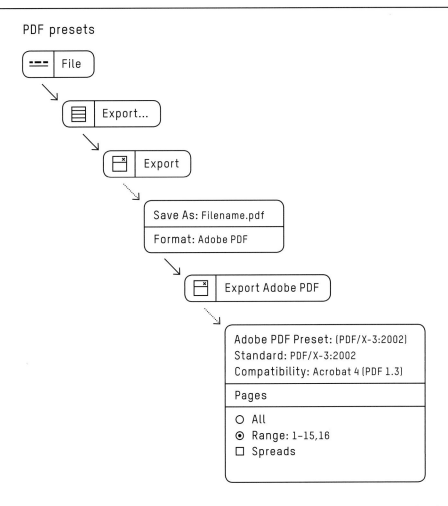

The choice of PDF preset, PDF default setting, and compatibility is the first step in creating a print PDF.

In theory printable PDF files can be created with RGB or Lab colors when a color management system converts the PDF to the correct inks during output. In general, however, one expects a PDF to meet all the printing conditions. The final artwork must be done, and the colors should already be adapted to the printing method.

Prior to sending the PDF to the printing press or publisher, one should make another proof of the print PDF, to check for any last errors before printing. If, for example, colored objects overprint by accident, black fails to overprint, or a transparency reduction is not good enough, one will see it on the proof at the latest. It is also useful as a color- and position-accurate reference at the printing press.

A PDF can be created in different ways. It is comparatively easy to export one from the respec-

tive application. The other possibility is to first create a PostScript file, and then write a PDF from it with Adobe Acrobat Distiller. This has the advantage that different PDF files may be created from the same PostScript file.

Making a PostScript file first makes sense when a PDF with embedded fonts needs to be extremely reduced in order to fit all of the type in. Exporting via PostScript is technically more precise, but much slower because of it.

One can simply export a print PDF from InDesign (File > Export...). The subsequent process is similar to the settings for printing. The following pages explain step by step what to watch out for, although for the sake of simplicity we will not look at other possible settings.

Step 1: General

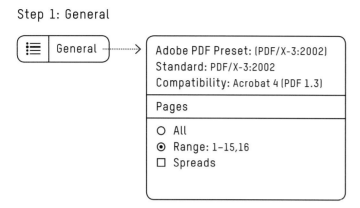

Adobe PDF Preset: (PDF/X-3:2002)
Standard: PDF/X-3:2002
Compatibility: Acrobat 4 (PDF 1.3)

Pages

○ All
◉ Range: 1–15,16
☐ Spreads

Step 1: General When one exports a file as a PDF, the first thing to do is to determine what kind of PDF it is and which pages of the document are for output.

One can choose previously installed presets, such as Press Quality, or a PDF/X preset. That way one has chosen a professional starting point, and any subsequent settings will only have to have minor changes.

One can choose None, PDF/X-la, or PDF/X-3 as the PDF standard. A printable PDF does not in fact necessarily need a predefined standard. What is important is that all subsequent settings are correct, and that the data from which the PDF was created matches the requirements of the print result.

The PDF compatibility should be as low as possible for output. A compatibility with Acrobat 4 (PDF 1.3) means that all transparencies are flattened to one layer. This is good for an imagesetter or color copier because such devices cannot print transparently. Therefore one must flatten the transparency before output. To avoid leaving the transparency flattening to the output devices, one should flatten all transparencies to one layer during PDF output at the latest, so that the PDF and proof results match the actual print result.

In general, one should create print sheets for multipage brochures with four pages at the most. Brochures or books that have more pages have to be imposed at the printer's and cannot therefore be output as double spreads. The other options in the window at the bottom are not relevant for print PDFs.

Step 2: Compression The next step for exporting a PDF covers the compression and resolution of the images. Compressing the data has the advantage that the file size is relatively small, which makes sending it per e-mail or uploading it to an FTP server easier.

The resolution of the images must not be interpolated when the PDF is written. As previously explained in the chapter "Image Editing" (see p. 246ff.), a bicubic interpolation of the image resolution may lead to undesired blur. The best way to calculate the image resolution is in Photoshop, so that blur can be corrected with an unsharp mask.

Top-quality compression causes no visible loss in quality; in some processes the quality is totally lossless. It makes sense when one wants as small a file as possible.

Step 3: Marks and bleed A print PDF should also include formatting marks and bleed.

One can do without the formatting marks when, for example, one sends artwork for an advertisement to the printing press or publisher, and the advertisement is only a part of the whole page. The trim marks for the advertisement would not be printed anyway because they are only indicated after page composition at the printer's.

When one creates a print PDF for the printing press, one should have all the necessary marks available, or at least crop and registration marks. One can select the type and weight of marks. Offset indicates how far the marks are from the edge of the page. This is

Step 2: Compression

≣ | Compression ┈┈┈┈>

Adobe PDF Preset: (PDF/X-3:2002)
Standard: PDF/X-3:2002
Compatibility: Acrobat 4 (PDF 1.3)

Color Images

Do Not Downsample   300 pixels per inch
for images above: 450 pixels per inch
Compression: Automatic (JPEG)   Tile Size: 128
Image Quality: Maximum

Grayscale Images

Do Not Downsample   300 pixels per inch
for images above: 450 pixels per inch
Compression: Automatic (JPEG)   Tile Size: 128
Image Quality: Maximum

Monochrome Images

Do Not Downsample   1200 pixels per inch
for images above: 1800 pixels per inch
Compression: CCITT Group 4

☑ Compress Text and Line Art
☑ Crop Image Data to Frames

Step 3: Marks and bleed

≣ | Marks and Bleeds ┈┈┈┈>

Adobe PDF Preset: (PDF/X-3:2002)
Standard: PDF/X-3:2002
Compatibility: Acrobat 4 (PDF 1.3)

Marks

☑ Crop Marks
☐ Bleed Marks
☑ Registration Marks
☑ Color Bars
☑ Page Information
Type: Default
Weight: 0.25 pt
Offset: 3 mm

Bleed and Slug

☑ Use Document Bleed Settings
☑ Include Slug Area

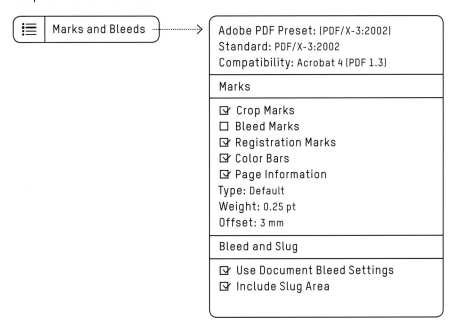

Step 4: Output

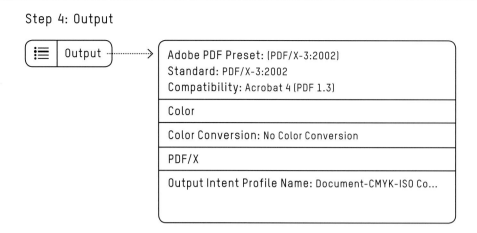

Step 5: Advanced

usually 3 to 5 mm. The color bar is often only placed on the print sheet at the printing press. However, it does not hurt to include it in the PDF.

Sometimes the trim also has to be indicated. The page information must be enclosed in case manually set fold marks are placed there, for example.

Step 4: Output
This step is about handling the colors and the output intent profile. Here one defines whether the colors of the document are to be converted and which color profile to use when the PDF is displayed.

It is recommendable to prepare a document with the correct colors, in order to make the result previewable. It is best not to convert the colors when the result has to meet corporate identity specifications or other special requirements. In such a case, one would ideally choose No Color Conversion. Under Output Intent Profile Name the profile with which the document was created is normally chosen automatically. Colors from other color spaces can be converted here to the desired destination profile. This has to be defined. Under Profile Inclusion Policy one can specify that all source profiles of objects in the document are included. This is not necessary when the colors no longer need to be converted for output.

Step 5: Advanced Next, one must regulate the font embedding and transparency flattener. Under Subset Fonts Below one can keep the default setting of 100%. This setting ensures that only the font data that is really needed is embedded.

The transparency flattener preset should be set to High Resolution for a print PDF. When one chooses a higher compatibility than Acrobat 4 in the pop-up menu, the transparencies would not be flattened to one layer. The transparency should, however, be flattened in a print PDF, as previously explained in "PDF compatibility" (see p. 274, Step 1).

Step 6: Security Here one can prevent the document from being printed by entering a password. An encryption or a password would not be part of a printing contract, however.

Step 7: Summary In the presets summary, all the applicable settings are listed and can be checked again where needed.

Step 8: Export In the final step, one must name the PDF after clicking on Export. InDesign will normally suggest the document name.

<u>7.3 Output preview in Adobe Acrobat</u> Every PDF that one creates must be opened and checked with Adobe Acrobat before sending the file on to the printing press. This ensures that no errors have crept into the artwork or the PDF. Part of the control is the output preview of the separations. The various color separations are listed, and one can also click away individual inks in the view.

Check PDF in Acrobat:
Output preview

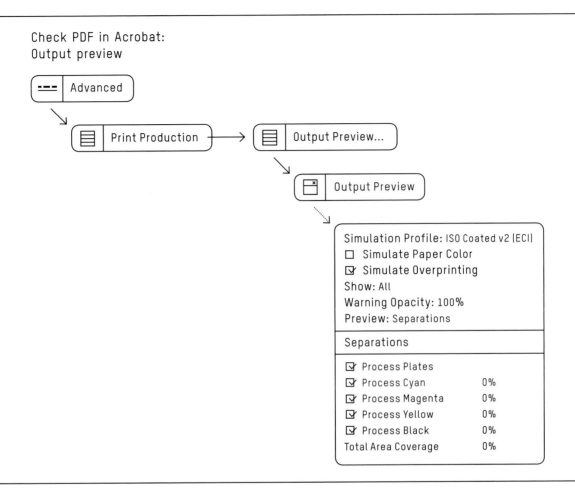

In Acrobat's Output Preview (Advanced > Print Production > Output Preview...) there is a list of the inks, which can be clicked away individually in the view. In the preview, one should check whether the PDF only contains the inks that will be used for printing, or whether there might be incorrect inks in the PDF.

The Output Preview also makes it possible to recheck the color composition. When one moves the cursor over the PDF, the component percentage appears next to the color descriptions. Thus one can do a final check to see that the colors correspond to the specifications.

One can also check the properties of the black ink here. By clicking away Process Black one checks that black really is only composed of black and whether it can print over its background.

The two options Simulate Black Ink and Simulate Paper White offer the possibility of seeing the PDF in the soft proof view, to simulate the print result as closely as possible on-screen.

8. Glossary

Additive color mix In additive color mixing, colors are produced by mixing the light colors red, green, and blue. All three base colors add up to white.

Adobe Systems John Warnock and Charles Geschke founded the American software company in 1982. Adobe designs programs for prepress, among them are InDesign, Illustrator, and Photoshop.

AM screen Amplitude-modulated screening is conventional periodic screening.

Baseline grid When lines of text are oriented around a grid, it is called a baseline grid.

Binary In the binary system, two digits, 1 and 0, represent number values. It is also called the dual system.

Bit A bit is the smallest displayable amount of data. A bit is the term for a binary digit and is the unit of measurement for data.

Bitmap Images in the bitmap mode have a color depth of 1 bit. This means that a pixel can only have two states—black or white.

Bleed Elements that go over the edge of the page or sheet must have a bleed, i.e., an area beyond the final trimmed size.

Book paper Book paper has a particularly high paper volume.

Broadsheet An unfolded sheet is also called a broadsheet.

Brochure A brochure is a bound work without a hard book cover.

Butt splicing Multiple-ups can be placed next to each other on a sheet without any space between them.

Cache A cache is a temporary storage in computing.

Calender A calender is a machine in which paper is glazed between cylinders.

Calibration Calibrating a technical device ensures that it will indicate the correct measurements. Monitors, printers, or scales may be calibrated, for example.

Chrominance Chrominance defines color tone and saturation.

CGATS The Committee for Graphic Arts Technologies Standards is the umbrella standard committee for printing, publishing, and converting technologies formed in 1987 by the Image Technology Standards Board (ITSB) of the American National Standards Institute (ANSI).

CIE CIE is the International Commission on Illumination—the "Commission Internationale de l'éclairage". It is one of the non-profit organizations recognized by the ISO, who discuss scientific topics regarding illumination. It developed the CIE standard color system.

CIE Lab CIE Lab is a color system developed by CIE. It is based on the CIE XYZ base colors and on the opponent color process that indicates the saturation and tone of a color in a coordinates system. This consists of a red-green axis a and a yellow-blue axis b, and can have positive as well as negative values on a brightness scale.

CIE Standard The CIE Standard allows colors to be converted from one color space to another.

CMM (color management module) Color management modules are operating system software components that are needed for converting colors to different color spaces.

CMS (color management system) A color management system standardizes colors for different output devices and print materials.

CMYK CMYK are the print colors cyan, magenta, yellow, and black. The K is for key black.

Color cast A color cast is when one color shifts to another color space and causes a new tint.

Color depth Color depth is measured in bits per color channel. It is the possible number of colors in a channel.

Color profile Color profiles describe the different color spaces.

Color separations In color separations, the colors of the individual inks are output separately.

Color space A color space is a collection of colors within a specific, often device-dependent coordinates system.

Color system A color system determines the color space that is used; the Euroscale color space is one example.

Commercial printing Commercial printing refers to all manner of commercial products in reasonably small print runs, from business cards to newspaper inserts.

Complementary colors Complementary colors are those that are opposite each other in a color model. Blue and yellow, or red and green are examples.

Composite A composite contains all the colors on a page that have not been separated.

Composite PDF The pages of a composite PDF are not separated. All the colors are on one page.

Compression In data compression, the storage space a file requires is reduced to a minimum. There is lossless and lossy compression.

Continuous printing Continuous printing is on rotary machines, where the paper webs are punched and perforated in a zigzag fold.

Conversion Conversion is the transformation of files. The colors in an image can be converted to another color space, or a file to another file format.

Corporate design A corporate design is the visual image of a company.

Corporate identity Corporate identity is the entire outward image of a company, including corporate design.

Crease A crease occurs when an unprinted sheet is folded by accident and then printed.

Digital printing In digital printing, the original is sent from a computer straight to a laser printer without having to go via printing plates. For small print runs, it is cheaper than offset printing.

DIN The German Institute for Standardization.

Dithering Dithering is a digital FM screening method that prevents hard transitions between colors. It is mainly used for color reduction.

Dmax D_{max} is the maximum density of a photographic material. The difference between D_{max} and D_{min} is the gamut.

Dmin D_{min} is the minimum density of a photographic material. The difference between D_{max} and D_{min} is the gamut.

Dot gain The increase in size of halftone dots in print is called dot gain. It is caused by the printing machine when the ink is applied.

Double page When two pages are opposite each other, it is a double page.

Downsampling Downsampling is image resolution reduction.

Dpi Dpi stands for dots per inch and describes the resolution of pixel formats or output devices.

Dummy A dummy is usually a handmade sample of the layout for prepress.

Duotone In Duotone printing, a black-and-white image is printed together with a second color. The image colors must be specially separated.

ECI The European Color Initiative is an initiative of the publishing houses Bauer, Burda, Gruner & Jahr, and Springer for the standardization of media neutral color processing for digital data exchange.

Em quad An em is a typographical unit of measurement. Its width is the height of the body of a letter.

Endpaper Endpaper connects the book block to the book cover.

Euroscale The European color scale consists of the base colors cyan, magenta, yellow, and black for four-color printing.

Facsimile A facsimile is a copy or reproduction of a valuable document or work of art that is true to the original in size, color, and condition.

Final artwork The final artwork is a file in which all components are checked for printability.

FM screening Frequency-modulated screening is the non-periodic, stochastic screening process.

Fold The middle of an open bound work is called the fold.

Fold marks Fold marks are printer's marks that indicate the position of a fold on a paper sheet.

Format the format is the shape and size of a paper sheet.

Galley proof A galley proof is a proof made to check the layout before the page composition is complete.

Gamma Gamma is the gradation curve of a film material, and the measure of the contrast in the midtones of an image. Gamma correction is correcting the tonal distribution of an image, using the gradation curve in Photoshop, for example.

Gamut The gamut or tonal range describes the difference between the brightest point (minimum density or D_{min}) and the darkest point (maximum density or D_{max}) of an original.

GCR Gray component replacement means achromatic generation and is the generation of neutral colors through cyan, magenta, and yellow with the addition of black.

Glazing Paper is smoothed under high pressure to give it a closed surface.

Glyph A glyph is a written character.

Gradation curve A gradation curve is for correcting the tonal value of an image using a coordinates system. In photography it is also called a density curve. It shows the extent of the exposure and the reaction of the light-sensitive material. The curve connects the points of maximum and minimum density within a coordinates system. The steepness of the curve produces the gamma value.

Grain The grain is the position of paper fibers. They run in one direction when they are machine-produced.

Gray value The gray value is the appearance of text in relation to its tracking, word spacing, line spacing, and stroke widths. Expressed differently, it is the relation between ink and paper white.

Grayscale wedge A grayscale wedge normally contains ten gradations from black to white for checking reproductions.

Halftone dot A screen consists of several halftone dots. It is used to simulate continuous tones in print.

Halftone image Halftone images may contain colors in all possible tonal gradations. Halftone images are rasterized for reproduction.

Highlights Highlights are the brightest areas of an image, roughly from 0 to 25 percent of a tonal value.

Histogram A histogram shows the distribution and frequency of the gray values or color values of an image on an intensity scale.

HKS The HKS color system contains 88 colors for the printing industry. There are also varnishes and synthetic materials. This guarantees color accuracy throughout a corporate design. HKS stands for Horstmann-Steinberg, K + E, and Schmincke.

HSB HSB stands for hue, saturation, and brightness. Colors may be defined according to this HSB system.

HWC Heavyweight coated paper.

ICC ICC stands for the International Color Consortium. The ICC is a consortium of international manufacturers of programs for prepress, formed to unify a color management system for all software and platforms.

ICC profile An ICC profile is a color profile for describing color spaces.

IEC The International Electrotechnical Commission developed the sRGB color space, one of the smallest truecolor color spaces. The IEC defines international standards for all areas of electro-technology.

Imagesetter Imagesetters are prepress output devices with which one produces separated color films or plates.

Imposition Imposition is the arrangement of several pages on a print sheet so that the page sequence is correct for printing after folding and cutting the sheet.

Initial An initial is an ornamental initial letter.

Interpolation One can heighten the resolution of an image in an image editing program by interpolating image points. The existing image points are then reintroduced. The main methods are bicubic and bilinear interpolation.

ISO The International Standards Organization.

Justified composition In justified composition, all the lines in a text are set to the same width. This is generally achieved by variable word spacing.

Kerning Kerning is a typographical term that means shortening the letter spaces. Manual or automatic kerning optimizes the letter spacing.

Lab The Lab color system has the three coordinates *a*, *b* and *L*. On the *a*-axis red and green are opposite each other, and yellow and blue on the *b*-axis. The luminance axis *L* is vertical to these.

Laminate A laminate is a bond of several layers of the same or different material—often paper and a protective foil.

Layout A design for a print product is called a layout.

LCH LCH stands for luminance, chroma, and hue. Colors may be defined according to the LCH color space.

Ligature Ligatures are frequently used letter combinations that, in the era of hot metal setting, originally used to be cast together in order to close gaps that would occur between letters, particularly after a lowercase *f*.

Line graphics Line graphics are illustrations that do not need to be screened for reproduction.

Lithography In this, the oldest planographic printing method, a damp stone is painted with fatty ink. The non-printable areas are dampened with water and thus repel the fat-containing ink.

LLWC Light lightweight coated paper.

Long grain The paper fibers run parallel to the broad side.

Lpi Lpi stands for lines per inch—a unit of measurement for screen ruling.

Luminance Luminance is color brightness.

LWC Lightweight coated paper.

LZW LZW stands for Lempel-Ziv-Welch—an algorithm for data compression.

MF Machine finished paper.

MFC Machine finished coated paper.

Microtypography Microtypography deals with individual characters, while macrotypography deals with the fundamental typography within a layout.

Midtones Midtones are the middle areas of the brightness intensity of an image, roughly 25 to 75 percent of a tonal value.

Moiré The moiré effect is the pattern that occurs in overlapping periodic screening.

Multiple-ups Multiple-ups are the number of copy areas on a print sheet.

MWC Mediumweight coated paper.

Offset The offset printing process is an indirect planographic method in which the printing and non-printing parts of the printing form are on one level.

Optical density Optical density is the opacity of a color.

Overprinting When a color prints over its background, the unchanged background remains underneath the object or color.

Oversize format Oversize formats are print sheets that are slightly larger than the usual trimmed size and have to be cut after printing. There are A4 or A3 oversize formats, for instance.

Pagination Pagination is the arrangement of composition with multiple columns.

Pantone colors Pantone spot colors by the American company Pantone, Inc. were originally conceived for colors in the cosmetics industry. Today Pantone colors are a comprehensive color collection for the printing industry.

Paper fibers Paper consists of plant cellulose fibers. These fibers are made of dextrose molecules. In machine paper manufacture, the fibers all run in the machine direction.

Paper volume The paper volume indicates the ratio of its thickness to its weight in g/m^2. The more volume a paper has, the more slip-proof it is.

PDF The Portable Document Format was created by Adobe. It is used for data exchange during prepress.

Perforation Perforation consists of punching little holes along a line in the paper to make it easier to separate.

Perforation marks Perforation marks outside of the trimmed size indicate the position of a perforation.

PostScript PostScript is a page description language for prepress. PostScript can also be integrated in files such as EPS.

PPD A PPD is a PostScript printer description that describes the properties of the printer, and is necessary for the print dialog.

Primary colors Primary colors are the base colors of a color system, such as red, green and blue, or cyan, magenta, and yellow.

Print control strip The print control strip is used for checking the color reproduction of the printing machine or of a proof.

Process colors The print colors cyan, magenta and yellow are also called process colors.

Proof A proof is a print sample that simulates the print result and is used for checking colors and layout.

PSO PSO stands for process standard offset print.

Punch Certain shapes made of paper or other materials are die-cut or punched from metal using special cutting tools.

Quarter tones Quarter tones are the tonal values of a color that have a gradation of roughly 25 percent.

RAL RAL is a German color system that contains a scale of standardized colors used to define varnishes, for example.

Ragged composition In ragged type the lines in a text have different lengths.

Recto The recto side is the side that is printed first on a print sheet.

Rendering intent The rendering intent enables the user of a color management system to determine what method to use for converting an image from one color space to another.

Register marks Register marks are essential for the accurate composition of color films in multicolor printing.

Registration When the paper runs through the printing machine several times, the sheet must be perfectly aligned so that the colors print over one another precisely. Since the paper stretches during the printing process, misregister within certain tolerance limits is sometimes inevitable.

Resolution The resolution is the amount of pixels in relation to a specific unit of length that a graphic or a printer possesses. It is usually given in dpi (dots per inch).

RGB RGB are the three base colors red, green, and blue of the additive color system.

Rich black A black is described as rich black when it consists of more than black alone. Cyan is usually used, but all other process colors can be mixed in different quantities with 100 percent black.

RIP RIP stands for raster image processor, the printer computer, in which the PostScript page is converted to the printer screen.

SC Supercalendered paper.

Scaling Scaling is resizing, i.e., enlarging or reducing an object.

Screen ruling The screen ruling indicates how far the halftone dots are spaced from one another, or how many dots there are per inch or centimeter.

Screenshot A screenshot is an image of part or all of the screen content.

Shadows Shadows are the dark areas of an image between 75 and 100 percent color application.

Sheet The print sheet is the untrimmed print material.

Sheet assembly In sheet assembly, the individual pages are placed on the sheet according to an imposition scheme.

Sheet-fed offset In sheet-fed offset printing, one prints a paper sheet.

Sheet size The sheet size is the size of the untrimmed paper sheet.

Short grain The paper fibers run parallel to the narrow side.

Silkscreen printing In silkscreen printing, ink is printed onto the carrier material through a mesh.

Small caps Small caps is a type style in which the lowercase letters consist of small uppercase letters with the same height as lowercase.

SNAP The Specifications for Newsprint Advertising Production improve reproduction quality in coldset web newsprint production.

SNP Standard newsprint paper.

Soft proof A soft proof simulates the print result onscreen.

Spot color Colors that are not composed of process colors are spot colors. Unlike process colors one does not create them by screening inks, but rather by mixing separate inks before printing.

Subtractive color mix In subtractive color mixing, one creates colors by mixing colors on materials. Color perception is created when light is reflected off the body colors. As opposed to light colors, the perception of body colors depends on the ambient lighting.

Three-quarter tones Tonal values at a gradation of around 75 percent are described as three-quarter tones.

Tonal value reduction One can counter dot gain with tonal value reduction in order to achieve the desired tonal value in the print result.

Total ink coverage Total ink coverage is the total amount of applied ink. An ink made of 100 percent cyan and 50 percent magenta has a total ink coverage of 150 percent.

Trap color The trap color is the ink that is trapped. It is a mixture of the object and background color.

Trapping Individual colors trap each other in order to prevent white gaps from occurring due to misregistration in multicolor printing. In general the shape of the lighter color is slightly bigger.

Trim marks Trim marks indicate where a paper sheet is to be cut. Trim marks are generally at least 3mm outside of the trimmed size.

Trimmed size The trimmed size is the final size of a print sheet, trimmed and sometimes folded.

Truecolor Truecolor is a system of color representation that contains at least 16 million colors.

Type area The type area indicates the borders of the design elements on a page.

Typography Typography is the design process used on printed works with type, images, lines, areas, and typographical space. Typography encompasses layout design and typeface design, but also the right choice of paper or cover.

UCA Under coat addition is gray generation with chromatic addition in color reproduction.

UCR Under color removal is the reduction of cyan, magenta, and yellow, and the increase of black in the neutral tones, particularly in the shadows.

ULWC Ultra lightweight coated paper.

Unsharp mask The Unsharp Mask tool in Photoshop corrects undesired unsharp areas.

Untrimmed size The untrimmed and unfolded size of a print sheet.

Vector graphics A vector graphic is a curve graphic. It is created in vector programs such as Illustrator.

Verso The verso side is the second print process on the reverse of the print sheet.

Web offset In web offset printing, a roll of paper is fed through the printing press.

White gaps When one overprints colors in offset printing, registration differences may cause white gaps to appear. The colors need to be trapped to avoid this from occurring. The traps are slightly wider than the registration tolerance value of the printing machine.

Ready to Print

Handbook for Media Designers

Edited by Kristina Nickel

Preface by Erik Spiekermann
Translation by Dylan Spiekermann
Technical consultation on the English language edition
by Erik Spiekermann

Cover and layout by Daniela Burger for Gestalten
Software infographics by Michael Luther for Gestalten
Typefaces: T-Star Pro by Michael Mischler and
Bonesana Pro by Matthieu Cortat
Foundry: www.gestaltenfonts.com
Image samples by Sarah Illenberger ("Essen und Trinken,"
motif 1, p. 188 et. al.; motif 2, p. 257, "Fashion Flowers,"
p. 213 et. al.), Zoren Gold/Minori ("Exploradora," p. 158
et. al.; "Twins," p. 260 et. al.; "Tourist," p. 215 et. al.;
"Kahimi Karie," p. 215 et. al.; "Metamorphose," motif 1,
p. 215 et. al.; motif 2, p. 251) and Elias Wessel/Saria Atiye
("Falling in Love," motif 1, p. 96 et al.; motif 2, p. 261)

Project management by Julian Sorge for Gestalten
Production management by Janine Milstrey for Gestalten
Proofreading by Transparent Language Solutions
Special thanks to Steven Sears and Karen Fishel for their
input and support.
Printed by Sing Cheong Printing Company Ltd.,
Hong Kong. Made in Asia.

Published by Gestalten, Berlin 2011
ISBN 978-3-89955-325-3

Respect copyrights, encourage creativity!
For more information, please visit www.gestalten.com

Bibliographic information published by the Deutsche
Nationalbibliothek.
The Deutsche Nationalbibliothek lists this publication
in the Deutsche Nationalbibliografie; detailed bibliographic data is available online at http://dnb.d-nb.de.

This book was printed on paper certified by FSC®,
which ensures responsible paper sources.

Gestalten is a climate-neutral company and so are our
products. We collaborate with the non-profit carbon offset provider myclimate (www.myclimate.org) to neutralize the company's carbon footprint produced through
our worldwide business activities by investing in projects that reduce CO_2 emissions (www.gestalten.com/
myclimate).

Brickwork Level 3